THE CROWN
AND
THE RING

The Crown and The Ring

THE STORY OF THE QUEEN'S YEARS OF MARRIAGE AND MONARCHY

Graham and Heather Fisher

ROBERT HALE · LONDON

© *Graham and Heather Fisher Limited 1971, 1972*
First published in Great Britain 1972

ISBN 0 7091 2998 X

Robert Hale & Company
63 Old Brompton Road
London S.W.7

PRINTED IN GREAT BRITAIN
BY EBENEZER BAYLIS & SON LIMITED
THE TRINITY PRESS, WORCESTER, AND LONDON

For
Linda and Craig,
Janet, Brandon
and James

Contents

Illustrations

Foreword

On 20th November 1972 a wife some uninhibited Canadian students once greeted as Betty Windsor and a husband named Philip Mountbatten celebrate their silver wedding anniversary . . . in the same year that Her Most Excellent Majesty Queen Elizabeth II and His Royal Highness The Prince Philip, Duke of Edinburgh, commemorate twenty years as Sovereign and Consort.

This is the story of those two couples who are really the same two people, of those two anniversaries and the years which have led up to them. It is a story which goes back to, and even beyond, that first boy and girl meeting of a youthful Prince Philip and an even younger Princess Elizabeth in the pre-war summer of 1939.

It follows that in writing it we have necessarily drawn upon conversations and interviews which have taken place over many years. Sadly but inevitably, some of those who have helped us are now dead. Others with whom we have talked more recently would prefer not to be mentioned by name. But to all, our grateful thanks.

In particular, we would like to thank Mr. Peter Townsend, the editor of *Burke's Peerage*, and Sir Charles Petrie for their helpful guidance in certain areas; Mr. William Heseltine, C.V.O., Her Majesty's Press Secretary, and Miss Anne Hawkins, M.V.O., Assistant Press Secretary, for their kindness in supplying information on certain points; and Miss J. Barratt and Miss D. Olliphant of Bromley Central Library for their patience in tracking down research references.

In expressing our gratitude to these, and others who helped us to get at the facts, we would also make it clear that the interpretation of those facts is necessarily our own and that this book is in no way an 'official' or 'approved' biography.

Keston Park,   G. and H.F.
Kent.

The Leading Characters

The Wife

Her Majesty Queen Elizabeth II. Born 17 Bruton Street, London, W.1., 21st April 1926, elder daughter of the Duke and Duchess of York (later King George VI and Queen Elizabeth). Christened Elizabeth Alexandra Mary, but sometimes called Lilibet in the family circle. Educated privately, mainly at home. Became heir to the throne on the abdication of her uncle, King Edward VIII (Duke of Windsor) and the succession of her father as King George VI, 11th December 1936. Betrothed to Prince Philip (then Lieutenant Philip Mountbatten, R.N.) 9th July 1947, married to him 20th November 1947. Succeeded to the throne on the death of her father, 6th February 1952. Height, 5 feet 4 inches; eyes, blue; hair, light brown.

The Husband

His Royal Highness The Prince Philip, Duke of Edinburgh, Earl of Merioneth and Baron Greenwich. Born in Corfu, 10th June 1921, youngest child and only son of Prince and Princess Andrew (formerly Princess Alice of Battenberg) of Greece. Educated at the Country Day and Boarding School, St. Cloud, Paris; Cheam, England; Salem, Germany and Gordonstoun, Scotland. Then at the Royal Naval College, Dartmouth. Served in the Royal Navy 1940–51, mentioned in despatches at the Battle of Cape Matapan, commanded H.M.S. *Magpie* September 1950–August 1951. Naturalised British, 28th February 1947; created Royal Highness and Duke of Edinburgh by the late

King George VI, November 1947; created Prince by the Queen, 22nd February 1957. Height, 5 feet 11½ inches; eyes, blue; hair, fair.

The Children
H.R.H. The Prince of Wales and Earl of Chester, Duke of Cornwall and Baron Rothesay, Earl of Carrick and Baron Renfrew, Lord of the Isles and Great Steward of Scotland. Born Buckingham Palace, 14th November 1948. Christened Charles Philip Arthur George. Educated Hill House, London; Cheam; Gordonstoun; Timbertop, Australia (a branch of Geelong Church of England Grammar School); Trinity College, Cambridge (where he gained a B.A. (Hons) degree, and the University of Wales at Aberystwyth. Created Prince of Wales, 26th July 1958; invested as Prince of Wales, 1st July 1969. Awarded Preliminary Flying Badge, 2nd August 1969. Entered the Royal Navy under the Graduate Entry Scheme, September 1971. Height, 5 feet 11 inches; eyes, blue; hair, light brown.

Her Royal Highness The Princess Anne Elizabeth Alice Louise. Born Clarence House, 15th August 1950. Educated Benenden. Voted 'Sportswoman of the Year' after winning the European Three-day Event at Burghley in 1971. Height, 5 feet 6½ inches; eyes, blue; hair, fair.

H.R.H. Prince Andrew Albert Christian Edward. Born Buckingham Palace, 19th February 1960. Educated Heatherdown School, Berkshire. Eyes, blue; hair, light brown.

H.R.H. Prince Edward Antony Richard Louis. Born Buckingham Palace, 10th March 1964. Eyes, blue; hair, fair. Educated Gibbs Preparatory School, London.

The Supporting Cast
(in alphabetical order)

Alexander, Sir Ulick. Keeper of the Privy Purse in the early days of the Queen's reign.

Alexandra, Princess. The Queen's cousin.

Altrincham, Lord (later Mr. John Grigg, having renounced his title in 1963). Editor *National and English Review* 1954–60.

Anderson, Mabel. Nanny to the royal children.

Andrew of Greece, Prince. Prince Philip's father. Died 1944.

Andrew of Greece, Princess (Princess Alice of Battenberg). Prince Philip's mother. Died 1969.

Armstrong-Jones, Antony. *See* Snowdon.

Aubrey, Ronald. The royal chef.

Bennett, Ernest. One of the Queen's two principal pages.

Bertold, Prince. Margrave of Baden. Husband of Philip's sister, Theodora. Died 1963.

Bloomer, Dr. Thomas. Bishop of Carlisle 1946–66.

Brabourne, Baroness (Lady Patricia Mountbatten). Prince Philip's cousin.

Browning, Lieutenant-General Sir Frederick. Comptroller and treasurer to the Queen when Princess Elizabeth (1948–52) and Treasurer to Prince Philip (1952–59). Died 1965.

Cecilie, Princess. Philip's sister. Died in an air crash, 1937.

Charteris, Lieutenant-Colonel the Hon Sir Martin. Private secretary to the Queen when Princess Elizabeth. Now one of her two assistant private secretaries.

Christopher of Hesse, Prince. First husband of Philip's sister, Sophie. Killed in a wartime air crash.

Churchill, Sir Winston. Prime Minister during the first four years of the Queen's monarchy. Died 1965.

Colville, Sir Richard. Formerly the Queen's press secretary.

Crawford, Marion. One-time governess to the Queen and Princess Margaret.

Cunningham, Admiral Sir Andrew. Commander of the British fleet at the Battle of Cape Matapan.

Dalrymple-Hamilton, Admiral Sir Frederick. Captain of the Royal Naval College, Dartmouth, when Philip was a cadet there.

Dean, John. One-time valet to Prince Philip.

Diefenbaker, John George. Prime Minister of Canada 1957–63.

Eisenhower, General Dwight D. Former President of the United States. Died 1969.

Eisenhower, Mamie. His wife.

Elizabeth, the Queen Mother. Mother of Her Majesty.

Elphinstone, Reverend the Hon Andrew. The Queen's cousin.

Elphinstone, the Hon Mrs. Andrew (formerly Jean Gibbs). Lady-in-waiting to the Queen when she was Princess Elizabeth. Now an extra Woman of the Bedchamber.

Fyfe, Sir David Maxwell. Home Secretary during the early years of the Queen's reign.

George II of Greece, King. Philip's cousin. Died 1947.

George V, King. The Queen's grandfather. Died 1936.

George VI, King. The Queen's father. Died 1952.

George of Hanover, Prince. Second husband of Philip's sister, Sophie.

Gibbs, Jean. *See* Elphinstone.

Gloucester, Duke and Duchess of. The Queen's uncle and aunt.

Gottfried of Hohenlohe-Langenburg, Prince. Husband of Philip's sister, Margarita. Died 1960.

Hahn, Dr. Kurt. Philip's headmaster at Gordonstoun.

Hartnell, Norman. Designed the Queen's wedding dress and coronation gown.

Hicks, Lady Pamela (Lady Pamela Mountbatten). Philip's cousin.

Kent, Duke and Duchess of. The Duke is the Queen's cousin.

Knight, Clara Cooper. One-time royal nanny.

Lascelles, Sir Alan. Formerly private secretary to the Queen.

Legh, Sir Piers. Formerly Master of the Queen's Household.

Lightbody, Helen. Former nanny to the royal children.

Louis of Battenberg, Prince. *See* Milford Haven, 1st Marquess.

MacDonald, Margaret (Bobo). The Queen's dresser.

MacDonald, Ruby (subsequently Mrs. Ruby Gordon). Bobo's sister and one-time royal nursemaid.

Macmillan, Harold. Prime Minister 1957–63.

Margaret, Princess. The Queen's sister. Born 1930.

Margarita, Princess. Prince Philip's eldest sister.

Marina, Princess, Duchess of Kent. Philip's cousin. Died 1968.

Marten, Dr. (later Sir) Henry. Former vice provost (later provost) of Eton College and the Queen's tutor. Died 1948.

Mary, Queen. The Queen's grandmother. Died 1953.

Milford Haven, 1st Marquess (Prince Louis of Battenberg). Prince Philip's grandfather. Died 1921.

Milford Haven, Dowager Marchioness. Prince Philip's grandmother. Died 1950.

Milford Haven, 2nd Marquess. Philip's Uncle George. Died 1938.

Milford Haven, 3rd Marquess. Philip's cousin David. Died 1970.

Mountbatten of Burma, Earl. Philip's Uncle Dickie.

Mountbatten, Lady Pamela. *See* Hicks.

Mountbatten, Lady Patricia. *See* Brabourne.

Muggeridge, Malcolm. TV celebrity, journalist, author and one-time royal critic.

Nevill, Lord Rupert and Lady. Friends of the royal family.

Nicholas of Greece, Prince. Philip's uncle. Died 1938.

Nicholas of Greece, Princess. Philip's aunt. Died 1957.

Ogilvy, the Hon Angus. Husband of Princess Alexandra.

Parker, Lieutenant-Commander Michael. Private secretary to Prince Philip 1947–57.

Peebles, Katherine. Former governess to the royal children. Died 1968.

Simpson, Mrs. Wallis. *See* Duchess of Windsor.

Snowdon, Earl of (Antony Armstrong-Jones). Princess Margaret's husband.

Soper, the Reverend Donald (later Baron). Prominent Methodist and opponent of blood sports.

Sophie, Princess. Philip's youngest sister.

Taylor, John. One of the Queen's pages.

Theodora, Princess. Philip's sister. Died 1969.

Townsend, Group-Captain Peter. One-time close friend of Princess Margaret.

Walton, James. Deputy Palace Steward.

Watts, Maurice. Former royal page.

Wernher, Sir Harold and Lady Zia. Friends of the royal family. Lady Zia is also a distant relative of Prince Philip's.

William of Gloucester, Prince. The Queen's cousin.

Windsor, Duke of. The Queen's uncle. Formerly—and briefly—King Edward VIII. Abdicated 1936.

Windsor, Duchess of. His wife.

Brief Chronology

10th June	1921	Prince Philip born.
21st April	1926	Princess Elizabeth born.
21st August	1930	Princess Margaret born.
11th December	1936	King Edward VIII abdicates to become Duke of Windsor and Princess Elizabeth's parents become King and Queen
22nd July	1939	Princess Elizabeth meets Prince Philip when she accompanies her parents on a visit to the Royal Naval College, Dartmouth.
	1944	Prince Philip renounces right of succession to the Greek throne.
3rd December	1944	Prince Philip's father—Prince Andrew of Greece—dies at Monte Carlo.
28th February	1947	Prince Philip takes British nationality and becomes Lieutenant Philip Mountbatten, R.N.
9th July	1947	Princess Elizabeth and Philip Mountbatten are betrothed.
19th November	1947	Philip is created a Royal Highness with the titles Baron Greenwich, Earl of Merioneth and Duke of Edinburgh.
20th November	1947	Princess Elizabeth and Prince Philip are married.
14th November	1948	Prince Charles born.

15th August	1950	Princess Anne born.
12th August	1951	Prince Philip ceases active duty with the Royal Navy.
6th February	1952	King George VI dies. Princess Elizabeth becomes Queen.
9th April	1952	The Queen declares, "I and my children shall be styled and known as of the House and Family of Windsor."
2nd June	1953	Coronation Day.
22nd February	1957	The Queen creates her husband Prince Philip.
26th July	1958	Prince Charles is created Prince of Wales.
8th February	1960	The Queen decrees the name Mountbatten-Windsor for those of her descendants requiring the use of a surname.
19th February	1960	Prince Andrew born.
6th May	1960	Princess Margaret marries Antony Charles Robert Armstrong-Jones (created Earl of Snowdon 1961).
10th March	1964	Prince Edward born.
1st July	1969	Prince Charles invested as Prince of Wales.
5th December	1969	Prince Philip's mother dies at Buckingham Palace.
4th August	1970	The Queen Mother celebrates her seventieth birthday.
20th August	1971	Prince Charles awarded his R.A.F. 'wings'.
5th September	1971	Princess Anne wins European Three-day Championship.
15th September	1971	Prince Charles joins the Navy.
20th November	1972	The Queen and Prince Philip celebrate their silver wedding anniversary.

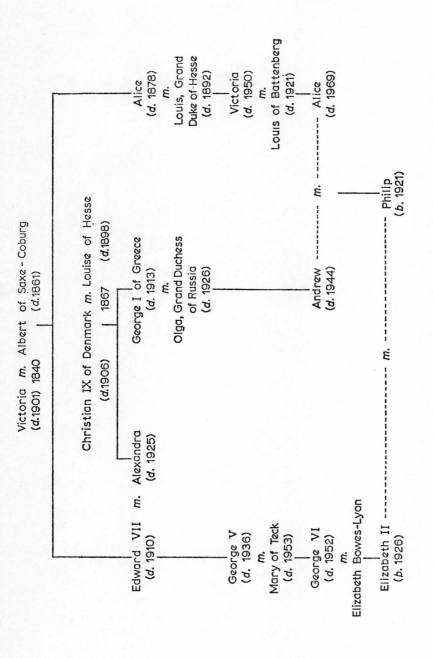

Victoria *m.* Albert of Saxe-Coburg
(*d.*1901) 1840 (*d.*1861)

Christian IX of Denmark *m.* Louise of Hesse
(*d.*1906) 1867 (*d.*1898)

Edward VII *m.* Alexandra
(*d.* 1910) (*d.* 1925)

George V
(*d.* 1936)
m.
Mary of Teck
(*d.* 1953)

George VI
(*d.* 1952)
m.
Elizabeth Bowes-Lyon

Elizabeth II
(*b.* 1926)

Alice
(*d.* 1878)
m.
Louis, Grand
Duke of Hesse
(*d.* 1892)

Victoria
(*d.* 1950)
m.
Louis of Battenberg
(*d.* 1921)

Alice
(*d.* 1969)

George I of Greece
(*d.* 1913)
m.
Olga, Grand Duchess
of Russia
(*d.* 1926)

Andrew
(*d.* 1944)

m.

Philip
(*b.* 1921)

I

The Crown and the Ring

Every year, on her wedding anniversary, the Queen can be sure
of receiving a large box of her favourite flowers: roses, carnations,
lilies-of-the-valley and others besides. The flowers are from
Prince Philip. Through all their years of marriage, he has always
marked anniversaries in this fashion. Even the year he was half a
world away from home, heading south for the Antarctic aboard
the royal yacht, his anniversary gift of flowers was still there to
greet the Queen when she walked through to breakfast that
morning.

The flowers her husband gives her may vary somewhat from
year to year, according to what happens to be available, but not
their colour. They are always white, a nostalgic echo of the spray
of white orchids the young Princess Elizabeth carried on her
wedding day.

What a panic there was over those orchids on the actual
wedding day! Picture the scene. The bride in her wedding dress
and on the point of departure. She looks round for the spray of
orchids she is to carry. It is nowhere to be seen and no one seems
to know where it is.

Hurried inquiries revealed that the orchids had been safely
delivered at the palace door. From there they had been sent up to
the second floor where the bride was getting ready for her big day.
From that point on, they have vanished.

A frantic search ensues. Royal servants scurry hither and

thither. The bride's father strides impatiently back and forth, looking at his watch. Nerves tighten and tension mounts.

Not until the young nursery footman returned from bagging a vantage point at one of the windows from which to watch the bride depart was the mystery solved and the situation saved.

"Oh, those," he says, when he hears of the missing orchids. "Just a minute and I'll get them."

He pops into the nursery kitchen and promptly produces the orchids from a small refrigerator in which he had placed them to keep them cool and fresh.

The orchids are whisked to where the bride is waiting, calm is restored, nerves settle, and the royal bride goes forth on her father's arm to her wedding in Westminster Abbey.

It was 20th November 1947. The Queen was a young princess, eager, excited and rather nervous, as young brides are apt to be. Prince Philip was 26, a dashing young naval officer, normally extrovert and uninhibited, but inclined to be edgy on his wedding morning, following a somewhat roisterous stag party the night before.

To both bride and groom, monarchy—if they thought about it at all—must have seemed a long, long way in the future. There was, as yet, no sign that the King's health was failing and no one could possibly have foreseen that in little more than four years that 21-year-old bride of 1947 would be Her Majesty Queen Elizabeth II.

Yet monarchy had already set its mark upon her. In a sense, the Queen was betrothed to monarchy long before her betrothal to Prince Philip; even before that childhood meeting at Dartmouth which was to lead to love, courtship and, after some delay, finally to marriage. She was betrothed to monarchy on that momentous day in 1936 when her Uncle David abdicated his kingship rather than give up the woman he loved and when her father, nervous and unprepared, reluctantly took over the vacant throne. She was 10 years old and only a single heartbeat now separated her from monarchy.

That she, and she alone, would be the next monarch was made clear in the House of Commons two months after her father's accession. All these years later it is difficult to realise that there was ever any doubt in the matter. But, in some minds, there was at the time. Legal purists had been arguing the matter back and forth ever since the birth of Princess Margaret, some six years earlier.

Had this second child born to the then Duke and Duchess of York proved to be a son, there would have been no cause for argument. A brother, though younger, would have taken precedence over the older sister. But when the second child turned out equally to be a girl there were some who held the view that, in the absence of a male heir, the two sisters should share the throne in the future as daughters share in land and property.

Constitutional experts debated the point, genealogists pondered the past, *Debrett* and *Burke's Peerage* had their say. But now, finally, the Home Secretary of the day was to settle the point.

He was asked in the House of Commons whether the Government proposed to amend the Act of Settlement.

"There is no need," he replied. "His Majesty's Government is advised that there is no doubt that in present circumstances Her Royal Highness The Princess Elizabeth would succeed to the throne as sole heir."

From then on the Princess was as surely committed to monarchy as later, and more personally, she was to commit herself to Philip. Carefully and painstakingly she was urged forward along the narrow, purposeful path which led to the throne. Everyone around her took a hand in her training. Her governess set her to read the youthful journal of her great-great-grandmother, Queen Victoria, so that she might know what was expected of her. Her nanny suggested sucking barley sugar as an antidote to nervous tension on public occasions and a cure for sickness when travelling. Latin was added to the curriculum of the nursery schoolroom against the future necessity to cope with state papers. Her grandmother, Queen Mary, hauled her off to Westminster Abbey, the Tower of London and other similar places designed to induce the correct sense of dynasty and destiny. Her father had her standing beside him on all manner of official occasions and, later, to sit with him while he went through the contents of the leather-covered 'boxes' which have arrived for successive monarchs in unending succession.

As the Princess grew from girlhood to womanhood, a young man named Philip and an age-old institution called monarchy were alike to woo her. Time and again highlights of her courtship by Philip were to be matched, and sometimes surpassed, by similar highlights in her apprenticeship to monarchy.

She was around 16 when she and Philip, separated by war, exchanged photographs to keep their features fresh in each other's memory while they were apart. But her sixteenth birthday was also the occasion of her first official appointment. She was made Colonel-in-Chief of the Grenadier Guards and took the salute at a wartime march-past at Windsor. She looked very much a schoolgirl (though she had never been to school) in her pleated skirt and woollen jacket.

She was seventeen, rising 18, when Philip's cousin, the King of Greece, met her father at a wedding in London and took advantage of the occasion to urge his young relative's suit. Her father brushed the suggestion quickly aside. It was not that he did not like Philip. He did. He considered him a young man of intelligence, with a good sense of humour, who "thinks about things the right way". But his daughter, he felt, was far too young to be thinking of marriage. Besides, she had never met any other young men of her own age and could not possibly know her true feelings.

"Philip had better not think any more about it for the present," he told the Greek king.

But if she was too young for marriage, the Princess was not, it seems, too young to become a Counsellor of State with authority to act for her father in his absence abroad.

Previously, no one under the age of 21 had been appointed a Counsellor of State. But now her father asked Parliament to amend the Regency Act so that she should become one immediately upon her eighteenth birthday. He wanted his daughter, the King said, "to have every opportunity of gaining experience in the duties which would fall upon her in the event of her acceding to the Throne".

Even the formal announcement of her betrothal to Philip, in the July of 1947, was preceded three months earlier by the solemn dedication she made on her twenty-first birthday:

There is a motto which has been borne by many of my ancestors —a noble motto—*I Serve*.

These words were an inspiration to many bygone heirs to the Throne when they made their knightly dedication as they came to manhood. . . .

I should like to make that dedication now. It is very simple.

I declare before you all that my whole life, whether it be long or short, shall be devoted to your service and the service of the great Imperial Commonwealth to which we all belong.

To a young woman of her serious, conscientious nature it was no lightly given pledge. They were not airy-fairy words to be quickly uttered and as quickly forgotten. She meant every word of what she said. The words of dedication may have been strung together for her by her father's private secretary, but they exactly paralleled her own deep feelings, and, reading through a draft of the speech beforehand, she was so stirred by her emotions that she was moved to tears.

In a sense, too, she was to marry twice, for the ceremony of coronation, where a queen is concerned, is surely by way of being a very special marriage service with monarchy as the bridegroom. Indeed, a ring which forms part of the ritualistic ceremony, a sapphire upon which the Cross of St. George is set in rubies, is sometimes referred to as 'the wedding ring of England' and is placed upon the third finger of the right hand, which is the finger on which the wedding ring used to be worn.

Like any other young bride of her generation, the future Queen, when she married Prince Philip, promised to love, honour, and obey him.

But on 2nd June 1953, at the coronation ceremony, it was Philip's turn to promise to obey her. He knelt before her, his hand in hers, to take the ancient oath of fealty:

"I, Philip, Duke of Edinburgh, do become your liege man of life and limb and earthly worship, and faith and truth will I bear unto you, to live and die against all manner of folks. So help me God."

The words are quaintly archaic; perhaps even ambiguous. But the meaning is plain.

The symbol of the first marriage was a wedding ring fashioned from a gift of Welsh gold. The major symbol of the second was the massive, ornately bejewelled Crown of St. Edward.

The crown and the ring ... and over the years since the Queen and her husband have had to learn to live with both; to adjust not only to each other as husband and wife but also to a third partner called monarchy. It has perhaps not always been an easy task.

Theirs was a love story which adhered closely to the concept of a child's fairy tale. A handsome, impecunious young suitor. A beautiful and perhaps lonely princess. Certainly one, as her father said, who had too little companionship of her own age and one whose young life was to spring from girlhood to womanhood, completely bypassing the exciting, carefree teenage era other youngsters know and enjoy. A chance—or perhaps not-so-chance —meeting which, if it did not result in love at first sight, assuredly sowed the seeds of love.

The Queen's father, eight years after that first meeting, was still shaking his head in puzzlement, still saying that he could not believe that Lilibet (as he called her) had really fallen in love with the first eligible young man to come into her life. Yet history is littered with the names of other princesses who have done the same. Indeed, Queen Victoria, when she decided to marry off her daughter, the Princess Royal, to Prince Frederick William of Prussia in the fond, if mistaken, belief that such a match would be the saving of Europe, contrived to engineer it in exactly this fashion. She had the pair of them at Balmoral and provided them with opportunities to be alone together. The prospective bride-groom was 24. The Princess Royal was 14, a susceptible and impressionable age in any girl and perhaps particularly so for an adolescent princess who had had little or no previous contact with the opposite sex. The outcome, as Queen Victoria had judged, was never in doubt. The 14-year-old princess fell hook, line and sinker for the first eligible young man she had really known.

That was in 1855. A little over eighty years later a benign fate— with perhaps just a little human help—was to lay a similarly romantic trap for another young princess. Like that Princess Royal of an earlier generation, Princess Elizabeth, at 13, had had vir-tually no contact with the opposite sex when Philip, noisy, excitable and a bit on the cocky side at 18, sprang athletically into her life.

Time has dimmed the memory of that first long-ago meeting, even for the two people whom it most closely concerned. Others who were present would seem to have confused and sometimes conflicting recollection of how it all came about and what actually happened. But most seem to agree that Philip's Uncle Dickie (better known since as Earl Mountbatten of Burma) had some small hand, however accidental or coincidental, in influencing the course of events.

As the King's equerry, he was with the royal family at Dartmouth the day the two young people first met. One version is that the meeting came about because Philip, on the suggestion of his uncle, was appointed captain's messenger on the occasion of the family visit to the Royal Naval College. Another version is that the Queen (now the Queen Mother) was worried that her small daughters might be bored; she confided in Uncle Dickie who suggested that Philip should be hauled out of chapel and charged with the task of keeping them amused.

There is similar confusion and contradiction about what happened subsequently. Surely one can discount the story that Philip suggested, "Let's go and have some fun jumping over the tennis nets." It simply doesn't stand up. A very small boy might have suggested something of the sort, but hardly an 18-year-old cadet, however brash and excitable. On the other hand, that does not completely negate the possibility that he did actually jump over a tennis net which chanced to be in his way, though Prince Philip himself has said that he does not recall the incident. It is exactly the sort of thing a young man of his extrovert nature and athletic ability might very well have done.

But in all the confusion and contradiction of what happened and how it happened, one thing stands out crystal clear and beyond dispute. For the girl destined to be queen, from the moment of that first meeting, there was never to be any other man in her life.

Of course, as her father pointed out to the King of Greece, she had very few opportunities for meeting eligible young men and perhaps no opportunity at all of meeting any other young man in the right place and at the right time, on the right footing and over a sufficient period of time for romance to develop. For a girl to fall in love, she must first meet the right boy then have opportunity to get to know him and come to like him. In consequence, most girls end up marrying the boy next door or a few doors down the street, a boy at college or youth club, a young man who works in the same factory or office or commutes back and forth on the same bus or train. There are occasional exceptions in the shapely form of the model girl who marries an earl or the show girl who becomes the wife of a millionaire, but this does not invalidate the overall rule.

As with ordinary girls, so with a princess. Perhaps more so. For the young Princess Elizabeth there was never any possibility of meeting someone outside her own circle. Brought up in comparative seclusion, she had few opportunities for meeting young men at all and certainly no opportunity for romantic experiment. Most girls, of course, lived more circumscribed lives in those non-permissive pre-World War II days of a generation ago. But her life was even more circumscribed than most. She never went to school, never went out to work, never went to a youth club or dance hall, never went window-shopping with a girl friend, never went on holiday other than to Sandringham or Balmoral with her family clustered protectively around her. Indeed, she never went out alone at all. Always there was some-one—governess, lady-in-waiting, detective—to keep a watchful eye on her.

Circumscribed by upbringing, she was hemmed in yet more by her high, unique—and lonely—status as heiress presumptive. Young men do not call up a royal princess—or they didn't in those days—to ask for a date. Not that Princess Elizabeth would have accepted if they had. She was a shy girl.

The war which broke out a few short weeks after that eventful visit to Dartmouth rendered the seclusion of her upbringing even more complete. Now she had to be guarded from German bombs and the possibility of German invasion in addition to everything else. Now, quite literally, she became a princess in a tower—in her case, the Lancaster Tower of Windsor Castle—with a company of hand-picked guardsmen to watch over her and her sister. While other girls of her generation, as the war ran its course, were finding the beginnings of a new emancipation at the work-bench and in the services, she was hemmed in more closely than ever. She did meet some young men: fresh-faced young Guards officers who served as partners for the impromptu dances held occasion-ally to brighten the monotony of wartime Windsor. But they, you may be sure, conscious of who she was, were careful to hold her at arms' length as they danced. Not that she minded or even seems to have noticed. By then, the romantic blinkers she had donned would permit her to see no one but Philip.

If it took her father almost eight years to realise that she was really in love with the first eligible young man she had ever met, others would seem to have been aware of it long before that. A bare eighteen months after that first meeting at Dartmouth, Philip's aunt, Princess Nicholas of Greece, was already confiding in friends that her tall, fair-haired young nephew was going to marry the daughter of the King of England.

Philip at this time was still only 19 and the Princess not yet 15. Since that first meeting at Dartmouth they had seen each other hardly at all, though there had been some boy-and-girl letter writing between them since Philip went away to war. How, then, did Princess Nicholas come to get such an idea—and so prophetic-ally accurate an idea—at so early a stage?

Not from Philip himself. Of that we can be sure. He was, then and later, a young man who kept personal things very much to himself.

But if not from Philip, who then? Perhaps from no one par-ticular person. Perhaps it was simply a case of the wish being father to the thought in the buzz of personal chit-chat which surely hummed back and forth between the marriage-linked families of Greek royalty, the Anglo-German Mountbattens and that section of Britain's royal family into which Princess Nicholas' daughter, the late Princess Marina, had married.

But whatever hopes may have risen in whatever breasts, then or later, certain it is that the Queen's marriage to Prince Philip, when it finally came about, was a true love match. There was nothing of an arranged marriage about it. Having married for love themselves, the Queen's parents, would never have dreamed of such a thing. Indeed, it was furthest from their thoughts. Their concern was not so much that their daughter should marry Philip or, indeed, anyone else, as to be quite sure that she knew her own mind in the matter and that Philip was the right man for her.

Such slight parental doubts as there were existed perhaps more in the King's mind than in that of his wife. The late King and the elder daughter who was to succeed him as Queen were always deeply devoted to each other and her devotion to his memory was shown soon after she succeeded to the throne and moved back into Buckingham Palace. The door by which her father had always entered and left the palace was known as the King's Door. It was suggested to her that, for the new reign, it would perhaps be more appropriate to re-name it the Queen's Door. She shook her head, and today it is still the King's Door. The desk at which

the Queen works today is the same desk that her father used.
Two photographs of him watch her from a folding leather frame
on one of the side tables as she tackles the contents of her boxes,
ever-present reminders of those earlier days when she sat at his
side while he went through the boxes and explained the workings
of monarchy to her. Between the two of them, as she grew to
womanhood, developed a depth of understanding which could
find expression in a quick flicker of the eyes, a fleeting exchange of glances. "It was", we have been told, "almost as
though they talked to each other with a silent language of the
eyes."

Like many another father, the late King was reluctant to lose
his daughter to another man. A touching letter he wrote to her
soon after her marriage reveals something of the mixed feelings
he experienced on her wedding day.

He was, he wrote, "so proud of you and thrilled at having
you so close to me on our long walk in Westminster Abbey".
But when he actually gave her hand in marriage he felt that he
had "lost something very precious".

Her leaving he continued, had "left a great blank in our lives".
The letter urged her to remember "that your old home is still
yours" and asked her to "come back to it as often as possible".

The King concluded: "I can see that you are sublimely happy
with Philip, which is right, but don't forget us."

If the King was perhaps reluctant to lose his daughter and
hesitated to give his consent to her betrothal, others were more
encouraging as the long courtship ran its course. Philip's cousin,
the late Princess Marina, acted as something of a fairy godmother
to the young lovers. Her Buckinghamshire country home, a short
drive from Windsor, served at times as a sanctuary where the two
of them could find a greater degree of privacy than was obtainable
elsewhere. Uncle Dickie was also helpful. His home in Chester
Street was always available if Philip wanted to stay the night in
London and later he was to be of no small help in smoothing a
path into public life for the nephew he perhaps looked upon
almost as a son.

The fairy-tale flavour of the love story continued right up to
the wedding and through into the first year or so of marriage.
The hard-up young naval officer was changed back into a prince—
or, at very least, into a Royal Highness (which the King regarded

as the same thing). The Princess was freed from her tower at Windsor by the ending of the war, brought forth from seclusion by her marriage to the prince and wondered at the marvels of the big, everyday world outside the walls of the palace. In a fairy tale it would have ended there—*and so they lived happily ever after.*

But for the Queen and Prince Philip, as for any other couple who fall in love and marry, the act of marriage is not an ending. It is only a beginning. For them, in the years which followed, there was to be sadness as well as happiness, doubts as well as hopes, disappointments as well as achievements.

No one can pretend, of course, that the royal marriage has known the sort of headaches common to less regal marriages. For the Queen and her husband, the pressures which exert strain on other marriages hardly exist and never have. When did Prince Philip have to worry about losing his job? When did the Queen have to empty out the contents of her piggy bank to see if she could afford Andrew's school fees or a new pair of shoes for young Eddy?

Mortgages, rates, heating and laundry bills, what to have for the next meal, getting the car serviced, keeping one's teenage daughter away from that suspect crowd at the local coffee bar . . . such worries, minor and major, have never touched the royal marriage, as Philip himself admitted when discussing the education of his children.

"There are a vast number who cannot afford to educate their children any way they like. We were certainly not limited in this way," he further conceded, "but there were many other considerations."

And just as there have been "many other considerations" to take into account in the education of the royal children, so there have been strains and stresses in the royal marriage peculiar to the unique positions occupied by husband and wife. It can surely have been no easy task to maintain the balance in a marriage in which the wife is so much more important than her husband and the husband, in turn, is perhaps not the type to sink complacently into second place.

Theirs was, and is, a marriage like no other. Other, more ordinary marriages are a straightforward relationship between two people who have to learn to live with and adjust to each other.

3

But in the married life of the Queen and Prince Philip, just as in courtship days, there has always been a silent but demanding third partner named monarchy to take into account.

All along it has made its presence felt. It accounted, in part, for the long wait before they could be formally betrothed. It was there, in a corner, at the wedding itself. In drawing up the guest list for that fairy-tale wedding of 1947 three names were omitted. Prince Philip's three sisters were not invited. They were married to Germans.

Philip's sisters had married during those between-the-wars years when the Greek royal family was living in exile in Paris. That they should have married Germans is hardly surprising. Originally a hotchpotch of smaller states, each with its own royalty, it has long been the European country in which royal bloodlines flow most freely. Queen Victoria knew that. She not only married a German herself, but married off six of her children to Germans.

A quarter of a century later, it perhaps seems rather petty that Prince Philip's sisters were denied invitations to their brother's wedding merely because they were married to Germans. But in those immediate postwar years when Mr. Norman Hartnell, in making the royal wedding dress, was so concerned that even the silk he used should have been spun by non-enemy silkworms, Philip's German connections, through his sisters, were seen by some people in high places as something to be soft-pedalled as much as possible. So the closest his sisters came to the wedding was when Princess Marina flew out to Germany with a batch of wedding photographs for them.

It was the start of the Queen's in-law problems. Hers have not been the same sort of in-law problems which plague some families, but they have been none the less real for all that. Through nearly twenty years of marriage she was obliged to draw a careful, if invisible, line between her personal self as a wife and mother and her official self as heiress presumptive and, later, queen.

In a personal capacity, she could invite her sisters-in-law from Germany to stay with her at Windlesham Moor, Birkhall, Clarence House, Balmoral, Windsor, Sandringham and Buckingham Palace. She could have one of them as godmother to Princess Anne. But she had to diplomatically sidestep any return invitations to visit them in Germany.

During the time when Philip was a naval officer in Malta and the Princess was out there with him as a naval wife, there was talk of spending one leave on a visit to Germany. They planned to travel through Italy and Switzerland. One of the German brothers-in-law, Prince Berthold, was to meet them at the Swiss border and conduct them to Salem. Then, suddenly, it was all off.

By 1953 British enmity towards Germany had dimmed sufficiently for all three sisters with their husbands and children to be officially invited over to their sister-in-law's coronation. They stayed at Buckingham Palace and the Queen arranged a family dinner party to celebrate the reunion. But because she was Queen, now more than ever she could not accept reciprocal invitations to visit them in Germany.

Philip could go. Charles and Anne, as they grew older, could also go. The Queen could send gifts of unwanted clothing to her husband's nephews and nieces in Germany, helping them out as various relatives had once helped him. But she could not go herself. And it was not until twenty years after the end of the war and eighteen years after she married their brother, coincidental with her state visit to Germany in 1965, that she was finally free to visit her sisters-in-law in their own homes for the first time.

The tragic death of her father and her own accession to the throne brought other problems to be resolved and other difficulties to be overcome in the delicate, three-cornered relationship involving wife, husband and monarchy. It was perhaps the husband for whom the problems were greatest and who was called upon to make the biggest sacrifices.

The Queen's father had foreseen that it might well be so.

The late King was talking to an acquaintance at the royal garden party which followed his daughter's betrothal. Something was said in jest about Philip having broad shoulders.

To this, the King replied that he was almost certainly going to need them.

"I'm not sure he knows what he's taking on," said the King. "To be a consort is much harder than to be a sovereign. I sometimes think it must be the hardest job in the world."

Philip was to find it by no means easy. As recently as 1969, commenting upon his roles as the Queen's husband, he said,

"There are a lot of problems and difficulties. Inevitably, it is an awkward situation to be in."

But the difficulties and problems were perhaps greater in the early days of marriage and monarchy. Philip's first big sacrifice came even before his wife succeeded to the throne. With her father's health failing, she was required to do much that he would otherwise have done in addition to all her own duties as heiress presumptive. She was still very young, relatively inexperienced for all her long apprenticeship, still shy and rather nervous for all her experience. She needed the help and support of her husband. But to give her that help and support meant that Philip had to sacrifice his own naval career and sea-going ambitions. Philip loves the sea. From boyhood he was drawn to it by both heritage and personal inclination. His heritage went back through Uncle Dickie, the naval officer who became like an adoptive father to him, to the shadowy dead figure of his Battenberg grandfather, Prince Louis, the German prince who became Britain's First Sea Lord. If the sea can be truly said to be in any man's blood, it was—and is—in Prince Philip's.

So the choice which confronted him must have been an agonising one. Either he could continue with his naval career while his young wife struggled through the most difficult phase of her life alone and unaided, or he must set his own dreams and ambitions firmly aside to support and sustain her. For a man of Prince Philip's sensibility there was perhaps not really a choice. But the sacrifice he made was no less meaningful on that account.

Initially, perhaps, he may have nurtured a lingering half-hope that he might yet be able to resume his naval career at some future date. But the King's health was to get worse, not better, and the break was to be permanent, not temporary. Any faint hope Philip may have had that he might yet return to the sea in a professional capacity was to die finally with the death of his wife's father.

Nor was his career the only thing he was called upon to sacrifice in those early days. There was to be another big sacrifice less tangible, but perhaps no less important to a man of Philip's pride.

Two months after her accession to the throne the Queen issued an Order in Council. In it she declared it to be her "Will and Pleasure that I and my children shall be styled and known as the

House and Family of Windsor and that my descendants, other than female descendants who marry and their descendants, shall bear the name of Windsor."

On the face of it, it seemed that the Queen was relinquishing her married name of Mountbatten and reverting to her maiden name of Windsor.

But was she?

In his book *Elizabeth and Philip*, published in 1947 to mark the royal couple's betrothal, Louis Wulff, the former Court correspondent, wrote that "marriage does not change Princess Elizabeth's surname". Similarly, Helen Cathcart, in her more recently published book on *The Married Life of the Queen*, takes the view that "the Princess [Elizabeth] specially retained her maiden surname of Windsor".

Not everyone agrees. The privately published work, *The Mountbatten Lineage*, which traces the history of Prince Philip's Mountbatten ancestors back through some forty generations, takes the contrary view: "Princess Elizabeth legally took her husband's name, Mountbatten, on marriage, for there was no legal provision for any female, not even an heir presumptive to the throne, to retain her maiden name on marriage."

An article by the late Edward F. Iwi in the 1965 edition of *Debrett* supports this view. In Mr. Iwi's opinion, "At the time of her marriage, Princess Elizabeth, in accordance with the custom followed by all the subjects of King George VI, took her husband's name of Mountbatten."

If so, then, as Mr. Iwi also stated, she succeeded to the Throne as "the last Sovereign of the House of Windsor and the first of the Family of Mountbatten". *The Mountbatten Lineage* concurs: "she succeeded to the throne as a Mountbatten".

In an attempt to resolve the riddle, we put the point to Buckingham Palace. The Queen's press secretary referred us to the Home Office. The Home Office, after pondering the point for four weeks, wrote back: "As a Princess of the Royal Blood there was no occasion for the Queen to use a surname either before or after Her Marriage and the question is academic. In the circumstances, the Secretary of State regrets that he is not in a position to give an authoritative opinion upon the views which you have quoted."

As a reply, it seemed to be avoiding the issue. Academic it

may be, but it is surely a point of historic interest to know whether the Queen came to the throne as a Mountbatten, a Windsor or both. And to say that the Queen does not 'use' a surname is not the same as saying that she does not have one. She had and 'used' a surname at the time of her marriage.

She was married, according to the Westminster Abbey marriage register, in the name of Elizabeth Alexandra Mary Windsor and her father's name was similarly given as Albert Frederick Arthur George Windsor, just as he before her used a surname on marriage and his father's name, on that occasion, was given as George Frederick Ernest Albert Windsor.

It was George Frederick Ernest Albert (King George V) who first decided that the family should have a proper surname like everyone else. He was born without a surname, as was his father before him. At least, if he had one, no one was quite sure what it was. Various surnames—Guelph, Wettin, D'Este—were attributed at various times times to the House of Saxe-Coburg and Gotha into which Queen Victoria had married, but no one knew which, if any, was correct.

King George V—"a very ordinary fellow", as he once termed himself—found this all very unsatisfactory and when, during the First World War, he relinquished the German house name handed down from Prince Albert, he took instead the name of Windsor both as an English house name and as a family surname.

It was in this name that the Queen was married. But did she then become a Mountbatten on marriage? *The Mountbatten Lineage* and the late Mr. Iwi seem to think she did; Louis Wulff and Helen Cathcart would seem to think that she did not. The Home Office sits on the fence.

The Queen herself, if one can form a judgement from the wording of her Order in Council, apparently thought she had become a Mountbatten. Otherwise why refer to "I and my children" when "my children" alone would seem to have been sufficient?

As the article in *Debrett* points out: "She did not expressly renounce the name of Mountbatten, but by implication did so."

And as *The Mountbatten Lineage* regretfully records: "So the House of Mountbatten only reigned for two months from 8th February to 9th April 1952."

What caused the Queen to make the change? It has been said that she did so on the "formal and insistent" advice of Winston Churchill, who was at that time her Prime Minister. It has also been said that she saw the continuance of the name of Windsor as another link with the dead father to whom she was so devoted. The truth is perhaps a bit of both.

There is no way of knowing what Prince Philip thought or how he felt. Outspoken as he has been in so many other directions, this is a subject on which he has never broken silence. It could hardly be otherwise, of course, and one is left to guess at his feelings on the basis of ordinary human judgements.

Rather like a man who marries a star actress, Philip thus found himself in the position of being married to a wife who preferred to use her maiden name for professional purposes, with the additional anomaly that even his children no longer bore his name. However, two other anomalies in his "awkward situation" as the Queen's husband were shortly to be ironed out in his favour.

In the October of her accession year the Queen issued a royal warrant ensuring that her husband "shall henceforth upon all occasions and in all meetings except where otherwise provided by Act of Parliament, have, hold and enjoy Place, Pre-eminence and Precedence next to Her Majesty". Thus Philip became the first gentleman of the realm.

The following year, in the interval between her coronation and leaving Britain on her 50,000 miles round-the-world tour, she also had the Regency Act amended so that her husband instead of her sister, Princess Margaret, would have responsibility for acting as regent to her son and heir in the event that he should succeed her on the throne ahead of his eighteenth birthday.

As the Home Secretary of the day, Sir David Maxwell Fyfe, explained to Parliament: "I cannot imagine anyone thinking that it could be right that, in the event of his child succeeding to the Throne, the Duke of Edinburgh should not be the guardian of the Sovereign.

"As soon as it is thought right that he should be guardian, we are faced with the position of the sovereign during the important and formative years before he assumes royal power. Only from the Regent will he receive practical instruction in the relative

problems he will have to face. . . . The interests of the prospective
Sovereign surely make a combination of regency, guardianship
and paternal influence, in the same hand, the most desirable
course."

It was, as events have turned out, no more than an academic
exercise. Yet it was surely, at the time, a source of paternal satisfaction to Philip that, should the necessity arise, he would at
least be guardian and regent to the small son who did not bear
his name.

But not for more than another six years was the anomaly that
his children did not bear his name to be resolved, and then only
in part.

It was perhaps the words of a provincial bishop which finally
caused the Queen to implement something she had been thinking
about for some time. She was at that time pregnant with her
third child, Prince Andrew, and in a sermon delivered just
before the Christmas of 1959, Dr. Thomas Bloomer, Bishop of
Carlisle, made pointed reference to the name the baby would
bear.

Taking as his theme, "Family Life", Dr. Bloomer said that
the royal baby would be in the unusual position of being born
not with the father's family name of Mountbatten but with the
mother's family name of Windsor and it did not seem right that
a child born in wedlock should be deprived of its father's name—
a right and privilege enjoyed by every other legitimate child in
the land.

"We in this country," he continued, "are accustomed to have
respect for titles, but a family name transcends these and stirs
deeper and more powerful emotions in the family circle."

The Royal Family, he added, set a noble example of family
life and he hoped that the Queen would make it her will and
pleasure to secure the same birthright for the royal baby that
other children enjoyed.

The Queen, in fact, had long wished to associate her husband's
name more closely with her own in family life. "Her Majesty
has had this in mind for a long time and it is close to her heart,"
a royal spokesman was to say later. So the Bishop's words struck
a responsive chord. But the problem was, equally, that she wished
also to continue the name of the Royal House established by her
grandfather.

She talked things over with Philip, with his uncle, Earl Mountbatten of Burma, and with the then Prime Minister, Harold Macmillan. From these talks a compromise solution emerged which met the Queen's wishes in both directions, and on 8th February 1960—just eleven days, as it turned out, before the birth of the new baby—the Queen issued another declaration in Council. In it, after making reference to the previous change of name, she went on:

"I have given further consideration to those of my descendants who will enjoy neither the style, title nor attribute of Royal Highness, nor the titular dignity of Prince, and for whom therefore a surname will be necessary:

"Now therefore I declare My Will and Pleasure, that, while I and my children, shall continue to be styled and known as the House and Family of Windsor, my descendants other than descendants enjoying the style, title or attribute of Royal Highness and the titular dignity of Prince and Princess and female descendants who marry and their descendants shall bear the name of Mountbatten-Windsor."

Purists have argued since as to the exact meaning of this cumbersomely worded and perhaps ambiguous declaration. One authority has taken the view that "the surname of the Prince of Wales' grandchildren (in the male line) will be Windsor, while that of Prince Andrew's grandchildren will be Mountbatten-Windsor". Another, on the contrary, has stated that "if for any reason Prince Charles were at any time to renounce his royal style and all his titles, he would then be known as Charles Mountbatten-Windsor".

The argument will doubtless continue until some Home Secretary of the future finally resolves it in the House of Commons, just as an earlier one, in 1936, settled the legal debate as to whether or not the Queen should share the throne with her sister. Even the simplest wishes of husband and wife, it seems, when they are queen and consort, can lead to complication and argument.

So while the married life of the Queen and Prince Philip may not have known the niggling money worries and depressing day-to-day problems of less regal families, it has been subject to strains and stresses of its own. Monarchy, the third silent partner, in their marriage, has from time to time created its own unique problems, and these have perhaps had their impact. For being queen and consort does not mean that royal husband and wife are not also human beings who, like any other human being, can sometimes feel disappointment, have hurt feelings, suffer from frustration and experience all those other emotions to which humanity is heir.

Like any other marriage, the royal marriage has doubtless had its ups and downs. The wind cannot have blown fair all the time and the sailing cannot always have been smooth. There has perhaps sometimes been rough weather, if not rocks ahead, along the way.

This was perhaps particularly so in those days when the wife first succeeded to the throne and the husband found himself in what must surely have been a frustrating and unenviable situation for a man of his outlook and temperament. It was the sort of situation very few men find themselves in on marriage, though it is common enough among women. They marry, give up their own worthwhile careers in order to make homes for their husbands and then find they are trapped between the food cooking in the oven and the baby's nappies piled up in the kitchen sink. Sometimes frustration sets in, and, while most marriages somehow survive it, some founder on it.

Prince Philip's situation was not all that dissimilar. The Queen, for a time, was almost totally immersed in her new role as monarch. But if she had too much to do, he had too little. He had sacrificed the career closest to his heart and had not yet established another. He was trapped, if not between the cooker and the sink, between tree plantings and foundation stones, neither of which can have been very meaningful to a man who once issued commands from the bridge of his own ship.

It was to be some time before the sometimes conflicting demands of the crown and the ring, of monarchy and marriage, were to be fully reconciled; before the Queen's absorption, in her regal heritage was to become less than total; before Prince Philip was to succeed in turning his nebulous role as the Queen's husband into the 'exacting task' Dr. Kurt Hahn, his headmaster in schooldays, had foreseen as essential to bring out the best in him. In the meantime, there was to be all the gossip and headlines of a supposed 'royal rift' between husband and wife.

If Philip was annoyed, the Queen was deeply upset at some of the things which were printed about them at that time. Yet perhaps those newspaper stories in 1957, wide of the mark and hurtful though they were, served a purpose, as did those much-publicised criticisms of the royal set-up which were to follow soon after. From then on, in public life, there were to be many changes along lines Philip had consistently advocated.

In their personal life, the Queen has always looked to her husband as the head of the family. To the children it has always been, "Ask Papa. He'll know." To relatives and friends, "I'll ask Philip. He'll know." And now, at this time, it was as though she was listening to him more and more also in matters of monarchy. Theoretically, of course, Prince Philip can have no say in such things. But common sense suggests that conversation between royal husband and wife, over the meal table or when they are alone together of an evening, is not entirely limited to such things as the length of Anne's skirts or how Andrew is getting along at school. And from 1957 on there was, clearly, a subtle readjustment in the relationship between royal husband and wife and a slight, but significant, change in course for queen and consort which has continued to the present day.

For the Queen and her husband, their years of marriage have been by no means uneventful. Indeed, because they are who they are, the passing years have perhaps been more eventful than for most of us. They have been years of much laughter and happiness, yet perhaps not without the occasional difference. Years touched by deep sadness and high emotion—as when the Queen's father died so tragically and she succeeded so dramatically to the throne. They have been years of bringing up a family, with all the joy and problems that that involves. And joy and problems alike are perhaps not yet over. They have been years of change, as there must be in all marriages.

That 21-year-old girl who was married in Westminster Abbey in 1947 is now a woman in her forties, a mother four times over, a monarch instead of a princess. Prince Philip too is similarly middle-aged. Two of their children are now older than he was when he first met the girl he was destined to marry. His naval career has long been a thing of the past. The naval officer of the immediate postwar years has turned into an extremely professional, and sometimes very outspoken, prince. But one thing assuredly has not changed. Their marriage, as they near the land-mark of their silver wedding anniversary, is as firmly rooted in love, affection, understanding and respect, one for the other, as ever it was.

2

Family Life

I   Husband and Wife

It is any day in any week between 6th February 1972, when Her Most Excellent Majesty Queen Elizabeth II celebrated her first twenty years as monarch, and 20th November, silver wedding anniversary of the wife whose name is Elizabeth Alexandra Mary Windsor. They are—the monarch who sits on the world's most stable throne and the wife who does not bear her husband's name—one and the same person.

It is not a day of high ceremony—such as that June day set aside for the ceremony of Trooping the Colour when the Queen rides on horseback at the head of her Guards, or that November day when she climbs into a coach which once belonged to her great-great-grandmother and sets out to perform the State Opening of Parliament. On the contrary, for wife and queen alike, it is just an ordinary, average day which begins with boiled eggs for breakfast in the royal dining room on the first floor of Buckingham Palace.

From the garden outside, where a kilted Scot paces back and forth as the Queen and her husband eat, comes the drone of bagpipes. Breakfast to the sound of bagpipes is a royal tradition handed down, like the coach in which the Queen rides to open Parliament, from the days of her great-great-grandmother. Inside the royal dining room there is a rustle of newspapers as husband

and wife skim through the day's news . . . and perhaps a sharp bark of annoyance from Prince Philip at something in one of them which is not entirely to his liking.

Breakfast over, the Queen, her corgis scampering ahead of her, walks briskly through to the comfortably cluttered sitting room which also doubles as her study. The corgis, after a brief sniff at the drinking bowl just inside the door, settle down and doze off. The Queen seats herself at the desk which is set at an angle to the bay window overlooking the garden. In a simple woollen or silk dress, with a triple string of pearls at her throat, she looks not so much a queen as a top female business executive.

For the next three hours she works steadily away, dealing with her correspondence, seeing her three private secretaries in turn, perhaps planning a trip to some of the remaining outposts of her dwindling Empire, and certainly coping with the contents of the leather-bound despatch boxes which have reached Britain's monarchs on a production-line basis for generations past. A glance at the diminutive face of her gold and platinum wrist-watch tells her it is time to move on. She freshens her lipstick and goes along to the high-ceilinged blue-and-white audience room at the end of the corridor where a new ambassador waits to present his credentials and other high-ups—a judge, a field-marshal and an archbishop among them—are to be received in audience.

Lunch follows, with Princess Anne for company. Prince Charles is away in the navy. Prince Philip is hedge-hopping by helicopter from one witty speech to the next, and the Queen may have reflected briefly that it is something for her husband even to be in the country.

After lunch comes a light spatter of engagements in one of the London boroughs . . . the inevitable hand-shaking, the inevitable speeches, the inevitable platitudes. The Queen collects yet another bouquet of flowers, perhaps an illuminated address, perhaps another jewelled brooch to add to the collection she already has. She is offered a glass of sherry, but says she would prefer a cup of tea. She takes it with milk but no sugar.

Then it is back to the palace in her Rolls-Royce with its St. George-and-dragon silver mascot. It is five o'clock, time for her to discard her unseen crown and revert to the less regal role of wife and mother. Edward, the youngest of her four children, comes down from the upstairs nursery and mother and son feed the dogs, nibble sandwiches, watch television together. Princess Anne returns from visiting a children's home and conversation, as so often when mother and daughter are together, turns to horses. Prince Philip comes in soon after, striding so briskly along the palace corridors he appears to be on the point of breaking into a run. He teases Anne about a new Marks and Spencer sweater she is wearing, but Anne, long-legged and volatile, can give as good as she gets. Philip and Edward go off together for a dip in the palace pool.

That evening, with Edward back in the upstairs nursery and Anne off to the theatre with a party of friends, husband and wife dine quietly together, serving themselves from silver dishes kept warm on the sideboard hotplate. Dinner over, they adjourn to the adjoining sitting room. The Queen glances briefly at her desk. A couple of official papers have been left for her to sign. She picks up her pen and executes a flourishing 'Elizabeth R' on each.

She crosses to the settee flanking the fireplace, nudges her shoes off and sits with her feet up. Philip perches himself on a footstool and talks animatedly of some incident that has happened during the day. The Queen caps it with a witty account of her own experiences that afternoon, mimicking an accent, chuckling with laughter. She picks up a newspaper and turns to the crossword. A word stumps her and she appeals to her husband. His flippant answer draws more laughter from the two of them.

Later the television set is switched on. Two well-known comedians are doing a skit on royalty. Royal wife and husband *ad lib.* their own jokes, talking over the top of the television. But the news which follows proves rather less amusing to them. A Member of Parliament has been criticising the monarchy. The Queen's face freezes and Philip gives vent to his favourite epithet. To both of them a joke about royalty is one thing, but criticism of the monarchy quite another.

All this, of course, is an imaginary picture of an imaginary day in the life of the Queen and her husband. But it comes very close to reality.

The difficulty in writing about the Queen and Prince Philip as husband and wife, as distinct from monarch and consort, is that very few people have seen them as such and those who have are not the sort to run round talking about it. No one has ever interviewed the Queen on her role as monarch, much less on her attitude as a wife. Prince Philip has been interviewed from time to time, but only on non-personal topics, though he has let slip the occasional unguarded remark about his role as husband and father: "I miss being able to walk in to a cinema, club or pub", "Now we are getting into middle age", "There are a lot of problems and difficulties". So any portrait of royal husband and wife inevitably has to be constructed rather like a jigsaw, carefully fitting together a lot of small pieces. Let us look at the sort of picture which emerges.

Today, the Queen and her husband are a long way removed from the shy young princess and dashing young naval officer who were married in Westminster Abbey a quarter of a century ago. In the years since they first met and loved, courted and married, a whole new generation has been born and grown up. Indeed, some who were not even born on that November day in 1947 when royal husband and wife were married, are now married themselves and may even have small children of their own into the bargain. Many of the Queen and Prince Philip's generation are now grandparents even if the royal couple themselves have not yet achieved that venerable status. But, counting the years, they are old enough to be grandparents. They are middle-aged, but a middle-aged couple who have contrived to remain young with their children. Neither marriage nor monarchy has made either of them old before their time.

Philip, his fiftieth birthday behind him—he was born on 10th June 1921—has long worn prescription glasses and has long given up trying to do anything about his thinning thatch. Equally, it is a long time since he played his last energetic game of squash, and the passage of the years has seen his polo go the same way through a recurring inflammation of the right wrist. The Queen, nearly five years younger—she was born on 21st April 1926— is yet able to put in a hard day's stalking on the heathery hills around Balmoral.

Married (at the time this book is published) for close on twenty-five years, monarch for twenty of those twenty-five years, the mother of four children, three sons and a daughter, born over a span of fifteen years, the Queen has not only contrived to remain young in heart but also younger-looking than her actual age. Her complexion is still good, her carriage briskly upright, her movements crisp; she walks with a swing and her statistics

Princess Elizabeth as Aladdin in the Windsor pantomime of 1943

(*above*) Lieutenant Philip Mountbatten giving a talk on current affairs at the Petty Officers' Training Centre, Corsham, while awaiting formal consent to his betrothal to Princess Elizabeth. (*left*) The first engagement picture

are better than her clothes would suggest. On the rare occasion when her clothes have done justice to her figure, the resulting photograph has gone round the world.

The longer look in feminine fashion which supplanted the mini (except among the very young and the very frivolous) in the autumn of 1970 suited the Queen remarkably well. While she never actually wore a mini, she did comply with the dictates of feminine fashion to the extent of shortening her skirts. That autumn, with fashion going into reverse and midis and maxis taking over, she was able to lengthen them again. The yellow silk coat she had first worn for her eldest son's investiture as Prince of Wales some eighteen months earlier, for instance, was brought out of storage and lengthened to the extent of having a band of matching embroidery tacked along the hem. The result was a style of her own which somehow contrived to make her look almost as young as she did in the so-called 'New Look' of a generation ago. She looked particularly youthful-looking, wearing black, at the Cenotaph on Remembrance Day. Black, though she seldom wears it, is a colour that seems to suit her, emphasising both her slimness and her complexion.

She is slimmer today than she was in her twenties, thanks to the smallness of her appetite. She is, and has long been, a small eater who prefers such protein-rich foods as fish, meat, eggs and cheese to potatoes and pastry, stodgy puddings, and fattening pies. Her height is 5 feet 4 inches, but she looks smaller, almost tiny, when she kicks off her shoes to sit with her feet up or run upstairs in stockinged feet at Balmoral after a long, hard tramp across the moors. In middle age, she remains attractively feminine, with hair which is naturally wavy, blue eyes which at times seem to hold just a hint of green, long eyelashes, slender feet and small, dainty hands. Her years with Philip have made her a lot less shy and tongue-tied in public than she was once, though no one could conceivably term her an extrovert. Even today, her public appearances as monarch seldom do justice to her as a woman. In public, because of the mainly serious nature of public occasions, she is often serious and unsmiling. In private, the reality can be different and the film *Royal Family* gave a few briefly tantalising glimpses of the woman behind the queen. As one U.S. columnist put it, the film revealed "a queen far merrier, prettier and cosier than we had imagined".

4

Yet the film still could not and did not show the real woman with her high-pitched, slightly girlish giggle when amused, her quick scream of distress if the royal corgis chance to knock over a vase of flowers. Only among family and friends is the real woman briefly revealed—the racing enthusiast hopping eagerly from foot to foot in the excitement of a close-fought finish; the dog-lover with the piercing whistle which brings her pets obediently to heel; the outdoor woman returning peat-streaked and bruised after a day's stalking; the comedienne with a mock-Cockney accent she has mimicked so often she sometimes does it without being aware of the fact; the chatterbox who, in the privacy of her home movie theatre at the palace, cannot resist predicting aloud what she thinks is going to happen next. Her father, in the middle of a tender love scene, was sometimes known to utter an impatient, "Get on with it, man," to the hero on the screen. The Queen may not go that far, but a good comedy will draw peals of laughter from her and she has even been known to let go a scream in a moment of screen suspense.

In most things, she is perhaps not an emotional woman and certainly does not permit her emotions to show in public. Yet the mystique of monarchy has emotional undertones for her. The Divine Right of Kings may be a thing of the past, but to her, her own relationship to the Crown has a sort of divinity about it, and moments of monarchical emotion have been known to move her to tears. As we have told, she cried when she read the declaration of dedication she was to make on her twenty-first birthday. There were tears in her eyes too when she drove through the streets of London to Westminster Abbey on the day of her coronation.

She believes in religion, monarchy, the ties of family—not necessarily in that order. By contrast, she is more than a trifle superstitious. Spilled salt must be tossed over the shoulder, crossed knives quickly uncrossed, clinking glasses as quickly separated, candles all lit from a single taper and thirteen people must not sit down together at the table. If mischance should result in a table total of thirteen she will increase the number by inviting Charles, Anne or an equerry to join the party or, if that is not possible, split the gathering between two tables pushed so closely together they appear as one.

Philip is more hard-headed and less emotional, an essentially

practical man. Save for his balding head, he—like the Queen—
has contrived to remain active and youthful-looking into his
middle years. His baldness is something he has long since learned
to live with. It has been going on now for more than twenty
years. Years ago, when it first became noticeable, a U.S. expert
on hair treatment sent him a bottle of so-called hair restorer.
It was promptly returned with a polite note that there was "no
cause for worry" as to the state of the royal hairline. In fact,
Philip at that time already had a lotion supplied by his own
hairdresser, but, either because he regarded it as 'cissy' or because
of his generally impatient attitude towards such things as clothes
and looks, quickly stopped using it with any degree of regularity.

But balding hair has not been accompanied by a spreading
midriff. At fifty, he is still a tall (5 feet 11½ inches), slim-hipped,
long-bodied man of quick, restless movements. He hardly ever
relaxes. Even at home, in the palace, he moves about, it is said,
"as though always on the point of breaking into a run". If he
no longer plays squash or pounds around the royal gardens
cocooned in sweaters, he yet retains the virile, fresh-scrubbed
look of an athlete straight from the shower. He is still a head-
turner where women are concerned, teenage dolly-birds and
middle-aged mums alike. Yet he remains what he has always
been, basically a man's man, most in his element amidst the sweat
and lather of a polo game, the gadgetry of the flight deck and the
uninhibited quarter-deck language of an all-male get-together.
He has penetrating blue eyes, a sharp brain and a tight, no-
nonsense mouth which can quickly give way to temper. Ruggedly
athletic though he always appears to be, there is also an inner
sensitivity, a touch of the artist. His stubby fingers have turned
out more than one oil painting in their time. If he poses no
threat to Annigoni, one at least of his works—a still life of
flowers in a vase—was judged good enough by his wife to adorn
their private sitting room at Windsor. And stored away somewhere in the royal closets is an intricate scale-model of Balmoral
Castle, complete to miniature knobs on the doors and a miniature
flagpole on the roof, which not only reveals artistry but suggests a
reserve of patience few would imagine he possesses.

Like many another married couple, the Queen and her husband
have widely different personalities. But the differences between
them are also complementary and this has been as beneficial to

their marriage as to their monarchical relationship as queen and consort. If the Queen is reserved, then Philip is out-going and over the years his more breezy, extrovert personality has often served to bridge the gap between a sometimes uncommunicative Queen and her awe-struck subjects. His aptitude for instant wit has helped equally. On more than one occasion when she has seemed more serious than the situation warranted, he has murmured to her, "Cheer up, sweetie—give them a smile," or something of that order and the remark itself has brought a smile to her face.

If the Queen in public is usually serious and formal, Philip can be and often is disarmingly informal. But at times and places of his choosing. No one would suspect him of possessing nerves, but they are there, beneath the surface and quickly apparent if he does not feel totally in command of the situation. Such was the occasion of a B.B.C. interview called "Let's Find Out". Philip's hands, it was noticed, literally shook with nerves.

By the same token, if Philip is an impatient, restless man who begins to fidget if even a haircut seems to be taking too long, the Queen is calmer and more relaxed. If he is quick tempered, she is slow to anger. Indeed, in public no one has ever seen her angry. Philip's outbursts, by contrast, are a matter of public record, magnified perhaps but not all that much. Less able than she is to control himself in public, it would be surprising if emotions running so close to the surface were switched off as though by some unseen electronic eye the minute he walked into his palace home. Ordinary human judgements suggest that they are not. More sensitive to criticism than he would perhaps care to admit, he can be quickly roused to anger by adverse newspaper comment, of which there has been no shortage over the years, giving vent to his anger in both blunt language and loud slaps on the surface of the desk or table at which he happens to be sitting.

Philip has always disliked the publicity which is an inevitable accompaniment to his role of royal consort and has sometimes jibbed against it, telling broadcasters to "stuff" their microphones or journalists to "muck off". And just as his extrovert wit has often spurred the Queen into a public smile, so has her more phlegmatic, does-it-really-matter attitude sometimes had a calming effect upon his more volcanic temperament. In fairness to Prince Philip, it should be added that his occasional displays of temperament have sometimes, though not always, been precipitated by what he considers unreasonable and excessive demands made upon his wife in her role as Queen.

The Queen may not see such demands as unreasonable or excessive. She is, as was seen in Canada when she was pregnant with Prince Andrew, prepared to undergo a great deal in the cause of what she conceives to be her duty. But Philip, like most really masculine men, is an essentially protective husband, resentful if he thinks that too much is required of his wife, inclined to fuss and worry if she is not 100 per cent fit (though he does not fuss or worry about his own health).

Equally, the Queen worries about him; quick to call a doctor on the rare occasion that her husband has been unwell, quickly turning pale if he takes a toss at polo, quickly restless if he is later home than expected. She has, of course, long come to terms with the lateness and uncertainty of his return which is a necessary part of the busy public role he has created for himself, but lateness in their leisure life—if he is out shooting or sailing, for instance—can and does worry her.

She is a person who is happiest if life is smooth, ordered, methodical. She was always like that, even as a child. Clothes had to be neatly folded and shoes lined up precisely before she tumbled into bed at night. Christmas and birthday gifts, as soon as they were opened, had to be compiled into lists ready for letters of thanks to be written and sent. Even the coffee crystals for which she developed a child-like addiction had to be sorted into little heaps, according to size, before being eaten. Today she is still the same. Meals on the dot; a place for everything and everything in its place. Her desk may look cluttered and untidy to the casual eye, but she herself knows where everything is. On her dressing table, the separate items of the silver gilt dressing set which was one of her wedding gifts are laid out with the precision of soldiers on parade. On her travels, the same order has to be maintained; hair brushes to the right, clothes brushes to the left on the dressing table; pencils to the right, scribbling pad to the left on her desk. On tour, too, she prefers to stick to the planned schedule so that everything ticks over with clockwork efficiency and her husband's occasional tendency to depart from the prescribed schedule if anything particularly interesting, unusual or offbeat happens along tends to dismay her. "He really is the limit," she remarked on one occasion in a tone of wifely resignation when things were held up because Philip broke away from the main party to chat with someone who had piqued his interest.

In all this, she is her father's daughter. He was a punctual, methodical, meticulous man. The Queen is the same. Her mother is the opposite, a woman with a complete disregard for time. Half an hour, this way or that, is nothing in the life of the Queen Mother. So if mother is coming to dinner and the meal is fixed for, say, eight-thirty, the Queen will send her word that it is at eight o'clock. In that way, she can be reasonably sure that her own keen sense of punctuality will not be disturbed.

Just as royal husband and wife are almost diametrically opposed in personality, so are their interests. Philip does not share his wife's enthusiasm for racing; she does not share his interest in sailing. Outside the monarchy and her own family, the Queen has only one real interest in life—horses. She breeds them, races them, rides them. On the subject of thoroughbreds, she is, according to a former royal trainer, a positive expert who can recite the pedigree of every horse she has ever owned—and most other leading racehorses, into the bargain—"backwards, forwards or upside down". It is perhaps the one subject on which she is never at a loss for words. On the racetrack, watching a close-fought finish, she becomes alive and eager as perhaps at no other time, springing to her feet, pounding the rail in front of her with a white-gloved hand. Even to watch a race on television is sometimes sufficient to wrench an exclamation of delight or dismay from her. Philip, by contrast, finds racing boring. He is a doer rather than a watcher. About the only time he consents to put in an appearance at a racetrack is during the week of Royal Ascot, an obligatory concession to his role as consort. Even then, it has not been unknown for him to forego watching the actual racing in favour of cricket on the television screen at the back of the royal box or to duck the last race in order to play polo.

Horses apart, the Queen, like her father before her, has no real hobbies. Interests perhaps, but not hobbies. She does not paint or knit or tackle the intricate embroidery her grandmother, Queen Mary, did so well. Tennis, swimming . . . these things do not appeal to her though she is a superb horsewoman and, what is not so generally known, a first-class shot. She loves walking—*real* walking—and at Sandringham and Balmoral is quick to slip into raincoat, head-scarf and a pair of stout walking shoes and set off for a brisk tramp across the moors which some-times takes her for miles. Philip, by contrast, prefers his walking to have point and purpose to it, as signified by a gun in his hand or his Hasselblad camera slung around his neck. The Queen dotes on her dogs—Heather, Buzz, Tiny and Brush—and is something of a crossword puzzle addict who thinks nothing of tackling two puzzles a day. But those are hardly hobbies. Even the amateur movies she takes on her world-wide travels are the result these days more of habit than of real enthusiasm. Having taken them, she sometimes does not always get round to showing them.

Prince Philip, on the other hand, is a man of many hobbies, a man with an inquiring mind and a quick interest in anything and everything. Middle age may have somewhat curtailed his prowess as an athlete, but he can look back on years of successful endeavour in almost every conceivable type of sport. Yet it would be a major mistake to picture him as all-brawn. Behind the ruggedly athletic exterior lurks a man of many parts: designer, inventor, artist, photographer, naturalist. Just as he once built a detailed scale model of Balmoral, so he designed the fountain which stands in the rose garden at Windsor and even the layout for the garden itself, planning it with the aid of pieces of foam rubber stuck on a wooden base. His 'inventions' have included a new type of boot scraper and the quick-release breeches he wears for polo. The swivel-mounted electric kettle with which the Queen makes her morning pot of tea was another of his ideas. He has tried his hand at oil painting and is a sufficiently expert photographer for some of his work to have been published in book form. Bird and wild-life photography continues to rank high among his hobbies, and these days, it is said, he is more often out with camera and binoculars than with gun and dog.

At Sandringham, certainly, he frequently goes off with his camera entirely on his own, a lonely figure against the wide background of sky and marsh, perhaps finding the silence and solitude a welcome antidote to the hustle and bustle of his workaday life, sometimes unrecognised by those who encounter him. There was such an occasion on nearby Snettisham marshes when Philip, out with his camera, came across a look-out who had been posted to keep stray passers-by from walking into an area in which wildfowl were being netted and ringed for future observation. The man did not recognise him and Philip, without revealing his identity, obligingly changed his line of walk to avoid the netting.

"Who was it?" the look-out was asked later when here joined the others of the netting party. He shook his head. "Looked like a worn-out Duke of Edinburgh to me," he said, joking. Then his grin faded and a look of embarrassment took its place. He had just realised that it was indeed the Duke of Edinburgh he had advised to "steer clear, mate" or something similar.

Though they are different in so many ways, there are other ways in which royal husband and wife are closely alike, including perhaps those things that matter most in family life. Both believe firmly in the family as a unit and the unity of the family, and while their workaday life may often take them in different directions, at weekends and on holiday there is nothing they enjoy so much as doing things together, with the children, as a family.

Yet clearly they are not a couple who find it necessary to live in each other's pockets. During the working part of the royal week, they each have their own different, but complementary, jobs to keep them busy and occupied. Indeed, the bustling, almost frenetic, round of public offices and engagements Prince Philip has built up for himself over the years frequently takes him away from home for days at a stretch; sometimes out of the country. "Prince Philip Visits Britain" one newspaper headlined his return home after one particularly hectic spate of flying visits to foreign parts. For a man of Philip's restless, impatient nature, such travels serve perhaps as a necessary safety valve. And the Queen surely knows and understands this, even if she did once remark to Prince Charles, in answer to a query as to whether his father would be in for lunch: "If he takes on much more, he soon won't be in for breakfast."

Even if Prince Philip is at home (in the sense that he is at least in or not far from London), wife and husband frequently do not see each other from breakfast time until dinner at night . . . and sometimes even later than that.

These days she usually has Anne, at least, for company over lunch, but earlier on, when Anne and Charles were both away at school, it was nothing unusual for her to lunch alone. If so, the lunch is usually no more than a simple two-course affair of meat (or fish) with accompanying vegetables and a side-plate of salad followed by biscuits and cheese.

The Queen is neither a gourmet nor a heavy eater. She prefers her meals to be light, plain and wholesome. In fact, she likes things like oysters so little that word is usually sent ahead to those who will be hosting her in the course of her travels to omit such items from the menu. Philip's taste is slightly more sophisticated and away from home he has been known to indulge himself with oysters, caviar, snails. "However can you eat those beastly things?" his wife asked him once as she watched him tucking into a plateful of snails.

Philip himself once remarked that he never gets any 'home cooking' at Buckingham Palace. If by 'home cooking' he meant meals actually prepared and cooked by his wife, then the remark was true enough. The Queen has hardly the time, even if she had the inclination, to toil over a hot stove. But the meals conveyed on a hot trolley from the royal kitchen to the private dining room are almost the equalivalent of 'home cooking' in their simplicity, with roast lamb and green salad seen far more frequently on the menu than delicacies such as lobster, pheasant or out-of-season strawberries.

Neither the Queen nor her husband smoke. The Queen, indeed, has never done so, though there are cigarettes in a silver box in her sitting room for visitors who do. Philip smoked the occasional cigarette and toyed with a pipe during his early days in the Navy, but was prevailed upon to give up both at the time of his betrothal. Today, his long nose is quick to wrinkle if he detects a sniff of stale tobacco smoke following a palace luncheon or dinner party and orders are promptly given for windows to be flung open and the room to be sprayed with air freshener.

Equally, both are no more than moderate drinkers. Indeed, the Queen can hardly be said to drink at all. She may toy with a pre-meal sherry or sip a glass of white wine at some official banquet, but in private she clings to orange squash or water. Philip enjoys a beer with his lunch, a glass of wine with dinner and, sometimes, a gin-and-something beforehand.

None of this, of course, means that royal guests ever go short. Official luncheons at the palace—even the so-called 'informal'

ones—are considerably more elaborate than private meals. There
are five courses, starting with prawn cocktail or melon and ending
with fresh fruit. There are at least two wines. There are brandy
and liqueurs to conclude and cigarettes and cigars for those who
indulge.

Prince Philip usually joins his wife for such official luncheon
parties, sitting across from her midway along the oval-shaped
table, vantage points from which they can more easily converse
with guests on either side and help to keep the conversation
flowing. But he is invariably missing when the five o'clock ceremony of afternoon tea comes around. He considers it a waste of
time.

The Queen, however, likes her afternoon cuppa. For her, it
marks the break between her workday role as monarch and her
personal life as wife and mother. It used to be the hour at which
the children came bundling down from the upstairs nursery to
join her for sandwiches, chocolate cake, children's television and
an hour or so of general playtime. One or other of them may
still join her at this time, but Anne and Charles are certainly no
longer children and even young Edward, the baby of the family,
will soon have outgrown children's television.

Even the royal corgis, for whom five o'clock is also feeding
time, have changed with the years. Susan, the favoured pet that
young bride of 1947 took on honeymoon with her, has been
dead these many years and is buried at Sandringham where a
small headstone pays tribute to her as the "beloved companion
of the Queen". Even Whisky and Sherry, puppies only a few
weeks old when Charles and Anne first had them as pets in childhood, are both dead and gone, and three other generations of
royal corgis—Susan's great-granddaughter, Heather, and her
brother, Buzz, Heather's daughter, Tiny, and granddaughter,
Brush—now have the run of the palace, frisking into the Queen's
bedroom each morning, sleeping in her sitting room while she
works and curling up under the table at her feet at mealtimes.

Perhaps no other part of her everyday life so points the difference between the Queen and the ordinary housewife as these few
minutes each day when she feeds her pets. Thousands share her
attachment to dogs. Thousands prefer to feed their pets themselves
whenever possible, as she does. But with this difference. The meat,
dog-meal and gravy the Queen mixes for her pets comes on a

tray borne by a liveried footman while the spoon and fork with which she does the mixing are of solid silver.

Just as she prefers roast lamb to pheasant, mint chocolates to chocolate liqueurs and orange squash to champagne, so the Queen, in her personal life, prefers tweeds to mink and a casual head-scarf to a fashionable hat. Even in her public life, she declines to be with-it or trendy in matters of dress, arguing that she is a queen and not a model girl or movie star. But the truth lies perhaps mainly in her own self-effacing nature. When it comes to trend-setting, she is more than happy to leave that to her more extrovert daughter. On holiday at Balmoral and Sandringham she often dresses so casually that she could pass unnoticed and has perhaps done so, just as her father once boasted that he had left Sandringham by a sidegate and walked unrecognised past the crowd of tourists gathered around the main Norwich Gates.

Had fate woven a slightly different pattern so that she never came to the throne, giving her a younger brother to succeed her father instead of a sister, she would almost certainly have matured into an attractively tweedy country matron, riding with the local hunt, ratting with her dogs, driving herself around in a Land-Rover instead of being chauffeur-driven in a Rolls, bothering little about make-up and not at all about fashion, visiting London as little as possible. She has never been one to hanker for the bright lights. Princess Margaret can have them. Her ideal is a quiet life in a country cottage. Well, perhaps not quite a cottage. Years ago, when she first came to the throne, she and Prince Philip had the idea of slipping quietly away from London at weekends and being on their own at Windsor. For one reason and another, it never quite worked out at that time. But in recent years they have resurrected the idea with rather more success. They have converted a farmhouse at Sandringham into a hide-away home to which they retreat occasionally at weekends. Only two servants—a maid for the Queen, a valet for Prince Philip— go with them. With village women brought in to do the cooking and the cleaning, they thus come as near as royalty can hope to get to the simple life.

Yet even at Buckingham Palace they try to keep their personal lives as non-fussy as possible. Except when they are entertaining guests, they do not dress for dinner. No servants wait on them during the meal. Instead, they serve themselves and so can talk more freely. They seldom entertain at midweek and go out only occasionally in a private capacity, usually to the theatre. Their taste in plays is fairly predictable. They went together to see *Vivat! Vivat Regina*, the Robert Bolt play about the Queen's Elizabethan ancestress, and, in Philip's absence, the Queen went with friends to see that horsy comedy *The Jockey Club Stakes*. Weekends often find them leading a full social life, particularly during the shooting season. Friends are invited to Windsor for a day's shooting or to stay the weekend. For day visitors there is always a high tea of hot soup, scrambled eggs, veal pie, ham, cheese and salad when shooting is over. For weekend guests there is a dinner party at night when evening dress is worn, liveried servants wait on table, and the cutlery and wine glasses are changed for each course. By way of an after-dinner divertissement, husband and wife will sometimes take their guests on a conducted tour of the state rooms with the Queen, in particular, acting as a knowledgeable guide.

By contrast, their mid-week evenings at the palace are relatively quiet. Philip may read while the Queen does a crossword. Or they may watch television together. Both enjoy a good play and like a good laugh. The Queen likes watching anything to do with horses. Major sporting events, whether to do with horses or not, are seldom missed. The Queen, in particular, was an enthusiastic viewer of the last Olympic Games in Mexico and the World Cup series.

For the Queen and her husband, such quiet evenings in front of the television have the same companionable contentment as in any less regal home. If the halcyon days of idyllic young love are now in the past, as for any other middle-aged couple, the royal marriage is firmly rooted in the mutual affection and understanding that comes with the years. Prince Philip long ago surfaced from that period of youthful frustration which dogged him in the early days of his wife's monarchy when she had too much to do and he had too little. All along he has dutifully abided by the ancient oath of fealty he took on the day of his wife's coronation. The Queen, for her part, has equally honoured her wedding day promise to love, honour and obey. If 'obey' seems a somewhat old-fashioned word in this age of equality and permissiveness, substitute 'respect'. Respect for her husband's ideas, outlook, opinions and wishes has always come naturally to her and still does. Today, in private, her conversation is still peppered with "Philip says..." and "Philip thinks..." just as it was in those days of courtship of a quarter of a century ago. And to the children it is still, as it has always been, "Ask Papa. He'll know."

After nearly twenty-five years of married life, the Queen and her husband have not yet reached the state when they have nothing to talk about to each other and sit glumly silent in each other's company. Nor are they ever likely to do so. On the contrary, they talk a lot, animatedly, amusingly. Typical of the sort of things they talk about was that snippet of family conversation on which camera and microphone eavesdropped in the film *Royal Family*.

Those who saw the film will recall the Queen's laughing account of how she was receiving a succession of official visitors when one of her aides murmured, "The next one in is a gorilla, Your Majesty."

The doors opened, said the Queen "and there he was . . . a gorilla—long arms, short legs, all hair".

It was not an incident rehearsed and staged specially for the benefit of the camera. It is the sort of story the Queen often tells to the delight of the family circle, sometimes enlivening it with actions, sometimes enhancing it with a mimicked Cockney or Scots accent. What the camera did not reveal was the way royal husband and wife sometimes dissolve into helpless laughter at such moments of recalled amusement. That they still find so much to talk about to each other, so much to laugh about in their private lives, surely speaks volumes for the happiness and contentment they have found in their marriage.

II Their Palace Home

Just like any suburban bank manager and his wife who occupy a flat directly over the bank, the Queen and her husband live on top of their work. In fact, the Queen's private sitting room also serves as her study. There are something like 600 other rooms in Buckingham Palace, many of which would serve equally well for working purposes, but she prefers the homely intimacy of her own room.

From a working viewpoint, it is, in fact, a highly convenient arrangement. The Queen has to walk only a few yards from the breakfast table each morning to be at her desk in the next room. She can and does pause to initial the occasional state paper or sign a few more gift photographs between finishing dinner of an evening and settling down with a crossword puzzle or in front of the television. Philip has a slightly longer walk to his own study, but it is still only a matter of yards. If either or both are going out, a car can be whisked round from the royal mews at the rear of the palace in a matter of minutes, while, as Prince Philip has demonstrated, the palace lawns can be used for helicopters as well as garden parties.

In a sense, the life the royal couple lead is a double one, or, if not that, certainly a life riddled with anomalies. They, of course, do not see it as such. The Queen could hardly be expected to do so. It is, by and large, a way of life to which she has been accustomed since childhood. Philip was brought up rather differently, but by now has lived with the anomalies for so long that, like the stains on the wallpaper in less regal homes, they are perhaps no longer visible to him.

Theirs is a life lived on two levels—regal and personal—as sharply contrasted as the flourishing 'Elizabeth R' with which the Queen signs her giveaway photographs and the hurried, sometimes almost illegible, scrawl she employs for more personal communications. Consider just a few of the anomalies. The Queen's eldest son buys himself a sports car capable of 150 miles an hour, but his mother, when she opens Parliament, goes there in a creaking, horse-drawn coach dating from her great-grandmother's day. For sea voyages, royal husband and wife have at their disposal a £2 million luxury yacht, yet not long ago they had to sell their much smaller racing yawl because they could no longer afford to run it. The wife, as Queen, is paid twelve times as much as her husband (or was when this book was written). Even the eldest son, after handing half of his income back to the State, is—or was—left with something like three times what his father gets. And father, with an income of over £750 a week, once found himself so hard pressed that he grumbled publicly that he might have to give up polo. In private, father and eldest son alike bang away at pheasants and grouse; in public, they combine to help raise around £400,000 for the World Wildlife Fund—and neither sees any contradiction in the fact. With upwards of 300 servants within call at Buckingham Palace, royal husband and wife yet prefer to serve themselves at mealtimes. At breakfast, a kilted piper paces back and forth beneath the window, the dining table almost groans under the weight of antique silver and even butter comes in dainty pats adorned with a miniature crown. But the marmalade which stands beside the butter is still in the pot in which it was bought. Of an evening, the Queen may kick off her shoes and sit with her feet up to watch the television like any ordinary woman, but she sleeps at night with a burly police officer keeping watchful vigil outside her bedroom door.

The Queen herself is perhaps not completely unmindful of some of the more curious contradictions of royal life, and sometimes, in the privacy of her palace home, able to joke about them. There was one occasion when she had been hosting a state banquet in all the glory of her regality . . . billowing state gown slashed by the blue ribbon of the Garter, glittering tiara, massive diamond necklace, the lot. The banquet over, she whipped off her tiara, removed her shoes, and, tiara in one hand, shoes in the other, padded off in the direction of her private apartment. On the way she ran into a member of her personal staff. Amused herself by the obvious incongruity of the situation, she faked a hobble, clapped a hand to her back and feigned a mock wince. 'It's me poor back,' she lamented, jokingly.

Philip apart, the first person to see the Queen each morning—and often the last to see her at night—is a remarkable woman named Margaret MacDonald. Remarkable because she has been close to the Queen longer than anyone else at Buckingham Palace—longer even than Prince Philip. Indeed, it was to Bobo, as she calls her, that the Queen first confided that she was in love with Philip. Over the years Margaret MacDonald has been the recipient of many such royal confidences. Yet Margaret Mac-Donald herself has no title. She is not one of the royal ladies-in-waiting; nor is her name to be found in the list of those officials, male and female, known as the Queen's Household. She is, in fact, simply a servant. But a very special servant. Between her and the Queen there exists that special relationship, a compound of two-way loyalty and natural affection, which grows sometimes between nanny and baby.

That was how the two of them first came together—as nanny and baby. Margaret MacDonald, the daughter of humble Scottish parents, was working as a maid for the Marchioness of Linlithgow when the Marchioness learned that her friend, the Duchess of York, was expecting a baby and was looking round for a strong, willing girl to help out in the royal nursery. She suggested Margaret for the post and the young Scottish lass travelled south to London and the York home at 145 Piccadilly. Not as nanny. That post was held by a Mrs. Knight. Margaret did the fetching and carrying with which a nanny could not be expected to soil her hands, washing the baby's nappies, laying and lighting the nursery fire, filling and emptying the baby's bath, running errands. Then came the birth of Princess Margaret. Mrs. Knight was fully occupied in looking after the new addition to the family and Elizabeth, just turned 4, was left more and more to the care of the young nurserymaid she called 'Bobo'. That childhood label has stuck over the years. Today Margaret MacDonald is still 'Bobo' to the Queen and others of the Royal Family. But to no one else. A palace official who once fell into the error of addressing her with such familiarity was quickly put in his place. "Only the Queen calls me that," Miss MacDonald informed him firmly.

Over the years since childhood, when they played games of hide-and-seek together in Hamilton Gardens and went for rides round Hyde Park in a carriage sent round from the royal mews, Bobo has been beside the Queen (or close at hand) throughout the highlights of her life. It was Bobo who draped a warm eiderdown round the young shoulders when the then Princess scuttled out of bed at the crack of dawn and stood at a window to watch the crowds gather for her father's coronation. It was Bobo who helped her into her coronation gown when that day came, too. In between, she had helped her also into her wedding dress and organised the hunt for that missing spray of orchids.

Wherever the Queen has gone over the years, Bobo has gone with her. To Australia and New Zealand, to Canada and the United States, to France and Germany, Norway and Sweden, and a score of places besides. Other royal servants take it turn and

The wedding of Princess Elizabeth in Westminster Abbey
in November 1947

On honeymoon at
Broadlands

turn about to accompany the Queen on her travels. But Bobo
goes everywhere. She was with her on that long-ago voyage to
South Africa which served as a final test of her feelings for Philip.
In fact, she was ill when the time came for sailing. But knowing
how upset the young Elizabeth was at being parted from Philip,
knowing that she would need all the comfort and companionship
she could get, Bobo had herself taken aboard on a stretcher rather
than remain behind. She was with her too in Kenya when word
reached them of the King's death. The baby girl with whom she
had once played hide-and-seek and hopscotch was now Queen
Elizabeth II and Bobo was among the first to curtsey to her.
"Oh, no, Bobo," the new, young Queen protested, "You don't
have to do that." She was one of the very few who knew that
the Queen was already pregnant when the royal party left for
Canada in 1959. Four years later she was the very first person to
know that the Queen was expecting Prince Edward. Philip was
out at the time and the Queen, her hopes of a playmate for
Andrew finally confirmed, felt that she had to tell someone. Bobo
was an obvious choice.

Over the years since babyhood Margaret MacDonald has
played no small part in helping to mould the Queen into the
woman she is today. As a young princess, carrying out her first
public engagements, the Queen suffered from both nerves and
travel sickness. Bobo helped her conquer both. "Suck barley
sugar," she suggested. It worked. Today, wherever she goes, the
Queen still takes a small canister of barley sugar with her and it
is one of Bobo's jobs to see that the canister is kept filled. Similarly, in the early days of her monarchy, the Queen jibbed
nervously at the idea of decking herself up in the required regal
finery of tiara and necklace, brooches, bracelets and ear-rings.
"But you must," Bobo persuaded her. "People expect it of you."

Nor is the Queen unmindful of all Bobo has done for her.
One of her first acts of monarchy was to appoint the one-time
nurserymaid as Member of the Royal Victorian Order "as a
reward for personal services", the only royal servant (as distinct
from members of the Queen's Household) to be so honoured.
That Margaret MacDonald ranks as no ordinary servant is seen
in other things too. She does not eat with the other servants. She
has her own small private apartment at Buckingham Palace. It is
an apartment with the luxury of a carpeted bathroom, a long way

5

removed from that Highland cottage of her childhood where bath night meant a tin tub in front of the kitchen fire. Alone among palace servants, she is free to come and go by any door. Alone among them, she has a royal car at her disposal if she wants to go anywhere.

In fact, she seldom goes out, seldom takes even a Sunday off. Her work is her life. Her official title today is the Queen's dresser. As such, she is up and about each morning in time to run the Queen's bath and lay out her clothes for the day before calling her at eight o'clock and is still working at nine o'clock at night when she lays out the royal nightwear and slippers while the Queen is at dinner. She looks after the Queen's jewellery, supervises the tidying of the Queen's bedroom and does much of the Queen's personal shopping for her. She accompanies the Queen wherever she goes. A small zip-fastened bag goes everywhere with her. In it are all the small essentials the Queen may need in a hurry—spare stockings, spare shoes, spare gloves. For travels further afield she ensures that the Queen is never without her favourite brand of toilet soap and her own special blend of tea. At each place and for each fresh function she ensures that the right clothes, pressed and bandbox fresh, and correct accessories are ready for the Queen to slip into. On a royal tour of any magnitude—of Australia, say, or Canada—this can mean masterminding perhaps as many as 150 different outfits. She has seldom been known to slip up, though there was one occasion when she did. The Queen was changing clothes aboard the royal train, between stopping points, when she realised that there was no hat to go with the new outfit. Rather than appear bareheaded or in a non-matching hat, she changed quickly back into the clothes she had been wearing earlier.

While Bobo is unique among palace servants in her relationship to the Queen, there are others who have served her almost as long. Ronald Aubrey, the royal chef, has been at the palace since the Queen was a girl of 11. James Walton, deputy palace steward, has been there as long. One of the Queen's two pages, John Taylor, was likewise with her father before her. Her other page, Ernest Bennett, has been with her since she was a newly married Princess living at Clarence House. Mabel Anderson, the royal nanny, has similarly been with her since the birth of Prince Charles. She was one of several applicants who answered a discreet advertisement for an under-nurse. For so personal a post, the young royal employer—the Queen was not yet 23—decided to interview them herself. She took an instant liking to the young woman from Elgin, perhaps because they were, employer and would-be employee, around the same age. Her choice proved to be well-founded. When Helen Lightbody, a nanny of the old school with whose ideas Prince Philip did not always see eye to eye, decided to leave the royal nursery in 1956, 'Mamba' Anderson, as the children called her, took over and has since looked after Charles, Anne, Andrew and Edward in turn.

Neither the Queen nor Prince Philip were particularly enamoured of Buckingham Palace when they first moved back into it from Clarence House on the Queen's accession to the throne, though they have settled to it since. Personal adjustments to their own apartment in the way of decor and furnishing have brought it close to the sort of home they always visualised. Philip's study has an air of streamlined, business-like efficiency, while the Queen's sitting room, which serves also as her study, is largely furnished with their own things, many of them wedding gifts, which they brought over with them from Clarence House.

The two of them live in a dozen or so connecting rooms spread out along the first floor of the palace, their windows looking north-east to Constitution Hill. The nursery is immediately above, with the rooms occupied by Charles and Anne on the same floor but just round the corner at the front of the palace.

The royal apartment is almost, though not quite, self-contained. Not quite because there is no kitchen or, at least, not one in regular use. Soon after they moved into the palace as queen and consort, Prince Philip had the idea of installing a small, new, modern kitchen on the same floor and close to the royal apartment. For their private meals, he thought, it would eliminate the long haul needed to bring food from the old lofty kitchens a quarter of a mile away at the far corner of the palace. He was keen on the idea and proud of the result. Friends who came to call were given a quick tour of the new kitchen, with Philip extolling the virtues of its pressure cookers and rotary spits, automatic controls and deep-freeze. "It was rather like the sort of steamlined galley you would expect to find aboard a luxury yacht," one visitor recalls. But for one reason or another, those who did the cooking soon drifted back to the old kitchen from where the food still takes so long to reach the royal dining table it has to be trundled there on a heated trolley to keep it warm.

But if it lacks its own kitchen, the royal apartment has everything else—his and hers bathrooms, his and hers dressing rooms, double bedroom, a second, smaller bedroom for Philip to use if he is late back, dining room, sitting room, central heating. The sitting room, as we have said, serves also as the Queen's study and Philip has a separate study of his own. Most of the rooms are large, multi-windowed and high-ceilinged in the tradition of those more spacious eighteenth-century days when they were originally laid out for the Duke of Buckingham. Only in Prince Philip's study has a noticeably more modern note been introduced by the installation of a false ceiling to give the room a lower, more streamlined appearance. Portraits of his mother as a young woman, his father and his Battenberg grandfather, Prince Louis, hang on the walls; a model of his old command, the frigate *Magpie*, remember his sea-going days. All else is workman-like in the extreme . . . window curtains which can be opened or closed at the press of a button, radio and television to bring him news of the outside world, an intercom system linking him with all parts of the palace and a tape machine on which he can record his speeches in advance and so get an idea of how things will sound.

The Queen's room, by contrast, is as fussy and feminine as Philip's is masculine and workmanlike. Used by her mother as a sitting room in the days when her father was King, it still looks far more like a sitting room than a study. It is cluttered with family photographs, china knick-knacks, vases of flowers. A couple of drinking bowls for the corgis are dotted here and there and one or more of these royals pets is usually to be seen curled up on the Persian rug in front of the marble fireplace. The desk set at an angle to the bay window, the intercom system beside it and the inevitable despatch box labelled 'The Queen' are almost the only signs that this friendly, family room is also the focal point of monarchy.

It is, in fact, very much a multi-purpose room . . . not only sitting room and study but also television room, playroom and, most of all, perhaps, a private sanctuary. Here, except when public engagements take her out and about, the Queen plugs away at the contents of her despatch boxes. Here she plans her world tours with the aid of maps so large they sometimes have to be spread out on the carpet with her and Philip crawling on all fours around them. Here she has afternoon tea with the children. Here the children, in turn, have played with their toys. Here she entertains her personal friends of an evening, with Philip fixing the drinks, or, if the two of them are on their own, sits with her shoes off and feet up to watch the television. It is a room which only a few people—family, friends and top aides—have ever seen. Others who have dealings with the Queen, including the Prime Minister, get to see her in the designated audience room just round the corner to the rear of the palace.

For the rest, Buckingham Palace remains vast and impersonal, part palace, part offices, part domestic quarters, part living quarters for servants. It is not so much a single, vast building as a village in the heart of London with its own police station, post office, telephone exchange, petrol pumps and blacksmith's shop, a labyrinth of corkscrew corridors, echoing, high-ceilinged rooms and heavy, dark antique furniture. There are servants the royal couple never see except when they hand out the traditional gifts at Christmas; parts of the palace the Queen has never visited even if Philip has. When they first moved in he made it one of his tasks to tour the whole palace, from basement to attics, though we cannot vouch for the story that he also counted the number of rooms in the course of his progress and came up with a total of 611.

If the Queen and her husband disliked the palace when they first moved in, they were not alone in that. Royal distaste for the palace goes back several generations. William IV flatly refused to live there. Queen Victoria grumbled that it was too small for her fast-growing family. George V once suggested that it should be demolished and he would go to live at Kensington Palace. Royal inmates, in turn, have labelled it "a sepulchre", "musty" and "an icebox". Queen Victoria preferred Balmoral. The Queen's father and grandfather preferred Sandringham and both died there. The Queen prefers Windsor. At Windsor, as at Buckingham Palace, she and her husband have succeeded in creating a home within a castle, remodelling rooms in what is now known as the Queen's Tower into a private apartment to their own taste. It has been a task requiring no little ingenuity and imagination. Windsor is a

real castle, not a mock one as Balmoral is, with corridors almost
wide enough to serve as a motorway and walls so thick that the
Queen's father, when he did some renovating before her, actually
had a bathroom constructed within the thickness of a single wall.
His daughter and her husband have displayed similar ingenuity in
creating a light, airy, essentially modern apartment which includes
two bedrooms, sitting room, dining room, study and kitchen for
themselves as well as bedrooms for the children and a shared
sitting room for Charles and Anne. Just across the corridor from
the main apartment is the Queen's drawing room. Once a gloomy
dining room with walls of blackened oak, it is now light and
bright with a decor of white and gold. Gold-coloured curtains
hang at the windows and the floor is close-carpeted in a cheerful
shade of cherry. A small gold statuette of Aureole, the Queen's
famous racehorse, stands in one of the windows; comfortable
sofas and armchairs are dotted about the room as well as some
antiques which are not quite what they seem. One of a pair of
matching antique cabinets is really a small cocktail bar while the
other conceals a record player.

While the Queen and Prince Philip may sometimes see comparatively little of each other during the course of their working
week, they can and do enjoy a considerable degree of togetherness
and family life at Windsor over the weekend. Their roles as queen
and consort temporarily forgotten, they are free to relax with
each other as husband and wife, mother and father. For a short
time the Queen can forget the necessity for dressing up and
queening it. Instead, she can relax in her favourite tweeds while
Philip can prowl around in nothing more dressy than a sports
jacket and flannels. They may stroll together beside the Thames
or take a walk over to the Home Farm. They may go riding
together. For Philip there may be a polo game, with his wife
watching and helping to stamp down the divots between chuk-
kers. On Sunday mornings they go to church together.

When they first started weekending at Windsor, the royal
couple hoped for an even greater degree of informality. Perhaps
not quite down to the level of the ordinary couple with a bunga-
low by the sea or a cottage in the country where the wife does the
cooking while the husband potters about the garden. But almost.
Two or three servants, no more, a minimum by royal standards
Unfortunately, it didn't work out. Just as Victoria and Albert

before them found that while the Lord Steward might lay the
fires in Buckingham Palace, he would not light them (that was a
job for the Lord Chamberlain), and while the Lord Chamberlain,
in turn, might have the windows cleaned inside, he would not
touch them on the outside (that was the responsibility of the
Woods and Forests Department), so the Queen and her husband
found that the chef who cooked their meals would not lay the
table and the man who laid the table for them equally jibbed at
cleaning the silver—and so *ad infinitum*. So what started out as
a quiet weekend in the country quickly turned into another of
the many anomalies with which the royal couple have to live and
which they now take largely for granted. The same goes for
Balmoral. When the Queen and her family journey north for their
two-month summer stay in Scotland, several dozen servants must
needs go with them. Officials too, for the work of monarchy goes
on even at Balmoral.

Just as so many other couples of their generation go to Brighton
or Scarborough, Torquay or Bournemouth, or, these days, to
Malta or Majorca with almost monotonous regularity each
summer, so the Queen and her husband go to Balmoral. They
could, of course, as easily afford to fly out to the Bahamas or the
Greek islands, but for them it would be no more than a busman's
holiday. All picture postcard views tend to seem the same when
you have seen so many of them. Besides, as they soon discovered
on their earlier trips to Greece, Italy and elsewhere, for royalty
such holidays can never be completely private. Always there must
be the inevitable official welcome, the inevitable official banquet,
the inevitable crowds. But at Balmoral there is no official welcome
and no crowds. Heath and woodland, mountains and the River
Dee (plus a small quantity of camouflage netting) combine to
keep them safe from rubbernecking sightseers.

Balmoral—which, like Sandringham, is the Queen's private
property (Buckingham Palace and Windsor Castle are state residences)—affords them almost complete privacy. Here the Queen
can roam around in tweeds or a tartan skirt, as the mood takes
her, Andrew and Edward can romp around in jeans and sweaters,
getting cheerfully grubby as small boys will, Anne can virtually
live in her riding things, while Philip and Charles can stride about
in free-moving kilts in one of the three tartans the Royal Family
is traditionally entitled to wear. We cannot vouch for the story

that Prince Philip, on his first-ever visit to Balmoral, had the Royal Family in stitches of laughter by appearing in a kilt belonging to the Queen's father. If true, the King's kilt must have looked rather like an early version of the mini-skirt on Philip's taller, more lanky frame. Less apocryphal is the story that when Charles was a small boy a wordy battle developed between him and his nanny on one occasion as to what went under a kilt. His nanny wanted him to wear a pair of tartan shorts. Charles resisted on the basis that "Papa doesn't wear them". But whatever Prince Philip may or may not wear under his kilt, Charles on that occasion ended up doing as he was told.

Balmoral Castle was originally built by Prince Albert for Queen Victoria. The hallmark of that devoted royal couple is still stamped indelibly upon it. Much of the tartan carpet, tartan curtains and tartan-covered furnishings date from the days of Victoria, as do the portraits of her many offspring, the paintings by Landseer, some of the ornaments and even some of the wallpaper with its VRI cypher. So do the traditions—the solitary piper who paces back and forth on the terrace during breakfast, the whole gaggle of pipers who parade round the dining table after dinner. As though all that was insufficient reminder of the great-great-grandparents from whom they are both descended, the Queen and her husband can contemplate portraits of Victoria and her husband as they sit at dinner while a marble statue of Great-great-grandpapa Albert in full Highland rig dominates the front hall.

Even at Balmoral, on holiday, neither husband nor wife are lie-abeds. They are usually up by eight o'clock and by half-past nine, with breakfast over, the Queen is busy with her correspondence or tackling the contents of her boxes, which pursue her even on holiday. She works in jodhpurs and riding jacket ready to go for a morning canter later, perhaps with Princess Anne, beside the River Dee. Meanwhile, Philip and the boys have already gone out for the day, perhaps with guns, perhaps fishing rods, perhaps cameras. Often enough they will spend the whole day in the open air, walking, stalking, shooting, fishing, swimming or sailing a boat on Loch Muick. Sometimes the Queen, too, will take off on her own for a day's stalking, as she did at least half a dozen times in the summer of 1970, her forty-fifth year. Failing that, she and Anne will usually join the men of the family for an out-door lunch, perhaps a picnic in the hills or a barbecue beside the loch with Philip doing the cooking. Sometimes, for father and sons, such outings take on a spirit of high adventure with a night spent rolled up in sleeping-bags in a seldom-used cottage on the shore of the loch and a cowboy breakfast of bacon-and-beans. Anne too, when she was younger and more of a tomboy, knew what it was to spend a night in this fashion. But not the Queen. She prefers Balmoral Castle and the comfort of her own bed.

Just as they continue the old royal tradition of summer holidays spent at Balmoral, so the Queen and her husband maintain the other royal tradition of the big family Christmas. It used to be at Sandringham, because the Queen's father loved the place so. But Sandringham is off the beaten track, a difficult spot for everyone to get to for just a few days at Christmas and no longer large enough for a family with so many growing children and so many servants. Windsor is larger, closer to London, more convenient. And the Queen likes it better.

Christmas is about the only time of the year when the Queen gets to do any personal shopping. For close relatives she likes to choose specific gifts she thinks will appeal to them. It is not always easy in a family which has almost everything . . . but she usually manages to find something—perhaps a new set of barbecue tools for Prince Philip or a new shotgun or something such as a paperweight for his desk. One year it was a set of model (not toy) soldiers in period uniforms carefully handpainted. For those fractionally less close she buys whatever catches her eye and takes her fancy. Sometimes she will buy two or three of the same thing, deciding later who gets what. Each gift is accompanied by a small card bearing her good wishes, hand-written just as she signs all her Christmas cards by hand.

Gifts for her staff are bought for her, either by the palace housekeeper or the head of the particular department. They range from small gifts like panti-hose, gloves and handbags for newly-hired maids all the way up to cutlery sets, dinner services and even armchairs for those who have worked for her a long time. And though someone else may do the actual buying, the Queen herself, helped by Philip and the children, likes to hand out the gifts personally.

To leave themselves ample time for church-going on Christmas

morning, the Queen and her family exchange their personal gifts
on Christmas Eve. Trestle tables are set up round the Christmas
tree and each member of the family has a section of table marked
off with coloured ribbon. Gradually each section fills with gifts
until the whole thing looks like nothing so much as a Christmas
display counter in some regal department store. For the younger
children, of course, some toys are held in reserve for Santa to
deliver and there is also a bulging stocking for each of them
when they wake on Christmas morning. There is a stocking, too—
filled with such doggy delicacies as chocolate drops and chewy
rubber bones—for each of the corgis.

The pre-taping of her Christmas telecast has enabled the Queen
to relax and enjoy Christmas Day in the same way as everyone
else. The live telecasts of earlier years were always something of an
ordeal for her. Nervous and tense at the prospect ahead of her,
she did considerably less than justice to her Christmas lunch before
dashing away to be made-up and have a last-minute rehearsal.

With the exception of those children who are still so young
they are better off eating in the nursery with their nannies, the
whole family—including, usually, the Queen Mother, the Snow-
dons, the Kents, Princess Alexandra and her husband, Angus
Ogilvy—sit down together for Christmas lunch in a Dickensian
atmosphere of holly and mistletoe, trinket-filled crackers and
cotton-wool novelties. Dinner at night has the additional touches
of candlelight and evening dress. The royal steward carves the
turkey and the royal chef brings in the holly-capped pudding in a
splutter of brandy-blue flame.

After dinner, as in thousands of less regal homes, there are
party games, practical jokes—the squeaking cushion is a perennial
favourite—and a singsong round the grand piano. The Queen
and Princess Margaret will sometimes team up in a duet just as
they did in those childhood pantomimes of wartime years. And
sooner or later they are almost certain to play charades. It is a
game the whole family plays with zest, donning comic masks and
false moustaches, aprons and overcoats, diving into a large box of
props for a walking stick or umbrella, pipe, riding crop or long
string of beads to enhance a particular role. The Queen Mother,
once when it was her turn to play, made a spectacular entrance
wearing a false beard. Through at least three generations—from
the Queen Mum to Charles and Anne—it has been the Royal

Family's favourite game. As Prince Charles says, "Charades? Great fun. I love it."

III   Parents and Children

In one aspect of family life, the Queen and her husband have been, and are, more fortunate than most in this day and age. Yet 'fortunate' is perhaps not quite the right word. In the upbringing of their children, they have surely worked towards and deserved the happy outcome they now enjoy in their middle years.

They had their first two children when they were comparatively young. The Queen was only 22 and Prince Philip 27 when Prince Charles was born. They were both still under 30—indeed, the Queen was only 24—when Anne came along. Over the years since, as Charles has grown to manhood and Anne to womanhood, the royal parents have contrived to remain young with them. As a result, they not only enjoy the love and affection of their children but equally their respect and confidence.

It was Prince Charles himself who spoke of the Queen as "A marvellous person and a wonderful mother. Terribly sensible and wise". His father he has termed "a great help" and "a strong influence".

Between the royal parents and their children there is no generation gap, or hardly any. "A united family" the Queen herself has called them, and this they are. In the privacy of the family circle, the royal parents and their two older children talk and behave more like brothers and sisters than parents and offspring. And how they talk! As one small sequence in the film *Royal Family* briefly revealed, they are considerable chatterboxes in their personal lives, laughing, talking and joking together, and sometimes even enlivening family conversation with a touch of mimicry. The Queen, in particular, is famous in the family circle for her witty lightning impersonations.

In these four—mother and the son who will one day succeed her, father and daughter—the generations meet and mix. Charles and his father not only play polo together, but often swim, fish, shoot or go bird-watching together. The Queen and Anne ride together; talk clothes together, with the mother sometimes displaying more enthusiasm over some new with-it outfit Anne has bought than ever she does over her own less trendy clothes, almost as though, in the big-sister relationship she has with her daughter, she enjoys at secondhand the youthful independence she never knew herself.

The close, almost brother and sister, relationship the four of them enjoy reveals itself in other ways too. It was to be seen in the quick grin of reassurance Philip flashed his son when Charles was undergoing the ordeal of his installation as Prince of Wales; in the quick, flickering exchange of glances often glimpsed between Charles and his mother; in the admitted way Charles and Anne often have to avoid meeting each other's eyes in public for fear of bursting out laughing at some moment of over-solemnity.

It is, above all, a relationship which has enabled the two elder royal children to grow up as completely independent human beings yet also secure in the knowledge that their parents are there in the background, ready to help and advise if need be.

Of course, like most young people, there have been times when they have needed parental help without being aware of the fact, as Anne did soon after leaving Benenden.

She found herself, at that time, at something of a loose end, though not perhaps a dead end. She was far from clear where she was going in life. She was fed up with schooling and had no wish to go on to university, as Charles had done. But she was not yet mature enough to undertake a full round of royal engagements on her own. She was out of touch with most of the friends she had made at Benenden and, because she was who she was, not in a position to make new friends. For her, there was no job to bring her into contact with other young people, no bus or train journeys to and from work, no youth club, Saturday night dances or coffee bar get-togethers. It all sounds slightly reminiscent of her mother's young days and so it was. But with this difference. Her mother, at the same age, was already in love with Philip and had Margaret for company. Anne had no one. True, she did meet other young people, including eligible young men, from time to time at private dances, riding gymkhanas or while watching her father or elder brother play polo, but mostly at insufficient length for the unseen barrier between royalty and the rest of the world to be broken down and for friendship to result.

Not all parents, involved in busy lives of their own, would have realised that their daughter had a problem. The royal parents did . . . and decided to do something about it. Prince Philip had a quiet word with one or two of his polo-playing and yachting friends who had youngsters of around the same age. As a result, Anne found herself going out and about with a small, lively group of young people.

Prince Charles probably had his own parents very much in mind when he talked about the responsibilities of parents a year or so back.

"Parents," he said, "should be responsible for explaining to their children the complexities of life in a large modern society."

They should do so, he added, by "reasoning, logic and persuasion. But don't for God's sake let the children find out totally by themselves.

"And if your children want to alter society, listen to their reasons and the idealism behind them. Don't crush them with some clever remark straight away."

In the upbringing of their children, the royal parents have consistently used reasoning, logic and persuasion, and have never tried to crush them, either with some clever remark or in any other way. Quite the contrary. As Charles has also said, his parents have never insisted dogmatically that their children should do this, that or the other. But neither have they taken the line of least resistance, as some parents do, and left their children entirely free to 'do their own thing'.

Their policy as parents has been somewhere between these two extremes. They have tried never to force an issue, but rather to guide and influence in the right direction. They have not said "You will do this" or "You will do that". Their approach has been more along the lines of "We think this might be a good idea, but what do you think?" Then child and parents have talked things over, with father sometimes taking a sheet of paper and listing the pros and cons of the subject under discussion. More and more, as Charles and Anne have grown up, the final decision as to what they should do or should not do has been left to them.

That way, as Anne has put it, "you can't very well blame your parents if you make a fool of yourself".

Of course, the royal parents, like any other parents, have made mistakes in the upbringing of their children. Being royal is not to be all-wise and all-seeing. Looking back, the earlier attempt to mould Charles in his father's more rugged, more athletic image was perhaps a mistake. But it was surely a mistake which did no great harm. Charles may have been unhappy for a time at the sort of school to which he was sent, but there can be little doubt that both his character and physique benefited as a result. He was, of course, too young at the time for his own, sometimes tearful, protests to be taken very seriously. But later his own wishes and inclinations were taken very much into account.

"He was keen to go to university," his father has revealed, "so we tried to figure out a way."

In the upbringing of the royal children, Philip has always played a leading role. In their private life, the Queen regards him as the head of the family and bows to his judgement. She feels that his own, more ordinary upbringing has given him more knowledge of the subject than she has herself.

Philip would like each of his children to achieve something in life, quite apart from their royal status, on which they can look back with pride and satisfaction. Charles has already done well in this respect, gaining a B.A. degree and learning to fly. His spell in the navy may yet add to the list of youthful achievements. If so, nothing would please his father more. "If I have a son," Philip remarked once, years ago, "I would like nothing better than for him to be a sailor." Well, he has got his wish, though Charles, like his father before him, will eventually have to abandon a sea-going life.

Anne has perhaps not yet quite matched up to her brother in the matter of youthful achievement. Schooldays over, she had no real wish to go on to university and try for a degree, and her parents, true to their policy of guiding but never forcing, did not make her. Of course, they may also have had in mind, the brouhaha which resulted when it was first announced that Charles was going to Cambridge and had no desire for a repetition.

Anne has, of course, done well enough on horseback, winning the European Three-day Championship at Burghley in September 1971, but that is not quite the same thing. She can hardly make a career of eventing, though she would perhaps like to have done so. "It's the one thing I can do really well," she told her parents on one occasion. This is doubtless true, but because she is who she is, because of the public demands made upon her time, she can no more make a career of it than her father could make a career of polo. It can be a satisfying spare-time pursuit, but not more. And this she realises.

To the upbringing of her children the Queen has always brought that same warmth of family life and sense of security that she knew herself in childhood. If she has perhaps sometimes been in danger of overdoing the security and thus diminishing childhood initiative and self-confidence, father has been quick to apply the remedy, as when he jerked Charles out of the royal nursery and buzzed him off to boarding school.

Prince Philip, who hardly ever saw his own father in boyhood, has consistently ensured that his own children should not suffer from lack of fatherly companionship and guidance. It was Philip who gave each of the royal children their first swimming lessons in the palace pool. He was teaching Charles and Anne to handle a car on the private roads of the Balmoral estate long before they were old enough to qualify for a driving licence. By the time he was 12, Charles was already able, under parental supervision, to drive a Land-Rover from Balmoral to Birkhall, some miles away. It was similarly his father who taught him to fish and shoot, who gave him his first cricket lessons and played bicycle polo with him at Windsor when he was still too young and too small for the real thing. Nor was this simply a case of a father's natural pride in his firstborn. Today a similarly close father-son relationship exists between Philip and his two younger sons, Andrew and Edward.

All the royal children, because their parents are also third cousins, tend to have features and facets which stem from both. Edward, the youngest, for instance, will some times look exactly as the Queen did in childhood while at other times, seen from a different angle, he will equally seem to look exactly like those biscuit-munching pictures of his father which were taken when Philip was a small boy in Paris. And one feature runs through the whole family—blue eyes.

Charles, the eldest, is now in his mid-twenties, and, to outward appearance, a dead ringer for his father. He holds himself as

Philip does, walks like him, talks like him. He has inherited all but the last half-inch of his father's tallness. But there are other, perhaps less noticeable things about him—like his naturally wavy hair—which come down from his mother. He has also inherited her trick (which she, in turn, inherited from her father) of twisting a ring round and round on his finger in moments of tension. The Queen does it with her engagement ring, Charles with the signet ring his parents gave him for his twenty-first birthday. And his eyes, like the Queen's, never leave the face of anyone to whom they are talking, a habit which some people find mildly disconcerting.

Like his mother, he is painstaking and conscientious, perhaps slightly over-serious at times and, on his own admission, still slightly on the shy side, though you would perhaps never suspect it. Certainly on public occasions—as those who saw him when the Freedom of the City of London was bestowed upon him will know—there is no longer any trace of his earlier gawkiness and uncertainty. Instead, he radiates an air of quiet, good-humoured confidence. If he seems more patient and less quick-tempered than his father, he can yet be stubbornly obstinate upon occasion it is said, as his mother can. And if he lacks his father's aptitude, for instant wit, he clearly possesses another quality of which his father gives little sign—a sense of humour. Prince Philip has frequently demonstrated the sharpness of his wit, but gives few signs of a real sense of humour. Charles, by contrast, can see the funny side, as he demonstrated when the *Tailor and Cutter* ribbed him for his "cult of studied shabbiness". Charles riposted by turning up for the annual dinner of the Master Tailors' Benevolent Association with a well-worn tweed jacket over his white dress shirt. He continued the joke, having changed into tails, in his after-dinner speech: "I am often asked whether it is because of some generic trait that I stand with my hands behind my back, like my father. The answer is that we both have the same tailor. He makes the sleeves so tight we can't get our hands in front."

If he has inherited something of his maternal grandfather's shyness, he has also inherited his grandmother's kindness and consideration. "A very warm-hearted boy," the Queen Mother once called him in childhood and the years have not changed him. He was only 8 when his first nanny, Helen Lightbody, left Buckingham Palace, but he has never forgotten her. He has been frequently to her flat in Kennington for a cup of tea and a chat and was personally responsible for ensuring that she was sent a V.I.P. invitation to attend his investiture in Wales. Similarly, spending a private weekend in Paris in the autumn of 1970, he popped round to see the ageing Duke of Windsor, something neither of his parents has ever done.

The first and second children of a family are often totally different from each other, and so it is with Charles and Anne. There has always been an essential difference between them. In childhood Charles was shy, serious, placid, nervous. Anne was none of these things. On the contrary, she was a bit of a tomboy, climbing trees, and on one occasion, on to a roof at Balmoral, while Charles looked on, urging her to be careful, calling her to come down. Far more quickly than her older brother she was confidently at home in a boat at sea or on the back of a horse. Charles had to work at achieving many of those qualities which seemed to come natural to her and it was perhaps fortunate that one of his own qualities was a plodding, determined, refuse-to-be-beaten nature. But if he was—and is—painstaking, she was—and is—impatient. As a child, he would patiently crayon or paint home-made cards to be sent to friends and relatives at Christmas. "Why can't we just buy them?" Anne wanted to know. Charles would sit quietly and contentedly while his portrait was painted. Anne fidgeted all the time. "She was difficult to paint, so active, like quicksilver," one artist recalls, diplomatically.

As in childhood, so today. Charles, like his mother, seldom permits his feelings to show. Anne does. If she likes someone, it shows. If she is displeased or upset, that shows too. "She never reacts tamely to anyone or anything," one acquaintance has summed her up.

While Charles is more like his mother, Anne would seem to take after the father she so obviously adores. When younger, she was so attached to him that she was not above staging the occasional display of tantrums if nothing else would gain his attention. The process of growing up has toned down that childhood attachment to its proper proportion, but even today she is seldom happier than when in her father's company and it is said of her that she is sometimes inclined to judge the young men she meets by how far they seem to measure up to or fall short of Prince Philip.

Plumpish in schooldays, when she was inclined to gorge too many fattening things, she has slimmed down a lot since. Twenty-one in 1971, 5 feet 6½ inches tall, long-legged and full-bosomed, she has inherited not only her father's fair hair, but eyes which, like his, are sensitive to strong sunlight. She has also inherited his dash, his restlessness, his impatience and, it would seem, something of his temper. Like him, she is sometimes intolerant of what goes on around her and not slow to voice her opinion.

Yet to term Anne "a wild one", as a friend reportedly did a year or so back, is surely to overstate the facts. She may be temperamental, but that is hardly the same thing. To date, as far as we are aware, she has not run off to live with a married man, announced from the Windsor battlements that she is about to be blessed with child while still unwed, thrown eggs at the police or indulged in any other of the fringe benefits of the so-called permissive society. Those, surely, are the wild ones. What Anne has done, by comparison, has been comparatively tame. She went twice to see the way-out musical *Hair* (which has since been left well behind by some other stage shows) as well as the fractionally nude *Abelard and Heloise*, danced her feet off at a Soho discotheque, visited some quite respectable night clubs with a bunch of friends, been seen around with the occasional long-haired boy friend, dressed herself in trouser suits and mini-skirts, and been shopping at Marks and Spencer as well as at Fortnum and Mason. All of which hardly qualifies for the adjective 'wild', and the friend who thinks it does is evidently out of touch with present-day attitudes.

Even the small adventure of going on to the stage at *Hair* to join in the end-of-show dancing was not really the 'wild' spontaneous act some people may have seen it as. On her own admission, Anne was very much in two minds as to what she should do. Should she stay put and risk being labelled a fuddy-duddy or should she join in the dancing and devil take the inevitable publicity? In the end, she did what most young girls would have done in her place. She conformed to the prevailing sub-culture.

Both the Queen and Prince Philip feel that they are being more successful in the upbringing of their 'second family'— Andrew and Edward—than they were with Charles and Anne. This is due to a number of factors. Experience, for one. They have the experience gained from the upbringing of Charles and

Anne to look back on and go by. With Andrew and Edward, too, they can plan their upbringing free from the pressures of monarchy which so preoccupied them when Charles and Anne were younger and which also had a bearing on Charles' upbringing as heir to the throne. Other factors have also played a part. The public spotlight, partly because the royal parents have taken steps to shield the glare, has shone less fiercely upon the youngsters of the 'second family'. Press and television are by now accustomed to the idea that small princes play football with other kids, learn tennis and skating, do physical jerks and go to school. Such things are no longer the novelties they once were. And the royal parents have become more adept at keeping the details to themselves. Prince Charles, when he first wielded a cricket bat and punted a football about, did it where he could be easily observed and photographed in the process. But when Edward's time came he was whisked back and forth to an army sports ground where a greater degree of privacy could be ensured. As a result, the youngsters of the 'second family' can enjoy a freer, less formal childhood than Charles and Anne knew. Palace officials see Andrew and Edward, apart from their background, as two 'very ordinary youngsters'. This assessment, of course, is only partly accurate. How ordinary can a boy hope to be when his mother's image is on the coins he spends in the school tuckshop and the stamps he uses to mail letters home, when 'home' is a 600-room palace stuffed with liveried footmen and holidays are spent in a castle in Scotland or on a yacht the size of *Britannia*? Yet certainly present-day royal upbringing is 'ordinary' compared with what their mother knew in childhood.

Within the limits of their vision (which is conditioned, of course, by their own upbringing and the lives they lead at the present time), the royal parents have always tried to ensure that as little pomp and ceremony as possible has touched the upbringing of their children. Charles and Anne, as children, were not allowed to see photographs of themselves in newspapers and magazines. Their mother did not want them to get a wrong idea of their own importance. They had to be polite not only to those in their own circle, but equally to servants. They had to say "please" if they wanted something and "thank you" when they got it. Indeed, such childhood courtesies were insisted upon to such an extent that Anne, for a time, even developed a habit of saying "please" when training her pet corgi. They were taught to do things for themselves, and Philip, on one occasion, was quite irritated when a servant hurried to close a door which Charles had left open. "Leave it alone, man. He's got hands. He can go back and do it himself." When addressing servants, they had to employ the polite prefix of "Mister". Servants, in turn, addressed the children by their Christian names, and not until Charles was nearing his eighteenth birthday—the age at which he could succeed to the throne, should circumstances require, without his father acting as regent—was word passed round that for the future he should be more formally addressed as "Your Royal Highness" or "Sir".

While the royal parents could by no means be classed as strict, they have been firm about the things they felt mattered. Princess Anne can recall being ordered from the table in childhood because she had sat down without bothering to wash her hands first. Both she and Charles have known what it is to be spanked by Papa. "No television tonight" has been another punishment which has served its turn.

At Buckingham Palace, as in many less regal homes, television has long been a distracting influence. Charles and Anne—and Andrew and Edward, in turn—have sometimes been inclined to sit watching it when their parents felt they should have been doing other, more worthwhile things. Particularly in the case of Prince Charles, his parents felt that he was often watching television when he might have been reading or studying.

Of all the royal children, Charles has had the stoniest path to tread. Almost from birth he was being brought up, even if he did not realise the fact, as a future king. Long before he went to school he was being taken to such functions as his mother's coronation, the annual ceremony of Trooping the Colour and the annual service of the Knights of the Garter in their chapel at Windsor, so that, even if he did not understand what he watched, he could at least absorb a sense of destiny. He was bugged, too, by the Windsor trait of shyness which so plagued his grandfather and has made public life no easier for his mother. Had he been brought up as his mother was before him, restricted to the close confines of a royal palace and the cloying atmosphere of a nursery schoolroom with a succession of nannies, governesses and tutors dancing attendance upon him, he might perhaps have found future public life a painful, almost unbearable, ordeal. Fortunately, his father saw the danger if his mother did not.

If it was Prince Philip's idea that the future king would benefit from being tossed in at the deep end of boarding school life, the Queen raised no objection. While she might not have thought of such a thing herself—it was, after all, something outside the range of her own upbringing and experience—she was quite willing to concede that her husband knew far more than she did about such things.

The decision to send their son to school had already been taken by the royal parents when Lord Altrincham came out with his trenchant look at royal life in the *National and English Review*.

"Will she, above all," the article asked concerning the Queen, "see to it that Prince Charles is equipped with all the knowledge he can absorb without injury to his health and that he mixes during his formative years with children who will one day be bus-drivers, dockers, engineers, etc., and not merely future landowners or stockbrokers?"

The royal parents, initially at least, were not quite prepared to go that far. At Cheam and Gordonstoun Charles did not mix with future bus-drivers or dockers, and, indeed, it is doubtful if he had at that time the temperament to have survived such an unusual experiment had it been tried. In any event, life at a reasonably exclusive boarding school proved to be no less tough than at a state school. There are in all walks of life, as his grandfather, George VI, found out before him, those who delight in pounding and pummelling a royal prince for no other reason than to boast that they have done so. So Charles had his head held under a tap on one occasion, was dunked in a bath of cold water on another, and while at Gordonstoun found himself the most heavily-tackled player on the rugby field. Later, at university, where seventy-five per cent of his fellow-students came from grammar schools, he found himself mixing with youngsters from the sort of background Lord Altrincham had advocated and was by then perhaps sufficiently mature to derive real benefit from such associations.

As a father, it was perhaps natural that Philip should want his son to go to his old schools and see him, at first, as an extension of his own rugged, thrusting, athletic image. To an extent, Charles suffered in boyhood because of that. But if he lacked his father's ebullient, extrovert nature, he had inherited his mother's determination and obstinacy, and these saw him through. So he played rugby at Gordonstoun, and broke his nose in the process, not because he really enjoyed the game—he didn't—but because he felt it was expected of him as his father's son. In the same way, he messed about in small boats at Gordonstoun not because of the pleasure he got from it, as his father had derived pleasure in boyhood, but because, again, he felt it was expected of him.

But to try being his father's son was also to gain something in the process. As a small boy he was inclined to be nervous of both the sea and horses. Today, as his polo playing and entry into the Navy have shown, he is nervous of neither. Yet looking back, he cannot truly say, as his father can, that he enjoyed his schooldays. His was not really the sort of nature to revel in the rough and tumble of schoolboy life. He made few friends and was sometimes lonely, sometimes unhappy. But sticking it out was surely the making of him.

Gondonstoun, in particular, was the anvil on which his character was forged. But Timbertop in Australia, to which he went for a couple of terms, did the essential tempering while Trinity, in turn, was responsible for the buffing and polishing. The two terms in Australia gave him an entirely new outlook on life. A naturally shy youngster, his years at Gordonstoun, despite his efforts at rugby, amateur theatricals and other school activities, made him, if anything, even more shy and introspective. At Timbertop, by contrast, he found himself looking outwards instead of inwards for perhaps the first time. Not that Timbertop, as a scholastic establishment, was all that different from Gordonstoun, on which it was loosely modelled. The difference was in the masters and boys he met there. Gone was that mixed atmosphere of awe-struck reverence and sickly sycophancy he had felt at Gordonstoun. For the first time in schooldays he could relax, settle down, be himself. If he still made few close friends—he is not one to make friends either easily or quickly—he was certainly less of the lone wolf he had been. He was also, when the time came to return home, less shy, less tense, much more self-confident.

In a sense, he grew up at Timbertop and the process of growing-up was seen in his changed attitude towards the opposite sex. Previously he had always been shy and nervous of girls. He returned from Australia with a distinct eye for a pretty girl.

He had already passed his O-levels in English language, English literature, history, French and Latin, though not in mathematics (which he found difficult) or physics. Now he took his A-levels in history and French. And so to Cambridge.

Cambridge was good for him and he enjoyed his time there. There he could mix or not, as he chose, without the necessity for living cheek by jowl with others. Buoyed by the new-found confidence he had gained at Timbertop, he emerged from his shell fully for the first time, going out of his way to mix with others, doing his best to get his fellow-students to accept him as one of themselves despite the fact that royal status necessitated a private bathroom instead of sharing the communal baths.

"He really worked at it," a fellow student recalls. But there was still, Charles found, an unseen barrier between himself and most of the others, though not now of his making. Many, though not all, of his fellow students fought shy of him on the basis that "you don't want him to think you're talking to him just because he's the Prince of Wales, now do you?" But his own shyness was no longer so noticeable to others nor so painful for him, though it was still there, if hidden more deeply. "I am still fairly shy," he confessed towards the end of his time at Cambridge. Fellow students did not all agree with his own assessment of himself: "Much more at ease than he used to be"; "Quite relaxed, or appears to be. If he isn't, then he makes a good job of pretending that he is." And he was less shy, it seemed, with girls than with men. Unlike his father, who is most at home and at ease in the officers' mess atmosphere of an all-male get-together, Charles, at Cambridge, seemed to shine brightest and be at his best if there was a pretty girl in the offing.

A spell at university might have been similarly beneficial to Princess Anne, perhaps toning down her natural effervescence in the same way that it bolstered her brother's increasing self-confidence. But Anne, as we have said, had no desire to go to university and, in any case, her academic qualities hardly justified it. Academically, she is a sprinter rather than a long-distance runner, bright, sharp and quick, but lacking patience and losing interest when it comes to too much studying.

Charles worked hard at Cambridge, both in studying for a

degree and in fitting himself for his future role as Prince of Wales. From the age of 18 there were matters concerning the Duchy of Cornwall, which provides him with his income, to deal with from time to time. With the aid of a record player, he began learning Welsh in preparation for his investiture. He also learned to fly. As with any other student, it was by no means a case of all work and no play, though the proportions, in his case, were weighed in favour of work. "The average student goes to about half the lectures he might attend," a fellow student recalls. "Charles went to nearly all." But there were pleasurable diversions, shooting at Sandringham at weekends, playing the cello, acting in student revues. He may not have been a brilliant actor, but he certainly enjoyed it. On stage, playing a part, he found that he could really let himself go and shed his inhibitions. He wrote an article for the student newspaper which, on his own admission, "received an unfair proportion of publicity for its literary and descriptive quality". As a result, he was offered £10,000 a year to write occasional newspaper articles. Sensible enough to realise that the offer was made because he was who he was rather than because of the brilliance of his writing, he did not pursue the matter. He went out with a few girls and surprised one by taking her home from a dinner party in a travel-stained Land–Rover instead of a royal Rolls or, at very least, the M.G. sports car he was running at the time. He also took part in one or two relatively mild student pranks, including a midnight bicycle race round Trinity's seventeenth-century courtyard following an evening spent wining and dining with a bunch of student friends.

He graduated finally with an average B.A. (Hons.) degree in history. More important perhaps, he graduated also as a human being, a young man in whom regal dignity and ordinary human nature are well balanced, more modest than his father, less remote than his mother.

He and his sister are now both in their marriageable years. Indeed, so good has royalty become at keeping its romantic secrets, that either or both could be betrothed in the interval between writing this book and its ultimate publication. So speculation is risky. But there is no harm in recalling something Charles himself said on the subject of marriage around the time of his investiture as Prince of Wales.

"When you marry in my position," he said, "you are going to marry somebody who perhaps will one day be Queen.

"You have got to choose somebody very carefully who could fulfil this particular role and it has got to be somebody pretty special.

"The one advantage about marrying a princess or somebody from a royal family is that they do know what happens."

His father later added a footnote. "People," said Prince Philip, also on the subject of his eldest son's possible marriage, "tend to marry within their own circle."

Was it just talk, or was it talk with a purpose? Were son and father perhaps both serving discreet notice that Charles already had his eye on someone? Or was it a royal smoke-screen?

There is, as they must both know, something of a shortage of princesses in the modern world. Allowing for age, consanguinity and religion—a Catholic princess could not become Queen—there is very little choice.

Yet if not a princess, who then? Princess Anne, like her aunt before her, could perhaps marry a photographer. Or a stockbroker. Or an airline pilot. With three brothers between her and the throne, she is hardly likely to become Queen. But Charles, barring accidents or a sudden spate of republicanism, will one day be King. So he could hardly marry a photographer's model, a stockbroker's secretary or an airline hostess.

Yet one thing seems certain. Neither Charles nor Anne will have their marriages arranged for them in the Victorian tradition. That is not their parents' way. But that is not to say that a little parental advice may not be forthcoming, a quiet nudge in one direction or a quick frown against taking another. Yet that is no more than happens in less regal circles, with middle-class mums and dads hoping their daughters will marry well and discouraging their sons from becoming too serious about what they consider to be the wrong sort of girl.

But whoever and whenever the royal youngsters marry, they can surely hope for no greater happiness than their parents have so obviously found in their own love-match marriage.

3

Courtship

I The Boy

He was an afterthought baby, conceived in exile, born nearly seven years after the youngest of his four sisters. In the tradition of the family, he was given only one name—Philip, Prince of Greece and Denmark. He was a Greek prince without a drop of Greek blood in his veins, born several rungs down the shaky ladder of succession to that most precarious of thrones, so often toppled pell-mell from its perch only to be hoisted back again after a decent interval of time in readiness for the next upset.

In him flowed the royal blood-lines of Denmark and Russia, Germany and Britain. His father, a dashing 6 feet 4 inches of moustached and monocled banter, was a younger son of Prince William George of Glucksberg, the Danish prince who became King George I of the Hellenes after Queen Victoria's second son, an earlier Duke of Edinburgh, had rejected that doubtful honour. His paternal grandmother was Russian, a Romanov, the Grand Duchess Olga. His mother was born a Battenberg, daughter of Prince Louis of Battenberg (later the first Marquess of Milford Haven), the German-born prince who joined Britain's navy as a 14-year-old midshipman and rose finally to command it.

Through his maternal grandmother he was descended, like so

many of Europe's royalty, from Queen Victoria. On his father's side he came down from King Christian IX of Denmark and one of the oldest dynasties in Europe. No mean combination.

He was born within sound of the sea, amidst the mingled scents of cypress and citrus, eucalyptus and magnolia, in a villa with the quaintly suburban name of Mon Repos on the island of Corfu. The date was 10th June 1921.

He was born to troubled times. His parents had only just unpacked after returning from a three-year spell of exile in Switzerland where, along with others of the Greek royal family, they lived an uncertain existence dependent on borrowed money and funds remitted by distant relatives, waited upon by servants whose loyalty was such they worked unpaid for weeks at a stretch. Scarcely had they unpacked than his father was packing again and off to command the Third Army Corps in that disastrous Greek campaign against Turkey which was to end in defeat, rout, the slaughter of 40,000 Greek troops, the massacre of Smyrna, insurrection and abdication.

Prince Andrew returned briefly to his island home to be with his wife, his four young daughters and his baby son. Then he was summoned to Athens, where a revolutionary junta was now in power. He was seized, imprisoned, charged with negligence and desertion. The result of his trial was a foregone conclusion. Three ex-premiers, two former ministers and the commander-in-chief had already faced a dawn firing squad following the equivalent of a drumhead court martial. Prince Andrew would assuredly have suffered the same fate but for the last-minute intervention of two kings, those of Britain and Spain, and the Pope. After a nail-biting night of suspense while they considered their verdict, the tribunal pronounced him guilty. But this time they did not impose the death penalty, though the alternative, for a man of Prince Andrew's pride, was hardly less bitter. He was stripped of both rank and nationality and banished from Greece.

Today, his son can remember nothing of those strange and uncertain times. They happened too long ago, too soon in life, beyond the reach of memory. He knows them only at second-hand and it was perhaps that second-hand bitterness which accounted for his angry "I don't speak Greek" of a few years ago.

Philip's mother, Princess Alice, had hastened to Athens to

be with her husband. Released but still not safe, he took refuge
with her in the British legation. Three days later they were hurried
aboard the cruiser *Calypso* which Britain had despatched to
extricate them from their still perilous situation. The cruiser called
at Corfu to pick up the children and their English nanny, and
the baby conceived in exile sailed again into exile. He was still
only eighteen months old, too small and too young to sleep
safely in an ordinary bunk. Cots are not among the normal
equipment aboard a British cruiser and some of the crew
ingeniously contrived one out of an old orange box.

So began Philip's years of wandering and insecurity.

The family, now holders of Danish passports, settled for a
time in Paris, living in what was formerly a staff lodge in Rue du
Mont Valerien. Paris in the 1920s was an exciting colourful city,
full of writers, artists, bohemians of all sorts, crammed with
refugees from Greece, Russia and elsewhere. For Philip's parents,
the years which followed were seldom easy. They may not
have been impoverished by the ordinary standards of the day—
millions in France and elsewhere had to subsist on a much lower
level. But they were no longer affluent by the standards to
which they were usually accustomed. Fortunately, as in Switzerland, help was again forthcoming from time to time from more
well-to-do relatives elsewhere and a little money still trickled
through from holdings in Greece. Others, faced with the same
problem, overcame it in various ways. Philip's uncle, Prince
Nicholas, gave painting lessons to augment his slender resources,
while his daughter, Princess Marina, who later became the
Duchess of Kent, made many of her own dresses, developed a
happy knack for turning cheap little hats into quite eye-catching
creations and became quite ingenious at ringing endless changes
with the only evening dress she possessed.

It was the sort of insecure, uncertain upbringing which either
makes or breaks a child. It made Prince Philip. He grew up
independent and self-reliant, high-spirited and energetic. At the
age of 6 he was sent to a school for the children of American
businessmen and diplomats in the Paris suburb of St. Cloud
where, among other things, he learned to box and swim, to swing
a baseball bat and utter American football chants. The English
he spoke at the time was not unnaturally tinged with an American
accent.

It was a curiously contradictory upbringing, at one and the same time both royal and down-to-earth. When he first went to school he was conveyed back and forth by car. But the clothes he wore in class were sometimes darned, sometimes patched. Later he saved up to buy himself a bicycle, starting his cycle fund with a Christmas box sent to him by one of his uncles. The uncle in question was the King of Sweden. He was brought up to think of himself as 'Philip of Greece', the name he wrote at the top of his school essays, but on a day of pelting rain he was unable to cycle home until the downpour ceased. He had no raincoat.

He was some three years at the Country Day and Board School, as the St. Cloud establishment was known. Again he found himself uprooted. This time he was shipped off to Britain where another uncle—Uncle George, the second Marquess of Milford Haven—sent him to school at Cheam along with his own son, David. Schooldays with David marked the beginning of a close friendship which was to continue into adult life—until Philip took umbrage at a magazine article detailing what happened at the stag party he and David (who was his best man) attended the night before his wedding and its sequel the morning after.

But that was a long way ahead for the schoolboy cousins who once spent a night sleeping on a Thames grain barge and another time scaled the roof of a riverside hotel so that they could peer in through the skylight. Philip, in those days, was a considerable young rip who more than once during his years at Cheam knew what it was to experience the thwack of a cane and was once caught by the police while climbing on to the roof of his grandmother's home at Kensington Palace. Holidays from school were spent sometimes at Kensington, sometimes at Uncle George's country home, sometimes with relatives in Romania and elsewhere, and sometimes with his parents in Paris.

But presently there was no longer a home for him to go to in Paris. Gradually his once close-knit family was to split up and drift apart. One by one, within the short space of two years, his four sisters all married German princelings. Sophie, the youngest, was the first to marry. She was only 16 when she became the bride of Prince Christopher of Hesse, who was subsequently killed in a wartime air crash. Then Cecilie, at 20, married the Grand Duke George of Hesse. Margarita, the eldest, married Prince Gottfried of Hohenlohe-Langenburg, while Theodora, the second eldest, became the wife of Berthold, Margrave of Baden.

With the marriages of their four daughters, Philip's parents drifted apart. They lived separately for a time in Paris. Then Prince Andrew moved south to the sunshine and pleasures of Monte Carlo, while Princess Alice followed her daughters to Germany. The question remained: what was to be done with young Philip?

Theodora's marriage to the Margrave of Baden provided a possible solution. Under the patronage of her father-in-law, Prince Max of Baden, a progressive educationalist named Dr. Kurt Hahn had founded a somewhat unusual school at Salem in Germany. Theodora's husband himself had been educated in that group of ancient monastic buildings at Salem, on the shore of Lake Constance. Now it was Philip's turn. At the age of 13 he went there as one of the school's 400 to 500 pupils. But not for long.

The year was 1934. The Nazis had come to power and Germany was now as unsettled and dangerous as Greece had been at the time of Philip's birth. Salem was of particular interest to the Nazis. With its emphasis on leadership through service, it was already famous as a character-building establishment. The Nazis wanted it under their control and forming part of their image. Kurt Hahn was arrested and deported. He fled to Britain where he continued his successfully unorthodox educational principles at a new school he set up on the shores of the Moray Firth— Gordonstoun.

Philip, during his brief period at Salem, found it an unusual establishment. The school day started with a cold shower (even in the depths of winter), physical jerks and a share of the domestic chores. There were, in addition to normal lessons, periods devoted to such classical athletic pursuits as throwing the javelin (at which Philip was quickly adept) and hurling the discus as well as compulsory rest periods when the boys stretched out on their beds while a master read to them.

As always, Philip was a high-spirited youngster, always sky-larking, sometimes in trouble. To him there was an amusing parallel between the raised hand of the Nazi salute and the raised hand of the schoolboy wanting what he has since called "a widdle". He mocked it accordingly, perhaps not realising how dangerous such mockery could be in the Germany of those days.

But if he did not appreciate the danger, his sisters did. Worried for his safety, and perhaps their own, they decided it would be better for everyone if he left Germany. So the boyhood travels which had already taken him from Greece to France, to England and Germany, now took him to Scotland, to Kurt Hahn's new school at Gordonstoun.

Gordonstoun, at the time Philip first went there, was in its infancy, a small, close-knit community of a few score boys and masters who shared not only lessons and games, but also in the task of converting the existing school buildings and constructing new ones. In one letter to his father around this time Philip wrote that he was helping to build a pig-sty.

He was always closely attached to the father he saw so seldom. He wrote to him at intervals from Gordonstoun and sent him photographs to show how he was growing up. In 1936, when Philip was 15, they were briefly united in Greece when Philip was given time off from school to attend the ceremonies marking the restoration of the monarchy there. There was at the time some suggestion that he should return to Greece permanently and enter the Greek Nautical College. Philip toyed briefly with the idea, but finally decided that he preferred to stay on at Gordonstoun.

His love of the sea had already begun to reveal itself, and was to grow even more in the years ahead. At Gordonstoun he helped crew the ketch *Diligent* on a trip round the Orkneys and Shetlands. He acted as cook and lamp-trimmer on a trip to Norway aboard the old three-masted hulk the school had acquired and renovated, renaming it *Prince Louis* in honour of Philip's Battenberg grandfather. "Not afraid of dirty or arduous work," wrote his sailing instructor of his efforts aboard ship. He helped build and man the school coastguard station. In his time off, he made model boats and was constantly to be found hobnobbing with the local fishermen at nearby Hopeman Harbour.

He was in those days, if the recollections of friends and relatives can be relied upon all these years later, hungry for

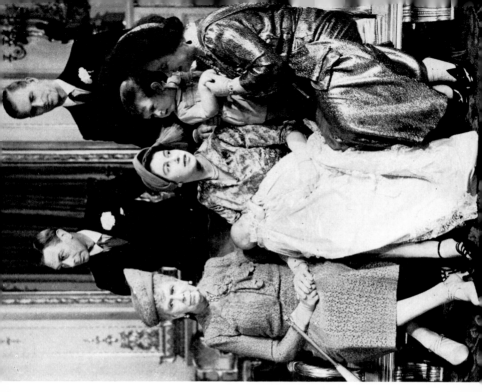

(*left*) After the
ceremony of Prince
Charles' christening in
January 1949. (*right*)
A 1950 family group
at the christening of
Princess Anne

(*left*) Prince Philip as commander of H.M.S. *Magpie* in the Mediterranean

(*right*) Princess Elizabeth taking part in a square dance during her 1951 Canadian Tour

security, reassurance, affection, running round in circles like a pup chasing its tail if admiration or praise came his way. Praise him for doing something and he would repeat the performance on a more exaggerated level in the hope of meriting further praise. He was a big eater, as small boys and insecure people often are; self-willed and quick-tempered; as restless then as he has proved since, always wanting to be up and doing. He feigned an unemotional shell, but others noticed that it could be quickly pierced by joy or sadness alike. Physically he was tough and revelled in his own toughness, though inclined to look down on those of lesser fibre than himself. In him, qualities of leadership were quickly noticeable, but marred, as Dr. Hahn noted, by "impatience and intolerance". His seamanship instructor added that he was cheerful, conscientious, trustworthy.

Academically, he seemed to exert himself no more than was necessary in order to get by. His best subjects were mathematics, geography and modern languages. His early years in Paris and his months in Germany got him off to a good start in French and German. Greek he did not take, though he could have done so. During his period in the middle school he got into a fair number of schoolboy scrapes through wildness and recklessness. He excelled in all forms of outdoor activity, representing the school at rugby and in the Scottish schools' athletics championships, captaining it at both hockey and cricket. He became, in turn, a colour bearer (equivalent to a prefect in more orthodox schools) and guardian (school captain).

Fate, however, had not yet finished playing its cruel tricks on his divided family. He was summoned one day to Dr. Hahn's study and there given the tragic news that his sister Cecilie, her husband and their two small sons had all perished in an air crash while flying from Germany to England to attend a wedding. He was just 16.

Another death around this time was to bring a new and lasting influence into Philip's life. With the death of Uncle George, cousin David became the third Marquess of Milford Haven and another uncle took over responsibility for Philip's welfare. This was 'Uncle Dickie', as Philip called the naval captain who was later to become famous as Earl Mountbatten of Burma. To Philip, Uncle Dickie was very much more than a mere father-figure who paid his school fees. He quickly came to hero-worship

7

him as the epitome of mature masculinity and was never more thrilled than when he could visit that fabulous London penthouse where his uncle's bedroom was laid out exactly like a ship's cabin. Uncle Dickie, for his part, perhaps saw the fair-haired young Philip, so Battenberg in so many ways, as the son he did not have. He had followed his own father, Prince Louis, into the Navy and was delighted to learn that Philip envisaged the same career. Both then and later he was perhaps the biggest single influence in Philip's young life.

Philip was not yet 18 when he left Gordonstoun for Cheltenham where he took a cram course with a naval coach before sitting the entrance examination for the Royal Naval College, Dartmouth. There were thirty-four entrants for the examination and he came sixteenth.

Dr. Kurt Hahn, in his final report on the youngster who was to prove his most famous pupil, had this to say of him:

> Prince Philip is universally trusted, liked and respected. He has the greatest sense of service of all the boys in the school.
> Prince Philip is a born leader, but will need the exacting demands of a great service to do justice to himself. His best is outstanding; his second best is not good enough.
> Prince Philip will make his mark in any profession where he will have to prove himself in a full trial of strength.

In the years which lay ahead Philip was to find his "greatest sense of service" tried and tested to the full.

II The Girl

She was a first and much-wanted child, born on almost the third anniversary of her parents' wedding in the Georgian mansion at 17 Bruton Street, which was the London home of her maternal grandfather. The date was 21st April 1926.

She, too, was descended from Queen Victoria and—through her great-grandmother, Queen Alexandra, sister of that Danish prince who became King George I of the Hellenes—from King Christian IX of Denmark. Her father was the Duke of York, second son of King George V. Her mother was the youngest-but-one child of the fourteenth Earl of Strathmore and Kinghorne.

She was born third in line to the world's most secure throne. Between her and it stood her Uncle David, the then Prince of Wales, and his brother, her own father, though marriage and fatherhood for the former or the birth of a son to the latter could yet alter the order of succession. Because of this, there were some who would have preferred her to have been born a boy instead of a girl. But her parents were content enough. "Our happiness complete," her father wrote to his father, the booming, bearded King George V. Indeed, her mother was overjoyed. She had always said that she wanted a girl first.

She was christened Elizabeth Alexandra Mary in the family tradition of handing down names from one generation to the next. Elizabeth was her mother's name, Mary her grandmother's and Alexandra that of her Danish great-grandmother. Grandpapa George V wondered whether they should not also include another generation by tacking on Victoria, the name of her great-great-grandmother, but finally decided that it did not really matter. In any event, her family was to call her by the pet name of Lilibet and her as yet unborn sister, Margaret, was to contract this still further to Lil upon occasion in the years ahead.

Her parents, until the day of her father's death just over a quarter of a century later, were utterly devoted to each other and never more so than during those early days of marriage before the abdication of Uncle David thrust monarchy upon them.

For her there were to be no years of exile, no divided family, no being constantly shunted hither and thither, never sure of where the next stopping place would be or for how long. Hers was a warm, happy, secure childhood lived within a close-knit family circle enlivened in a few short years by the arrival of a small chubby sister who was finally named Margaret Rose after Grandpapa, again fussing over names, had flatly rejected the initial choice of Ann Margaret. It is interesting to speculate all these years later that if that second baby had been a boy instead

of another girl, it would have been a king and not a queen who
would eventually have succeeded to the throne.

For her, there was never any patched or darned clothing. Toys
and playthings were showered upon her so abundantly that
many were passed on to charitable institutions. There were
budgerigars to feed, a corgi to play ball with, a pony to ride,
with one of Grandpapa's carriages always available for jaunts
round the Serpentine. There was never any shortage of money,
not even after Grandpapa and Uncle David volunteered substantial pay-cuts because of the difficult economic times through
which the nation was passing. There was never any trouble about
where to go for holidays. Christmas at Sandringham and summer
at Balmoral, surrounded by battalions of protective royal relatives,
came round with clockwork regularity. The only small dis-
turbance in her young life came with the occasional move back
and forth between London and Royal Lodge, the pink-walled
country home Grandpapa had given her parents in Windsor
Great Park so that his small grand-daughter could escape at
intervals from the soot and fogs of London. Her home in London,
a tall, narrow, unpretentious town house at 145 Piccadilly was
within a stone's throw of Buckingham Palace. With a pair of
field-glasses, as she was to discover when she was only a little
older, you could stand at one of the windows and actually see
Grandpapa at one of the palace windows—looking back at you
through his own field-glasses. It became quite a game between
them.

Her young life was as content and secure as childhood can
possibly be. A squad of loyal retainers watched over the wellbeing of her and her baby sister. There was 'Alla' Knight, their
nannie; an under-nurse named Margaret MacDonald who was
to become her beloved 'Bobo'; Margaret's sister, Ruby, brought
down from Scotland to help out with the newborn baby sister;
and a nurserymaid with the prosaic name of Smith. Later came
a governess named Marion Crawford who was promptly nicknamed 'Crawfie'.

Her schooling, like everything else about her upbringing, was
safe, secure and unadventurous. The idea that she should go to
school in the ordinary way never occurred to her parents. While
Philip was shuttling about from St. Cloud to Cheam, Cheam to
Salem and Salem to Gordonstoun, Elizabeth was sitting quietly

in an improvised schoolroom at either 145 Piccadilly or Royal Lodge, listening to the gentle voice of Miss Crawford. Her mother left the educational syllabus to her father who left it to Miss Crawford. So she was taught writing, composition, poetry, history, geography and Bible study. Arithmetic was kept to a minimum. "She is unlikely to need it," said her grandmother, Queen Mary. Cleaning and tidying a miniature thatched cottage at Windsor gave her a slight smattering of domestic science. She was also taught to knit, but was never any good at it.

While Philip was learning to live and face up to life as it really is, she was being brought up in an old-world atmosphere that was already fading fast and was soon to vanish almost completely. Music, dancing, singing, drawing, riding . . . these were the accomplishments she gained from a succession of private tutors. Later came swimming and tennis to ensure that she got sufficient exercise.

While Philip was perhaps puzzling his schoolboy head as to why his parents were no longer together, she was playing tag and hopscotch with a doting father and learning the elements of good manners from a loving mother. While he was sleeping on grain barges and climbing hotel roofs, she was being solemnly conducted to places like the National Gallery and the British Museum. Her biggest adventures in childhood—and these much later—were a ride on the Underground and a trip on the top of a double-decker bus.

It was all very safe, secure and cloistered. If it was also dull, Elizabeth Alexandra Mary does not appear to have noticed it. She was not an adventurous girl. Brought up largely in the company of grown-ups with only her small sister for a playmate most of the time, it is perhaps not surprising that she should have tended to grow up older than her years, a serious, patient and most punctual youngster. Occasionally obstinate. But mostly methodical, dutiful and conscientious, carefully tidying her clothes at bedtime, making neat lists of what she was given at Christmas so that she could write the appropriate thank-you notes without difficulty or delay. Then, as later, she was the dutiful one; Margaret the playful, affectionate mischief.

She was a pretty child with rosebud cheeks and golden hair, a delightful little bridesmaid at the royal weddings of two of her uncles, the Duke of Kent and the Duke of Gloucester. Acting as train-bearer to Princess Marina, the beautiful exiled Greek princess who married the Duke of Kent, she cannot possibly have realised how helpful a part Philip's cousin was to play in the development of her own future love story.

For Britain's royalty, despite their volunteered pay-cuts, it was a golden age. Wherever they went they were surrounded by loyal emotion and dizzy enthusiasm (even from the tens of thousands of the unemployed), and never more so than in 1935 when King George V and Queen Mary celebrated their silver jubilee. The young Elizabeth accompanied her parents to the commemorative service in St. Paul's and later drove with her grandparents on a triumphal procession through London's flag-bedecked streets. The crowds went wild over her almost ethereal beauty.

But a few months later Grandpapa was dead and the small princess who had so enjoyed those triumphal jubilee rides now found herself dressed in mourning black for his funeral. With his death, she was second in the line of succession. She was 9 years old.

Her Uncle David, perhaps her favourite among all her uncles, was now King Edward VIII. The shortness of his reign had perhaps been foreshadowed a year before at the wedding of the Duke of Kent to Princess Marina. The wedding had been preceded by a reception and banquet at Buckingham Palace. Among the guests was a vivacious, slender, elegantly groomed American who chattered volubly and laughed a lot. Her name was Mrs. Wallis Simpson and the man Elizabeth knew as Uncle David had been almost inseparable from her.

The uncle who was now king brought his intriguing companion to have tea with the Yorks and their children at Royal Lodge one afternoon. Elizabeth could not help noticing that he was no longer the gay, playful, teasing Uncle David of old. Instead, he was serious and preoccupied. Perhaps it was all the new duties of monarchy. And perhaps it was something else.

Her Uncle David was, in fact, a king ahead of his time, and not only in his desire to marry a divorcée. He was a man who preferred living in her modern, sophisticated world to the gracious, old-style world of royalty. Indeed, he considered the traditional royal way of life and the court which revolved around it to be so old-fashioned as to verge still upon the Victorian.

Almost his first act of kingship, when his father died at Sandring-ham, was to order the clocks there to be put to the correct time. King George V had always insisted that they were kept fast in order to give him an extra half-hour of daylight in the shooting field. Such old-style royal shooting parties similarly held no appeal for the new king. To him, Sandringham was little more than an expensive white elephant. Balmoral bored him similarly. He infinitely preferred the more cosmopolitan playgrounds of Europe to what he considered the introverted shooting-yachting-horsy atmosphere of the traditional royal round.

All this, of course, was above Elizabeth's pretty little head and beyond her childhood understanding. Nor did she realise how fortunate she was perhaps to have been born in phlegmatic England rather than hot-blooded Greece during the weeks and months which followed. In Greece, such a crisis of monarchy could hardly have been resolved without bloodshed. In Britain it passed off in a quieter and more orderly Anglo-Saxon fashion. A few there were who talked of "standing by the King" and who would perhaps have welcomed the excitement of a little bloodshed in the process. But the overall British spirit did not go along with such heroics. So the King quietly took his leave, his brother took over the throne and the young Elizabeth was now irrevocably betrothed to monarchy—irrevocably because it was inconceivable, with her upbringing and outlook, that she would ever do anything even remotely approaching what her Uncle David had done.

Now, with the move to Buckingham Palace, the pattern of her life was imperceptibly changed. From then on, her upbringing was noticeably—though not to her—more disciplined than that of the younger Margaret. To her father, Margaret was the fun child, Elizabeth the daughter who would one day succeed him. He treated her accordingly and she responded in a manner which brought pride and joy to him.

But she did notice that her father, involved in duties he had neither sought nor desired, now had less time for raceabout games of tag, hopscotch and hide-and-seek. "I do wish Papa didn't have to see all those people," she complained once. "It would do him more good to play with us for a bit." She little dreamed of how quickly she herself was to be caught up in those same duties and ceremonies.

The Civil List for the new reign gave her an annual allowance of £6,000, rising to £15,000 on her twenty-first birthday. It made no change in her personal finance. Her pocket money, which started at one shilling (5*p*) a week, never rose above five shillings (25*p*) Dressed in a gown of lace and silver, a purple cloak trimmed with ermine, silver slippers and a pint-sized coronet, she was taken to Westminster Abbey to see her father crowned. The more volatile Margaret went along too, similarly dressed, and the serious and conscientious elder sister took a quiet pride in the fact that she had to keep the younger one in order. But there was still sufficient of the child in her, when she travelled north to Balmoral, to get a policeman at Euston station to buy her a comic to read on the journey.

If there were fewer games with her father, there were other respects in which she saw more of him. Almost as though he foresaw the shortness of his own reign, he quickly set about training her to succeed him. He had her standing beside him on all manner of official occasions. He arranged for her to accompany her mother on similar state occasions in Scotland. He arranged with his mother, Queen Mary, to take her on 'educational visits' to such places as the Royal Mint (where she saw his Royal Seal being made), the Post Office savings bank (where she was delighted to find she had a nest-egg of £30) and the Bank of England (where they jokingly offered her a gold brick if she could carry it away with her. She tried; she couldn't). French and Latin were added to the schoolroom curriculum, and, later, Dr. Henry Marten, the then vice-provost of Eton College, was roped in to supervise her studies. He gave her instruction in such specialised studies as constitutional history and the law of land tenure and set her reading such works as Muzzey's *History of the United States*, Chaucer's *Canterbury Tales* and Foucin's *Geographie Historique*. To encourage her to mix as well as give her some company of her own age, a group of Girl Guides was formed at Buckingham Palace. It was not, initially, a noticeable success. Public duties started early. She presented the prizes at the National Pony Show and was among the official guests at a luncheon held at Windsor Castle in honour of the visiting foreign minister from Poland. She was still only 12. She saw her parents off on their visit to Canada and the United States.

"Your handkerchief is to wave, not to cry into," she carefully cautioned the younger Princess Margaret.

III   Boy Meets Girl

It was soon after his return from America in that pre-war summer of 1939 that King George VI conceived the nostalgic notion which was to mark the beginning of his daughter's love story. As a lad of 15, along with his elder brother, the Prince of Wales, he had trained as a cadet at the Royal Naval College at Dartmouth, where he went down with measles, was sixty-seventh out of sixty-eight in his first end-of-term examinations, received a whacking for letting off fireworks, was awarded an hour's extra drill to be carried out at the double as punishment on three other occasions and was finally appointed a midshipman aboard the battleship *Collingwood* on which he saw action as 'Mr. Johnson' at the Battle of Jutland. Now, in middle age, he experienced a desire to recapture old memories. So he decided to start his summer holiday by re-visiting Dartmouth before going on to Balmoral, where, in a further concession to nostalgia, he planned to hold another of those famous 'boys' camps', with their mixture of privileged and not-so-privileged youngsters, which he had first started back in 1921.

It was all to be a family, rather than an official, occasion, and his wife and daughters were with him when he sailed for Weymouth aboard the old royal yacht *Victoria and Albert*, a coincidentally romantic name in the light of subsequent events. Though they were both totally unaware of the fact, the royal tapestries of Princess Eliabeth and Prince Philip, the one unblemished despite the Abdication, the other less patched and darned than it had been in early days, were about to intertwine.

At Dartmouth Royal Naval College there had been all the customary spit-and-polish which always precedes a royal visit.

The programme was now all arranged. The royal party would inspect the college and its grounds, attend service in the chapel and entertain the cadet-captains to dinner aboard the royal yacht. But like the best-laid schemes of mice and ordinary men, those of reigning monarchs can sometimes go astray.

Just as an outbreak of measles had stricken the college almost as soon as the king went there as a lad of 15, so now, coincidental with his return visit, mumps and chicken-pox joined forces in a combined operation which quickly filled the sick bay and dormitories alike. As a result, there was a hurried last-minute reshuffling of plans as the *Victoria and Albert* dropped anchor in the Dart on 22nd July 1939, and the royal family squelched ashore in a downpour of summer rain. Princess Elizabeth was a few months past her thirteenth birthday, a rather leggy youngster who had lately overcome an earlier tendency to nail-biting. Margaret, at 9, was plumper and inclined to giggle. Also in the party, attending the King in his capacity as royal A.D.C., was Philip's Uncle Dickie.

Neither of the princesses had had mumps or chicken-pox. Both were likely to get either if they were jammed into the college chapel along with a mass of young cadets. Rather than take the risk, it was decided that they should wait in the house of Admiral Sir Frederick Hew George Dalrymple-Hamilton, the captain of the college. Watched over by their governess, Miss Crawford, the two girls amused themselves for a time playing with a toy train set. Presently the door opened and a tall, fair-haired boy whom governess Crawfie described as "rather like a Viking with a sharp face and piercing blue eyes" came into the room. It was Philip.

Perhaps through nerves, he gave a first impression of being slightly cocky. He had just turned 18 and only ten days before had won the javelin event in the Devonport Port Athletics championships with a throw of 140 feet 10 inches.

It was not the first time he and Princess Elizabeth had seen each other. Both had almost certainly been guests at the same children's parties in earlier years. Both had been at the coronation of Elizabeth's father. But now they really met for the first time.

For a meeting which was to have such momentous consequences it was not a particular romantic occasion, though the young and impressionable Elizabeth may have seen it as such. Philip did not. Accustomed to the society of rather more mature young ladies when on holiday, he saw Elizabeth as no more than a small relative who had to be amused for an hour or two.

He got down on to the floor to help Margaret operate the toy train set. There was refreshment in the shape of lemonade and ginger biscuits. The sun came out and Philip suggested a game of croquet. He thought Elizabeth shy. He played well, she thought. Evidently he thought so too, for he seems to have rounded off the game with an exuberant leap over a nearby tennis net.

The chapel service over, the King toured the college. He was in good form. He called for the punishment book and, amidst laughter, read out details of his own misdemeanours.

Philip, as Uncle Dickie's nephew, was invited to join the royal family for lunch aboard the yacht. Later he showed the two small princesses round the college. That evening, along with the other cadet-captains, he dined with the King. But Elizabeth was not there. At 13, she was considered still too young to stay up for dinner and had gone to bed.

But the following day the two of them were again thrown into each other's company. They had lunch and tea together, the blushing Princess hovering solicitously around Philip as he consumed liberal helpings of shrimps as well as a banana split. Then the nostalgic royal visit was over and it was time for the Princess to accompany her parents back to the yacht.

It was "Up anchor" and the yacht set sail, with the college cadets giving it a right royal send-off, piling into a miscellaneous collection of small boats to speed it on its way. More than 100 small craft escorted it as far as the harbour mouth. As the *Victoria and Albert* steamed out into the Channel, most of the accompanying small craft turned back. But not all. The King became rather alarmed for their safety and ordered a signal to be flown for the remaining few to turn back also.

Presently only one was left. Princess Elizabeth, staring at it through her father's field-glasses, recognised the occupant as Philip.

Perhaps he had not seen the signal. Perhaps, like Nelson, he decided to turn a blind eye to it. Either way, he continued to follow the royal yacht out to sea.

The King was really worried now. Worry made him angry. He called Philip "a damned young fool".

Frantic hand-signals were made for him to turn back. A

megaphone was brought into use. "Go back. Go back," called the King.

Finally Philip did so. Elizabeth continued to watch him through her father's field-glasses until his small craft was no more than a dot in the distance.

IV   Boy Woos Girl

Among all the other monarchical necessities and personal knick-knacks—blotting pad and stationery rack, brass carriage clock and silver inkstand, calendar and engagement book, pens, pencils, pins, paper clips and rubber bands—which crowd the desk at which the Queen works in the bay window of her private sitting room are a number of treasured photographs. There is one of her mother, one of Prince Charles as a baby, one taken when she and her husband were on their honeymoon. And two of Prince Philip as he was in those wartime days when he first courted her by correspondence.

In one, youthful looking and clean-shaven, he stands crisply to attention in his naval uniform, his hand at the salute. It is the first photograph she ever had of him. He was 21 when he sent it to her and she was 16. She sent him a girlish photograph of herself in exchange, signing it "Lilibet", the pet name by which she was always known in the family circle.

In the other photograph he is also in naval uniform, but this time handsomely bearded. It is the photograph she took with her in her cabin aboard the battleship *Vanguard* when she sailed for South Africa with her parents early in 1947. She had been cautioned that the earlier photograph, which originally occupied a place of honour on the mantelpiece of her room at the palace, might lead to gossip. So the change was effected. "Now he's completely incognito," she said, laughingly. But even the beard could not completely disguise who it was.

It is now around thirty years since those photographs were first taken. The Queen has treasured them all that time. For her, from the moment of their first meeting at Dartmouth, there has never been any other man in her life. It was, in a sense, love at first sight, even if further time was required for love to blossom and flower.

But if she was to become a one-man girl from the moment of that first meeting, Philip, initially at least, was perhaps less single-minded. His life, after all, was less circumscribed than hers in those wartime days so soon to follow that first meeting and there were pretty girls in every port.

Philip, like many another young man, grew up quickly under the impact of war. The "noisy, over-excited young fellow" governess Crawfie had first thought him to be matured quickly into a young man with more masculine appeal and considerable charm. Tall, slim, fair-haired and blue-eyed with the profile of a young Greek god, athletic, witty, energetic and high-spirited, quickly expert at almost everything he undertook, from water-skiing to table tennis, it can hardly be wondered at if feminine heads were quick to turn wherever he went. Opportunities for flirtation were plentiful, and he proved he could flirt charmingly enough.

His upbringing, despite the relatively monastic nature of such establishments as Gordonstoun and Dartmouth, had not been without feminine contacts and the occasional youthful 'crush'. There was one occasion, during a pre-war holiday in Venice, when he took a sweet young thing out for a boat trip on the lagoon. The trip lasted a long time and Philip returned with the explanation that there had been "trouble with the sparking plugs".

Now, in wartime, wherever he went there were inevitably girls whose eyes radiated the age-old message and girls' mothers who hopefully contemplated the prospect of a son-in-law from the royal house of Greece. But Philip, though he may have flirted from time to time, also played hard to get. Though he went out with girls, he was careful not to become involved or even halfway committed. He might escort a girl to a dance, but there always seemed to be some reasonable enough excuse for not seeing her home afterwards. There was equally some excuse for not seeing the same girl more than once or at least not too often. The time-honoured excuse of the sailor—"I'm sorry, m'dear, but I have to rejoin my ship"—may have come in handy, however apocryphal the story of the seemingly designing young miss who rang his grandmother's home at Kensington Palace in the hope of persuading him to take her out. The man's voice which answered the telephone was sorry but Prince Philip had left to rejoin his ship. Only after she had replaced the telephone, so the story goes, did it occur to the young lady that the voice had sounded suspiciously like Philip's own.

Philip had done well at Dartmouth. He had won the prize for the best all-rounder of his year and the King's Dirk for the best special entry cadet. As at Cheam, Salem and Gordonstoun, there had also been one or two youthful scrapes. He was justifiably cleared of blame when his cutter collided with the commanding officer's boat on one occasion, but another misdemeanour resulted in an hour's extra drill and digging a slit trench into the bargain.

The early weeks of 1940 found him serving as a midshipman aboard the battleship *Ramillies*, at that time based in Far Eastern waters, a compromise solution to the somewhat tricky situation in which he found himself on the outbreak of war. He had qualified to serve in the Royal Navy. But, technically at least, he was still a Greek and a member of the royal house of Greece at that. And Greece was not at war.

Naturalisation would have been a simple way out of the dilemma, but naturalisation procedures, Philip found out on inquiry, had been abruptly suspended for the duration of hostilities. It was Uncle Dickie who came up with the idea of a posting to the Far East. Based on Ceylon, the *Ramillies* was at that time sufficiently remote from the real trouble spots to render it unlikely that Philip would fall into enemy hands, which would have been a delicate situation indeed. Philip saw and accepted the necessity for this move, though far from overjoyed by it. Like most young men, he would have preferred to have been where the action was, and the Indian Ocean, at the time, hardly seemed the place.

Before he left, Uncle Dickie organised a sort of going-away party which also included the King and Queen. They all went to see the musical *Funny Side Up*. Princess Elizabeth was not included in the outing.

Perhaps she was considered too young. In any event, she was not in London. With the outbreak of war and their own return to the capital, her parents had deemed it safer for her and Margaret to stay on for the time being at Birkhall on the Balmoral estate. From there, she travelled south to spend Christmas with her parents at Sandringham before going to Royal Lodge at Windsor. Lessons were resumed under Dr. (later Sir) Henry Marten and coloured flags stuck into a map fixed to the wall of the schoolroom enabled her to follow, if not understand, the progress of the war. But as the German panzers rolled back the map of Europe, as British troops extricated themselves from the inferno of Dunkirk and Operation Sealion seemed all but imminent, Royal Lodge was hardly the safest place in the world for the heiress presumptive. There was a suggestion that she should be sent to Canada, but her parents would not entertain it. Instead, she became a princess in a tower . . . the Lancaster Tower of Windsor Castle. It was perhaps not the most comfortable of residences, but the deep-down dungeons were relatively safe in the event of air attack. Blast and flying glass were a greater danger. To minimise both, sandbags were stacked against the thick stone walls, the huge chandeliers were taken down and glass-fronted cabinets turned to face the other way. At night the Princess slept with a siren suit beside her bed. When there was an air-raid warning she slipped it on over her nightdress and was whisked down to the dungeons.

The battleship *Ramillies*, with Philip aboard, sailed for Australia to act as a troop escort and from there to Alexandria. With the Italians poised to emulate the German sweep across Europe with a matching drive into Egypt, it looked as if Philip might get all the action his youthful heart desired. But the powers-that-be thought otherwise. Greece was still neutral and a Greek prince serving in the British Navy could not be permitted to fall into Italian or German hands. So he was hurriedly transferred, first to the cruise *Kent* and then to the *Shropshire* at Durban.

While Philip was shuttling around between Colombo and Australia, Australia and Alexandria, Alexandria and Durban, Princess Elizabeth, at Windsor, was knitting rather shapeless socks as comforts for the troops—she was never very good at either knitting or needlework—and helping to collect old metal for aircraft production. She took part in fire fighting and anti-gas drills. As always, she took such things seriously. To Margaret, they were more of a lark. Once the younger sister joked that she was going to sound the alarm which would turn out the guard. "You can't do it," cried the older sister, almost petrified with nerves as she dashed back into the castle. In fact, Margaret didn't.

A great letter-writer like her ancestress, Queen Victoria, the Princess penned letters of good cheer and encouragement in a scrawling schoolgirl hand to royal servants who were now in the forces. But if her handwriting was still unformed, in other respects she was growing up. She experimented with lipstick, coating her mouth so heavily it looked as though it was smeared with raspberry jam. She became a fan of such wartime folk heroes as 'Sailor' Malan, Stanford Tuck and Guy Gibson of Dambusters fame. Like Tuck and Gibson, Malan, despite his sobriquet of 'Sailor', was a flyer and it is interesting to note that the Princess' heroes were mainly to be found among this new young breed of fighting men.

It was around this time that she and Philip exchanged their first letters. It started with a Christmas card which Philip sent her. She had not sent him one and her first letter was perhaps to make amends for the oversight. He wrote back. In the years that followed, while the war ran its course, they corresponded with increasing frequency and growing tenderness.

The Italian invasion of Greece in the October of 1940 had meantime resolved Philip's tricky situation for him. Greece was no longer neutral and neither was he. Now he could go where the action was. Diplomatic string-pulling found him transferred yet again, this time to the battleship *Valiant* in the Mediterranean.

In the March of 1941 came the moment of action he had so long desired. A British Mediterranean fleet under Admiral Sir Andrew Cunningham intercepted the Italian main fleet off the toe of Italy. What followed was perhaps the most sweeping British naval victory since Trafalgar. For the British, the Battle of Cape Matapan was a victory won without a single British casualty and no material damage to the British ships. The only loss was a solitary naval aircraft. Against this, Italy lost three heavy cruisers, a 6-inch gun cruiser and two large destroyers. Another destroyer and a brand-new battleship were severely damaged. It was also a victory which started in the true Nelsonian

The Duke of Edinburgh kneels in homage to his wife as queen during the Coronation

In Portugal in the aftermath of the so-called 'royal rift'

tradition, with the light cruiser *Orion* acting as a decoy to lure the Italians towards the main British fleet.

At ten o'clock at night the trap was suddenly sprung. The British ships opened concentrated fire on a surprised and unsuspecting enemy at extremely short range. Philip was in the thick of it. Aboard *Valiant* he was responsible for operating the searchlights on the engaged side. So effective was his illumination of the Italian cruiser *Fiume* that *Valiant* and *Warspite* wrecked it with their opening salvoes. Philip then beamed his searchlights on *Zara*, another Italian heavy cruiser, and in moments that too was wrecked and sinking. Neither *Fiume* nor *Zara* had fired a single shot.

For his part in the action Philip was 'mentioned in despatches' by Admiral Sir Andrew Cunningham and was additionally awarded the War Cross by his native Greece.

This spell of service in the Mediterranean also afforded Philip the opportunity of a reunion with his mother, Princess Andrew. She had returned to Greece following the restoration of the Greek monarchy and now obstinately declined to leave Athens. With three daughters married to Germans and both a son and a brother serving in the British Navy, hers was an unhappy predicament. Her duty, as she saw it, was to Greece. Even after the German occupation, she stayed put, working in Greek hospitals, and acting as temporary foster-mother to a small group of war-orphans.

Indeed, at this time Philip seemed to be constantly bumping into one or other of his relatives. There was a brief meeting with King George II of the Hellenes, his cousin despite the more than thirty years which separated them in age. In fact, the *Valiant* served as escort when the King left Greece for Cairo following the German invasion. In Cairo Philip met other relatives who had escaped only in the nick of time, among them Crown Prince Paul and Crown Princess Frederika with their daughter, Sophie, and their baby son, Constantine. He ran into his uncle, Lord Louis, who turned up in Cairo after the sinking of his destroyer, *Kelly*, and in Alexandria there was a brief reunion with his cousin David, third Marquess of Milford Haven. He ran into Crown Princess Frederika and other relatives again in South Africa when he arrived there later that year on a troop ship. But he never saw his father again. The war was not yet over, though

8

in its closing stages, when Prince Andrew died in Monaco from a heart attack in December 1944. He was 62.

His correspondence with Princess Elizabeth continued—even if letters sometimes took a long time to reach their destinations in those wartime days—and led to an invitation to spend part of his leave at Windsor when he next landed in Britain. We can imagine with what warm delight the Princess welcomed him. To her, he seemed very much a young man of the world, on a par with those flying heroes whose exploits she read with such avid interest. He captivated her and amused her father with witty tales of his sea-going adventures, among them perhaps the story of how the Chinese stokers had deserted ship at Puerto Rico and it had been a case of "Who's going to shovel coal—you, you and you!" Characteristically, Philip had volunteered and was now the amused possessor of a certificate giving him status as "a qualified coal-trimmer". The episode had also given him sorely blistered hands at the time. Doubtless he kept silent about the grimmer side of war in front of the young Princess, even if he told the King in private that the Battle of Cape Matapan had been "as near murder as anything can be in wartime".

The King liked Philip. He liked his blunt naval way of talking and his breezy, sometimes slapstick sense of humour, in both of which he saw echoes of himself. But he was, as yet, a long, long way from seeing him as a prospective son-in-law. He saw him as a likeable enough young man, a distant relative, but no more. Indeed, with his elder daughter not yet 16, the King was a long way from thinking in terms of marriage and sons-in-law at all and it was to be a few more years before he was to bring himself to do so.

But perhaps others saw more than he did. During the course of Philip's leave, his cousin, the late Princess Marina, then Duchess of Kent, arranged a small dance at Coppins, her country home. The Princess was invited and it was there that she and Philip danced together for the first time.

It was around this time that Philip was first thrown into contact with the breezy wartime acquaintance who soon became a close friend and whose life was to be so interwoven with his own in the years following the war. Philip had been posted to the *Wallace*, a destroyer flotilla leader operating out of Rosyth with the task of escorting North Sea convoys through E-boat alley. He had taken his sub-lieutenant's course and promotion, for him as for other young men, came quickly under the exigencies of war. He became a sub-lieutenant in February 1942, and was promoted lieutenant in the October of the same year. He was still only 21.

Michael Parker, from Melbourne, Australia, was similarly lieutenant on a companion ship, *Lauderdale*. Like Philip, he loved the navy (though he was later invalided out). Like Philip, he was blunt-spoken and outgoing, breezy, boisterous and perhaps devil-may-care. The two of them met, became friends, got on like a couple of houses on fire, and a few years later when Philip felt in need of someone to bolster his morale in his newly married role as a member of the royal family, Mike Parker was the first person he thought of.

But if Philip was now a lieutenant, Princess Elizabeth outranked him. She was appointed colonel (honorary) of the Grenadiers, the senior regiment of the Brigade of Guards. It was her first fully official appointment, made to mark her sixteenth birthday, and provided a curious link with her great-great-grandmother, Queen Victoria, in that she succeeded Victoria's own son, the Duke of Connaught, who had died a few months earlier at the ripe old age of 92.

That same birthday was also marked by a well-publicised visit to the local employment exchange in Windsor town, where she registered for war work. She completed the same registration form as every other youngster of those wartime years, listing her education as "Private", answering "No" to the question as to whether she attended evening classes and writing "Girl Guides" as her youth organisation. But she was not dealt with like any ordinary youngster. Her father considered that training for monarchy was more important to her than routine war work.

That evening, in company with her parents, she popped into the sergeants' mess of the Grenadier barracks, where a dance was in progress. A 16-year-old drummer boy braced himself sufficiently to ask the King's daughter to partner him and they danced a fox-trot together.

The destroyer *Wallace* with Lieutenant Prince Philip aboard was sent out to the Mediterranean, where in July 1943 it helped to provide cover for the Canadian landing on Sicily. Three dive-bombers made repeated attacks on the vessel during the course of the operation, without scoring a single hit. Back at Windsor, the Princess was saddened by the news that her uncle, the likeable Duke of Kent, had been killed when the flying boat in which he was travelling to Iceland ploughed into a Scottish hillside and by a report that her cousin, the Master of Glamis, was "missing believed killed" in the Middle East. Equally naturally she wanted to do something concrete to help; to play her part, however, youthful, in the war effort. But her father, when she spoke to him again on the subject, still would not hear of it.

The *Wallace* returned to Britain towards the tail-end of 1943 for a re-fit. For Philip, there were further courses to undergo while the ship was laid up. There was also some leave due to him. Along with his cousin, David, he was invited to spend Christmas at Windsor, where he was amused to see that a replica of a ship's bridge, complete with compass, engine-room telegraph, speaking tubes and lifebelts had been rigged up. At 17, the Princess had graduated from the Girl Guides to the Sea Rangers and the mock-up enabled her, as 'bosun of the starboard watch', and the rest of the 'crew' to parade weekly in a suitably nautical atmosphere.

In the happy atmosphere of a family Christmas, the two of them, Philip and the Princess, danced together again and sat together in a darkened room, lit only by flickering firelight, telling ghost stories. Margaret played gooseberry. "We settled ourselves to be frightened—and were not," she lamented, disappointedly. Her sister and Philip, sitting close together in the firelight, had perhaps less cause for disappointment.

There was also another evening of that Christmas stay when Philip, weatherbeaten from his months at sea, sat with his future in-laws, the King and Queen, to watch one of the famous wartime amateur pantomimes in which the two princesses 'starred'. There had been two other pantomimes before this one—*The Sleeping Beauty* the previous year and *Cinderella* in 1941—and a nativity play called *The Christmas Child* the year before that. This year it was *Aladdin and his Wonderful Lamp* and the shilling programme which Philip nursed had an appropriate willow-pattern design on the cover. The royal portraits which had once adorned the windowless walls of the Waterloo Chamber, in which the show was staged, had been stored away for safety during those years of war and the massive gilt frames which had once held them now contained colourful posters of such pantomime characters as Mother Goose and Dick Whittington. "My ancestors," the King joked, pointing them out to Philip.

Both of them laughed heartily at jokes about 'the Castle' and other royal gags which had been worked into the traditional script. Margaret played the part of Princess Roxana and Elizabeth was Aladdin, popping up from a laundry basket to reveal a pair of shapely legs clad in silk tights. Something that evening gave the King his first inkling that the boy and girl friendship between his daughter on the stage and the young Greek-born prince who sat beside him in the audience had developed into something more. To test the truth of what he sensed he waited until Philip was not around and then dropped a jesting remark about him into the conversation. He was intrigued to see his elder daughter blush beetroot red.

Even so, the King did not realise how serious were the feelings of these two young people for each other. The Princess could talk of nothing but Philip. It was constantly "Philip this" and "Philip that". Close as she was to her father, she could not talk to him of love and marriage. So it was to governess Crawfie and her beloved Bobo that she confided the depth of her feelings. She asked the same question so many young girls in love have asked. "I wonder what it is that makes a person fall in love."

Philip, too, was now thinking seriously of marriage and it was his cousin, King George II of the Hellenes, who first raised the matter for him with Elizabeth's father. It was March 1944 when the two monarchs—George VI of the United Kingdom and George II of Greece—met at the Yugoslav Embassy in London. The occasion was the marriage of King Peter of Yugoslavia to Princess Alexandra, the daughter of another of Philip's many cousins, the ill-fated King Alexander of Greece who died from the bite of a pet monkey just before Philip was born. Britain's king was serving the bridegroom in the office of best man while the King of Greece was giving the bride in marriage. For the Greek king, the atmosphere seemed right and the opportunity perhaps too good to miss. But George VI, as we have related earlier, was quick to brush the whole suggestion aside.

Transfer to a new destroyer *Whelp* found Philip heading for the Far East. It is not difficult to imagine with what disturbed feelings Princess Elizabeth watched him go. If Philip's feelings were equally disturbed, there was plenty of action in the shape of diversionary attacks against Japanese-held islands to keep him occupied as well as some pleasurable shore-leave in Australia. In Sydney, however, there was the same trouble over his name as he had experienced in schooldays. Hiring a car for the period of his leave he signed the rental form with a solitary and legally correct "Philip", only to have a somewhat suspicious car-hire man accuse him of trying to take the mickey! There was a breezy reunion with Mike Parker, who, like Philip, was handsomely bearded in those wartime days. The beards came in handy during a day at the races. A bunch of Australian racegoers asked Philip if he had seen "Prince Philip" anywhere around. He promptly pointed to Parker—and Mike played up to the gag.

But Philip, around this time, was also doing some hard thinking about his future. He wanted to marry the Princess, but at that time saw that as no reason why he should not also continue with a naval career. But if he was to get a permanent commission once the war was over he would have to be a British citizen. He had discussed the matter with his Uncle Dickie and had also approached his cousin, the Greek king, for formal permission to renounce his Greek citizenship and his right of succession to the Greek throne. The request had been granted, but in Britain the normal processes of naturalisation were still in a state of suspension. There was, for the time being, nothing more he could do about either marriage or a permanent commission.

In his absence, Princess Elizabeth continued with her apprenticeship in monarchy. Her eighteenth birthday in April 1944 saw her appointed a Counsellor of State—the first time anyone under the age of 21 had held such an appointment—and two months later, while her father was away visiting Allied troops in Italy, she signed her first Parliamentary Bill for him. She now had a car of her own and her own lady-in-waiting, who acted also as her secretary. She made her first public speech, to the governors of the Queen Elizabeth Hospital for Children in Hackney after they had elected her president, and carried out a steady spatter of public engagements. She dined with the Commonwealth Prime Ministers when they met at Buckingham Palace, launched the new battleship *Vanguard* and visited a number of military establishments, including an American air base where she smashed a bottle of cider on the nose of a Flying Fortress being readied for its fourteenth raid on Germany and named it *Rose of York*. Sadly, the bomber was later lost during a raid on Berlin. In company with her parents, she watched a secret rehearsal for D-Day with paratroopers dropping from the sky in formation and Horsa gliders landing with their wingtips almost touching. She visited the docks in Swansea, mines and factories in Wales, schools and Service clubs in Edinburgh.

But more than anything she still wanted to make a direct contribution to the war effort, to share in some small way the discomforts and dangers she knew Philip must be undergoing. Once again, she spoke to her father. He still did not altogether agree, feeling that her duty to monarchy should come before everything else, but finally he was persuaded and gave way.

It was a month before her nineteenth birthday when the Princess at last found herself in uniform. She had been granted an honorary commission as a second subaltern in the Auxiliary Territorial Service. It was perhaps a rather feather-bedded spell of military training even if the Princess was unaware of the fact. But at least she could feel that she was doing something. Her company commander drove to Windsor to collect her on her first day and take her to Camberley. Each night she returned to Windsor to sleep in her own bed. Nevertheless, those weeks at No. 1 Mechanical Transport Training Centre taught her a lot. From 10 a.m. to 5 p.m. each day she clambered in and out of repair pits and worked away at the bench. She learned to change tyres, grease lorries, adjust carburettors, grind valves, decarbonise a cylinder head, and dismantle and reassemble an engine. She also got her first glimpse perhaps of life as it is lived on the other side of the counter. She found herself and her unit being inspected by her aunt, the Princess Royal, Controller Commandant of the A.T.S.

"You've no idea what a business it has been," she said when she got back to Windsor that day. "Spit and polish all day long."

There was the same spit and polish later when 'Papa and Mummy' inspected the unit. Clad in grease-stained overalls, she was working on her vehicle when her father came along. We cannot vouch for the story that he removed the distributor arm of the vehicle while she was not looking. If so, it was a practical joke in keeping with his character and certainly, later, as she struggled in vain to start the vehicle, there was a chuckle in his voice as he asked with apparent innocence, "Not got it going yet?"

VE Day came, providing another fleeting glimpse of life outside the circumscribed royal circle and the stereotyped royal round. In company with Margaret, and with two young officers as escorts, the Princess slipped out through the trade gate of Buckingham Palace at 11 o'clock on the evening of 8th May and mingled unrecognised with the cheering, celebrating crowds along the Mall and in neighbouring Whitehall. The following night they repeated the experiment, this time going in the opposite direction to Piccadilly. It was a novel and exciting experience. But how much more exciting it would have been in Philip's company! He, however, was still half a world away in the Far East.

But the young royal lovers had not long to wait before they were reunited. The holocaust of Hiroshima hastened the ending of the war against Japan and Philip was briefly transferred from *Whelp* to Admiral Halsey's flagship, *Missouri*, as one of the British officers who witnessed the final act of surrender in Tokyo Bay.

Soon afterwards he was back in Britain. He still had his blond Viking beard. The Princess did not like it and asked him to shave it off. He complied. He was now 24; she was 19.

Philip's destroyer *Whelp* was placed on the reserve and he was transferred first to H.M.S. *Glendower*, a shore establishment in Wales and then to H.M.S. *Royal Arthur*, a similar establishment at Corsham in Wiltshire, as an instructor. Here he found himself lecturing petty officers on naval warfare and current affairs, playing cricket as well as an occasional game of skittles at a local hostelry, the 'Methuen Arms'. Corsham was just under 100 miles from London and the young lovers could now meet more or less regularly.

Philip acquired a rakish-looking MG sports car (registration number HDK 99) for the weekend drive back and forth, sometimes stopping and popping into a pub for a quick beer on the way. Sometimes they met in London, at Buckingham Palace; sometimes at Royal Lodge at Windsor. Either way, they were relatively safe from prying eyes and possible gossip. But at neither place did Philip stay overnight. Instead, he stayed with either his grandmother, the Dowager Marchioness of Milford Haven, at Kensington Palace, sometimes climbing in through a window if he was late to avoid disturbing everyone by climbing the stairs (which were inclined to creak rather excessively), or at the Mountbatten home at 16 Chester Street, where Mrs. Cable, the cook, would bustle round preparing a meal for him and Jessie, the housekeeper, would quickly make up a bed.

Discreet though he and the Princess were, their budding romance quickly became the subject of public gossip and speculation. Just as the first whisper of their growing fondness for each other had been aired in Athens as far back as 1941, so now, towards the tail-end of 1945, an Athens newspaper speculated that a betrothal was imminent. The King promptly authorised the issue of an official denial and for the next twenty months his private secretary, Sir Alan Lascelles, was to be kept busy issuing similar denials as first one newspaper, then the other, resurrected the story. Such denials told the truth when they said that there was no formal betrothal, but not the whole truth which was that courtship was continuing with growing and tender affection.

Except that it took place against a more regal background and in more circumscribed surroundings, their courtship differed little from that of any other young couple. They went riding together in Windsor Great Park and walked hand-in-hand beside the Thames with the royal corgis frisking behind and ahead. Sometimes, to their dismay, a teenage chatterbox named Margaret insisted upon tagging along as well. They played croquet on the lawn of Royal Lodge, perhaps talking of that earlier croquet game which had first brought them together, and swam together in the green-tiled pool. There were outings in Philip's little sports car, sometimes in the direction of Coppins where his cousin, Princess Marina, could perhaps be expected to have more understanding of their occasional need to be alone together.

When the Princess and her sister returned to London from Windsor on Sunday evenings, Philip went along too, usually outpacing the stately royal limousine in his nippy little sports car. After having supper with them in the chintzy little apartment which had once been their nursery, he would take his leave of the Princess and drive back to Corsham in readiness to resume his lecturing duties the following morning.

Outside governess Marion Crawford and Bobo MacDonald,

few of the royal staff were aware of Philip's comings and goings. Fewer still linked them with the sudden fresh interest the Princess was showing in such essentially feminine things as hair styles, make-up, perfume and the clothes she wore. Indeed, among those who were not in the know, Philip at this time was far from being the front-runner for the hand of the Princess. Perhaps to keep her true love secret, perhaps because her parents wished her to have an opportunity of testing the strength of her feelings for Philip, she was suddenly surrounded by a whole battery of eminently eligible young men, among them the heirs to two duke-doms and the heirs to three earldoms. They were to be seen at nearly all the royal dances. They were invited, ostensibly for the shooting, to Balmoral in summer and Sandringham in winter. They were house-guests at Windsor for Ascot week. They were more in evidence than ever Philip was. The Princess walked with them, talked with them, danced with them. But her heart was fixed on Philip.

Occasionally the young couple ventured out into the public limelight together, though usually as two of a small group to avoid drawing undue publicity to themselves. The Princess' lady-in-waiting, a 23-year-old war widow named Jean Gibbs, and her cousin, Captain the Hon Andrew Elphinstone, often made up the party. It was as two of such a group that they visited places like the Bagatelle Club where they could dance together—though, again to avoid drawing undue attention to themselves, they danced more with others. Similarly, they went together to see the American musical *Oklahoma!*, which had just opened in London. One of the hit tunes from the show struck a responsive chord in the young Princess. Philip bought her a copy of the record and for the next few months the strains of "People Will Say We're In Love" could be heard constantly coming from her second-floor apartment. She played it over and over again until the recording was worn and scratched almost beyond further playing. For perhaps the first time in her life, she permitted herself the luxury of day-dreaming. For hours at a time she would sit alone in her room, playing the worn record, gazing absently into space or out of the window with eyes which saw only Philip.

Her parents by now, of course, were well aware of her feelings for Philip. But her father was still reluctant to give his consent to a formal betrothal. Partly this was personal, due to a desire to be certain that his daughter was absolutely sure of her feelings and perhaps due also to a father's natural reluctance to lose her from the family circle; and partly it was official.

Philip, for all that he had surrendered his Greek title and nationality, was still having difficulty obtaining British citizenship. His original desire for naturalisation had been in order to obtain a permanent commission in the Royal Navy. But now there was another, more important reason. There were those in high places who felt it highly desirable that the heiress presumptive should marry a Briton, even if only a naturalised one.

For Philip, however, the normal processes of naturalisation, in full working order though they were for others now that the war was over, seemed to be continually blocked by regal red tape. First there was delay because of doubts as to whether or not the monarchy would be restored in post-war Greece. For a Greek prince to seek British naturalisation, Philip was told, might upset the delicate negotiations which were in progress towards this end.

Finally the restoration of the Greek monarchy was confirmed by plebiscite. Now, it would have seemed, Philip could hope that everything would be plain sailing. But no. The Greeks, who had earlier urged his matrimonial cause even with the King, now took the view that it might harm the recently-restored Greek monarchy if he was seen to abandon his Greek nationality so soon afterwards. Again he was asked to stay his hand. Impatiently, he agreed.

V   Boy Wins Girl

Queen Victoria, when she lighted upon someone she thought might be suitable for marriage into her family, had the autocratic habit of requiring them to be presented to her at Balmoral for inspection and possible approval. Nearly half a century after her death, in the immediate post-war summer of 1946, King George VI similarly invited Prince Philip to spend a month there.

Not perhaps to inspect him in quite the way Queen Victoria would have done. He had already met him several times in the years since that visit to Dartmouth and knew him reasonably well. The King considered Philip intelligent, with a good sense of humour, a young man who "thinks about things in the right way". But before giving official approval to his daughter's betrothal, the King wanted to be quite sure that she knew her own mind and that her choice was a sound one.

Philip arrived at Balmoral with the slender wardrobe of any young naval officer in those immediate post-war years. "I am one of the generation", he has said since, "who started the war in nappies, spent the next few years in uniform and when peace broke out found myself without any other clothes."

Invited to Balmoral, he had neither the opportunity nor perhaps, on lieutenant's pay, the spare cash to equip himself with a full civilian wardrobe. The solitary valise he took north with him contained a pair of flannels, some sweaters, spare shirts and socks and a dinner jacket passed on to him by his Uncle Dickie. He took no pyjamas with him (he never wore them), no slippers (no need of them in the navy), no lounge suit, no tweeds for the grouse moors and no spare shoes. When the shoes he was wearing suffered from the hard going over the heathery moors they were whipped over to the local cobbler in nearby Crathie for running repairs.

But he was by no means alone in the economy of his wardrobe. Princess Elizabeth, making do—if not actually mending—on the same quota of clothing coupons as any other young woman of those austere times, often went out with him in London wearing an evening dress fashioned from one of her mother's old ones. A catalogue of her wardrobe, published around the time of her betrothal, lists it as including an ermine coat, a white ermine evening wrap, a belted camel-hair coat, two woollen coats, a tweed suit (on which she spent $15\frac{3}{4}$ of her precious clothing coupons), three or four dresses of wool or silk, an unspecified number of jumpers, skirts, head-scarves and shoes, and some half a dozen hats. Also a pair of sheer light-coloured nylons— one of the first pairs ever produced in Britain—which were given to her when she visited a hosiery factory. "They look as though they might be rather cold to wear," commented her grandmother, Queen Mary. Goodness only knows what the old queen would have thought of Princess Anne's latter-day mini-skirts.

Like nearly every other room at Balmoral, the ground-floor bedroom Philip was given, with its brass bedstead and vast marble-topped wash-stand, echoed the far-off days of Victoria and Albert, the great-great-grandparents he shared with the Princess. The floor carpet was tartan, the soft furnishings were tartan-covered and his great-great-grandmother's cypher was still to be seen on the fading wallpaper. It also adorned the gold-rimmed basin in which he washed each morning in hot water brought to him in towel-wrapped brass jug.

For the young royal lovers it was an enjoyable—indeed, unforgettable—holiday. Though seldom alone, for the first time they could feel really close to each other, saying their good-nights happy in the knowledge that they would see each other again over breakfast in the morning. The King took Philip shooting on the grouse moors. The Princess noted with pleasure how well the two of them got along together, though Philip, right up to the King's death, was always a little in awe of him and treated him rather as he might have treated a very senior officer in the navy. She, for her part, initiated him into the subtleties of stalking a stag and he bagged two. Stalking was, and is, one of her favourite outdoor pursuits and the previous year, wearing a pair of her father's plus-fours—Margaret thought them "inelegant" on her—she had shot her first Royal, a stag with twelve points. Of an evening, a sometimes blundering Prince Philip was taught the intricacies of Highland dancing.

For the young couple, there were doubtless tenderly romantic moments as that summer stay at Balmoral ran its course and it was perhaps the memory of such moments which moved the Princess, in a subsequent speech of unusually poetic content, to conjure up a vision of "some well-loved loch with a breeze ruffling its waters, the white clouds sailing overhead and a curlew crying just out of sight . . . a long hillside shimmering in the sun, with nothing stirring save the bees".

Certain it is that it was beside some such loch or on some such Balmoral hillside that the two of them arrived at their final understanding. Whether she proposed to him, as great-great-grandmother Victoria did to great-great-grandfather Albert, or he to her, there is no way of knowing. Not even their closest friends know. This, like the wording of the inscription Philip had engraved inside the Queen's wedding ring, is their own special secret. And who would have it otherwise.

Unofficially, they knew they had the King's blessing. But he still insisted on further delay and continued secrecy before there was any formal announcement. He hoped they hadn't thought he was being "hard-hearted", he said later.

Back from Balmoral, they were more and more seen about together—at weddings, parties, private dances, theatres. They were together at the wedding of Prince Philip's cousin, Lady Patricia Mountbatten, to Lord Brabourne. The shows they saw together were in keeping with their own romantic mood, among them *The Hasty Heart* and the Ivor Novello hit, *Perchance to Dream*.

The problem of Philip's naturalisation was still not resolved, though slowly chugging its way through what are known as 'the usual channels'. He had completed the customary questionnaire in which he certified that he was financially solvent, had an adequate knowledge of the English language and would either continue in the service of the Crown or reside in one of the dominions. This he forwarded to the Home Office with the required deposit of £1. (Later, when it was finally granted, he had to pay a further fee of £9 and the Commissioner of Oaths before whom he took the oath of allegiance charged him an additional 2s. 6d.)

He was invited to spend Christmas with the royal family at Sandringham. The King took him pheasant and partridge shooting. His markmanship had not yet attained its later proficiency, but he was willing to learn. His wardrobe had grown with the addition of some old suits of his father's which he had inherited and had altered to fit him. He also had his father's old shaving brush which he had fitted with new bristles for future use.

News of Philip's stay at Sandringham intensified the rumours of an impending betrothal. One newspaper polled its readers on the desirability of the rumoured marriage. Fifty-five per cent voted in favour of the match, 40 per cent were against it and there were 5 per cent who didn't know. A later poll saw a sharp increase among those who voted in favour. They now numbered 87 per cent.

But in high places—the Cabinet had been informed of the King's wish that his daughter should marry Prince Philip— there was no small degree of opposition. His German connections were held by some to be one strike against him. His membership of the Royal House of Greece was held (by some Socialists, at least) to be another. "Not being English—does it make any difference?" queried Princess Margaret after overhearing some family discussion on the point.

Conversely, the pro-Philip faction argued that Philip was a Greek with no Greek blood in him, did not speak a word of Greek, was more Danish than Greek and, by now, no less British than his Uncle Dickie. Philip himself became increasingly frustrated, impatient and irritated as rumour spread, one newspaper report followed another and the controversy continued to rage.

Things had still not been finally settled when the Princess, with her twenty-first birthday coming up, sailed for South Africa with her parents. She looked sad as she left the palace for the battleship *Vanguard* on which they were to sail, perhaps because her betrothal was still not official, perhaps because Philip was not coming to see her off. In an attempt to minimise public gossip, he had, in fact, been seeing her less frequently of late, though they talked on the telephone regularly each evening.

Two nights before her departure she and her parents dined with Philip and the Mountbattens at Chester Street. It was by way of being an unofficial engagement party. The following day the Princess asked her father if there could be a formal announcement before the family left for South Africa. But again the King said, "No".

But one thing had been settled—the name Philip would take when his long-delayed naturalisation finally came through and the status he would have. Schleswig-Holstein-Sonderburg-Glucksburg, the royal house from which he had sprung, was a bit of a mouthful as an ordinary surname. Something simpler and more easily pronounceable was required. Philip thought at first of calling himself Oldcastle, the anglicised version of the old Royal House of Oldenburg, from which he also came down. But finally, to the delight of Uncle Dickie, he settled upon the anglicised form of his mother's family name of Battenberg— Mountbatten.

The question of a title had also been discussed. The King was quite prepared to grant him the title His Royal Highness Prince Philip. The Prime Minister, Mr. Attlee, agreed and so did Uncle Dickie. But Philip did not. So far in life he had not infrequently found his Greek title more of an embarrassment than a help. At school he had written the name "Philip" at the top of his essays until his teacher queried, "Philip who?" "Philip of Greece," Philip replied. His schoolmates fell about laughing and, with ponderous schoolboy sarcasm, continued to address him as "Philip of Greece" for a long time afterwards. There had been other similar experiences over the years, right down to the brush with the car-hire proprietor in Sydney, Australia. Philip wanted no more such embarrassment at this delicate stage. So he thanked the King for his offer, but politely insisted that when his natur- alisation came through he would prefer to be known simply as Lieutenant Philip Mountbatten, R.N. The King was considerably impressed.

Initially, on that tour of South Africa, the Princess seemed detached and preoccupied, clearly missing Philip. She kept his photograph close beside her in her cabin aboard *Vanguard* and took time out from royal duties to write to him several times a week. Then, midway through the trip, she was suddenly gayer and more lighthearted, noticeably happier. One of Philip's letters informed her that his naturalisation had finally come through. Listed as "Mountbatten, Philip; Greece; serving officer in His Majesty's forces; 16 Chester Street, London, S.W.1", it was one of a batch of 817 all announced on the same day.

The Princess, telling her father, again raised the question of a formal betrothal. He agreed that the announcement should now be made as soon as possible after their return to London. She was overjoyed.

While her heart may have been dancing with happiness, she contrived to remain as regally diplomatic as ever, adroitly fending off questions about her matrimonial intentions.

"When are you going to get engaged?" one blunt old Afrikaner farmer asked her pointblank.

"Ah, that you'll have to wait and see," she said, smiling happily.

Back home, her grandmother, Queen Mary, was also asked

about the possibility of an engagement. "I know nothing," she said. "No one has told me. He seems a good boy."

It was a noticeably paler and thinner Princess—she has always found prolonged tours a bit of a strain—who scanned the shoreline through a telescope on her return to Britain and was disappointed to see that Philip was not included in the welcome-home party. Sensibly he had decided that their reunion should be a private one.

With the royal family's return home, Philip became a more frequent and more open visitor to Buckingham Palace. He was there for a family luncheon party arranged in honour of Queen Mary's eightieth birthday. Most of his visits were far less formal. He would drive through the wrought-iron gates, park his MG in the inner quadrangle and, scorning the lift, bound two or three at a time up the red-carpeted stairs which led to the sitting room the Princess shared with her younger sister. Once inside, he invariably tossed his jacket aside and sat around shirt-sleeved. There were more outings together. He took her to meet his mother, who was now in England and living with her mother at Kensington Palace. There was, on another occasion, a more impromptu outing to Richmond Park where they walked alone unrecognised, Elizabeth in a head scarf and Philip in dark glasses, just like any other young courting couple. Sometimes, with the Princess watching, Philip would spend his time cleaning and tinkering with his MG in the garages of the royal mews.

He was not included in the official guest list for the Royal Ascot house-party at Windsor Castle, as he had been the previous year, but he was there just the same, turning up on the last night for the end-of-week dance in the Red Drawing Room. The dancing went on until three o'clock in the morning and, safe for once from prying eyes, he and the Princess danced nearly every dance together.

But monarchy still laid its claim upon her and that year of 1947, when the annual ceremony of Trooping the Colour came round, she rode side-saddle at her father's side in her role as Colonel of the Grenadier Guards, looking decidedly fetching in her feminine-styled uniform.

As with most young people in love, pre-marital tension tended to build up on both sides. The Princess returned home in tears on one occasion from a public function at which the crowd had

greeted her with boisterous shouts of "Where's Philip?" She
was perhaps more upset than the occasion warranted and for
the next few weeks really dreaded making public appearances.
Margaret sympathised with her. "Poor Lil. Nothing of your own
—not even your love affair." Philip, for his part, quite lost his
temper—and had good cause to do so—with an acquaintance who
rudely joked that he was marrying the wrong sister . . . "Margaret
is better looking." On balance, the ever-increasing pressure of
publicity tended to upset him more than it did the Princess. He
was less accustomed to it and inclined to resent it.

July 8th found the Princess in a state of whirlwind excitement.
Not even her long years of training, for once, could enable her
to conceal her emotions. Nor did she wish to do so. That day,
for once in her life, she wore her heart on her sleeve, as, impatiently, excitedly, she awaited Philip's arrival.

He arrived at last and was shown to the first-floor Buhl Suite,
in which he was to stay, with its heavy mahogany furnishings and
outsize bathroom. His wardrobe had by now been reinforced by
the addition of a dinner suit and a lounge suit, but he was still
unencumbered by pyjamas, bathrobe or slippers. Even with the
additions, his wardrobe was clearly insufficient for the new, more
regal way of life which lay ahead of him, and the following day
a tailor arrived to measure him for further outfits. That was also
the day, as far as can be pinpointed, when he smoked his last
cigarette.

Almost his first act was to give instructions that his window
curtains were to be kept tightly drawn. The Buhl Suite is at the
front of the palace and Philip's naval training was quick to spot
that the Victoria Memorial would make a fine vantage point for
any photographer with enough nerve and a sufficiently long-range
lens.

He remained carefully out of sight the next day while the
Princess went to the International Horse Show at the White
City with her parents. Fleet Street was buzzing with rumour—
and had been ever since Uncle Dickie had invited a number of
newspaper editors to his Chester Street home to meet his nephew,
Lieutenant Philip Mountbatten—and royal protocol required
that they should not be pictured together until after the official
announcement.

The announcement was released finally at seven o'clock that

evening (though with an added embargo that it was not to be published, broadcast or transmitted overseas until half an hour after midnight): "It is with great pleasure that the King and Queen announce the betrothal of their dearly-beloved daughter the Princess Elizabeth to Lieutenant Philip Mountbatten, R.N., son of the late Prince Andrew of Greece and Princess Andrew (Princess Alice of Battenberg), to which union the King has gladly given his consent."

The King gave a small family dinner party in the Pine Room of the palace to celebrate his daughter's betrothal. Philip went up to her sitting room to collect her just before dinner so that they should enter the dining room together. As they entered her engagement ring glinted on the third finger of her left hand. The diamonds in it—a large square-cut diamond surrounded by several smaller stones—had come from a ring which Philip's father had given his mother years before. She, in turn, had now passed it on to her son for his bride-to-be. Philip had had the diamonds reset, but had got the size wrong. The ring was fractionally too large. It has been altered again since, but even today would seem to be a bit on the large size, judging by the ease with which the Queen can flick it round and round on her finger.

The celebration party was a strictly family affair. The King and Queen sat opposite each other at the oval-shaped table, with the Princess on her father's right hand, and Philip, a bit tense and nervous under his seeming exuberance, on the right of his future mother-in-law. Princess Margaret sat between Philip and her father.

The following morning the bridegroom-and-bride-to-be posed for pictures in the Bow Room—the selfsame room in which a youthful Victoria once proposed to her beloved Albert—and outside on the palace terrace. That evening they listened together to the nine o'clock news. It was dominated, of course, by news of the royal betrothal. "And now," said the newscaster, "we are taking you over to our commentator outside Buckingham Palace."

But the commentator outside the palace had nothing to describe but the waiting, singing, cheering crowds.

Like a star actress who waits for her cue, Princess Elizabeth knew instinctively that this was exactly the right moment. As the commentator tried desperately to spin out his words, making much of little, she stood up and held out her hand to Philip.

Together they went out on to the palace balcony.

VI   Boy Weds Girl

If the Queen did become a Mountbatten on marriage, as some authorities maintain, one thing is certain: she did not become plain Mrs. Lieutenant Philip Mountbatten. Her father saw to that. The day before she was married he bestowed upon her husband-to-be the style of Royal Highness along with the accompanying titles of Baron of Greenwich, Earl of Merioneth and Duke of Edinburgh.

"It is a great deal to give a man all at once," the King commented, "but I know Philip understands his new responsibilities on his marriage to Lilibet."

Clearly Philip did. A few months before he had protested that he wanted no title. Now he accepted.

But one thing the King seems to have overlooked. He did not make Philip a Prince, an omission which the Queen was to rectify after she had succeeded her father on the throne. It was perhaps not so much an oversight on the King's part as a misunderstanding. He took the view that the title of Prince was synonymous with the style of Royal Highness and certainly, as far as he himself was concerned, consistently referred to his son-in-law from that day on as "Prince Philip".

The King also bestowed on his prospective son-in-law the Most Noble Order of the Garter, the highest of Britain's Orders of Chivalry and one of the few still in the personal gift of the Sovereign. To ensure her seniority, the King bestowed the same order on his daughter eight days earlier. Prince Philip, on the day of his marriage, was wearing the insignia of the Garter, though the order of service for the ceremony, because the printing had necessarily to be put in hand before his new titles were announced, still referred to him as plain Lieutenant Philip Mountbatten, R.N.

In the weeks which preceded the wedding Buckingham Palace was almost in danger of vanishing under the avalanche of letters, telegrams and gifts which poured in. Other excited brides-to-be wrote that they were now planning to be married on the same day. Gifts ranged from an under-slip of handworked Victorian lace which the old lady who sent it wrote had been worn by brides in her family for generations to the thirty-piece set in silver gilt from the Diplomatic Missions in London which still graces the Queen's dressing table today. There was a mink coat for the bride and a sewing machine it was doubtful if she would ever use in person. A sailing dinghy for the bridegroom. An ivory table from a maharajah, a Persian carpet from the Shah of Persia. Philip's old skittles team, the Methuen Moonrakers, sent him a walking stick. There were hundreds of handkerchiefs for the bride; hundreds of pairs of nylon stockings. Lots of people, eager to help with the bride's trousseau, sent their clothing coupons. These were carefully returned whence they came—for a princess, as for any other girl, it was a breach of current regulations either to give or accept them—but in other respects convention was waived to permit the Princess to keep the hundreds of gifts which descended upon her. Normally, unsolicited gifts are always returned with a polite note of regret, though occasionally an exception is made. From Wales came a chunk of Welsh gold for the wedding ring. There was more than enough. "We must save a piece for Margaret," said the excited Princess.

Amidst all this pleasurable anticipation, there were almost inevitably, a few slightly discordant notes, among them the fact that no wedding invitations were sent to Philip's three sisters and their German husbands. He wrote to them ahead of the betrothal to tell them what was happening and sent them photographs of himself and his bride after the ceremony. But that was all he could do.

More alarming was the car crash in which Philip himself was involved a bare four weeks ahead of the wedding. He was returning to Corsham after visiting his bride-to-be at her palace home—it was said at the time that he could cover the 98 miles involved in 1 hour 40 minutes—when his MG skidded and smacked into a tree. He was perhaps fortunate to escape with no more than superficial injuries, scratches and bruises, and thumbed a lift from a passing motorist on the Cirencester road. Realising that the story might somehow find its way into the newspapers, he decided to call the Princess so that she should not be alarmed if she read about it later. She did not take the call herself. But she did chance to overhear part of what was being said and nothing would then satisfy her but she must speak to Philip himself and make quite sure that he was all right.

The wedding morning found Buckingham Palace in much the same state of excited chaos as exist in less regal homes as the bride prepares for her big day. Servants scurried here and there in a fine state of confusion from which order somehow emerged. The bridal spray, as we have related, was temporarily mislaid and came to light at only the last moment. The bride's tiara, the same one her mother had worn for her own wedding a quarter of a century before, came apart at the seams just as it was being fixed into position on her head. It was hurriedly rushed to a jeweller for repair. To top it all, the bride had a natural senti-mental desire to wear the pearls her parents had given her. But these were on display with the rest of the wedding gifts at St. James's Palace. The Princess despatched her private secretary to collect them. But he seems to have had some difficulty in convincing those responsible for guarding the gifts of both his identity and integrity. Finally, he was permitted to take the pearls, but only on condition he took a three-man police escort along with him as well.

There was perhaps less confusion, though something of a slight morning-after-the-night-before atmosphere, at Kensington Palace, the home of Philip's maternal grandmother, where the bridegroom was getting ready. Princess Elizabeth had gone to bed early the previous night. But excitement and nervousness drove sleep away. So she put on a dressing gown and stood at a window, peeping out at the milling crowds around the palace. "I can't believe it is really happening," she exclaimed. While she was at the window, her bridegroom-to-be was indulging in the high jinks of the traditional stag party with which old pals of the bridegroom usher him into married life. It was, judging by all accounts, a typically hilarious bachelor party at which the best man, Philip's cousin David, and his old seafaring chum, Mike Parker, were present among others, though we cannot vouch for the truth of the story that at one stage of the proceedings there was a boisterous attempt to debag the prospective bridegroom.

Be that as it may, Philip overslept slightly on his wedding morning. To those around him he seemed touchy and nervy. He breakfasted on toast and coffee, his habit at the time. In those days he seldom bothered with a cooked breakfast. Despite over-sleeping, he was ready ahead of time. He had a gin and tonic to steady his nerves, then walked out to the waiting car. He was too soon. The timekeeping police officer on duty outside gave a warning shake of his head and Philip went back inside again. He was dressed in naval uniform and wearing the dress sword which had once belonged to his grandfather, Prince Louis of Battenberg. With true naval thoroughness he had taken the precaution of getting his best man, who was equally in naval uniform, to make a small ink mark inside his cap so that there there should be no confusion between the two. It would never do for a roya! bridegroom to pick up the wrong cap and walk out with it down over his ears.

Back at the palace, the bride was being helped into her wedding gown of pearl and crystal encrusted satin. It had been designed for her by Norman Hartnell, a true patriot who had been at some pains to ensure that the material with which he worked was woven from silk spun by Nationalist Chinese silkworms rather than enemy silkworms from Japan or Italy. He had also taken security precautions worthy of a later James Bond film, white-washing the windows of the workroom in which the dress was being made, draping them with muslin as an additional precaution, locking the designs in his safe each night and having his work-room manager do guard-duty on a camp-bed in the same room.

Twenty-five years later it all sounds rather far-fetched and perhaps even a trifle hilarious. But on the patriotic count, in those immediate post-war days, there were many who thought as Mr. Hartnell did. On the secrecy count, the copying of royal designs was almost a major industry at that time and was to remain as such for many years to come.

It took three of Hartnell's assistants plus the indefatigable efforts of Bobo MacDonald to prepare that royal bride of 1947 for her wedding at Westminster Abbey. Like Philip, she suffered from pre-wedding nerves. If he was edgy and touchy, she was "pale and solemn" to an extent where those responsible for dressing her became "almost alarmed" at one stage of the proceedings. Ready at last, she stood briefly at the window, looking out at the crowds along the Mall. This had the effect of easing her tension and she was smiling when she finally left her room and walked slowly down the stairs leading to the Grand Hall of the palace on her father's arm.

It was 20th November 1947, a raw, grey day, and the royal wedding provided London with its first real slice of colour and pageantry since the pre-war era. "A joyous event," Winston Churchill called it. "A flash of colour on the hard road we have to travel." There were five kings, six queens, twelve princes and twelve princesses, not counting the bride and groom, in Westminster Abbey, though the Archbishop of York, curiously, saw the ceremony as "in all essentials exactly the same as it would be for any cottager who might be married this afternoon in some small country church".

The King, in the uniform of Admiral of the Fleet, thought that his daughter was "pale but composed" during the service. Inevitably, there were the usual small mishaps. One of the pages, Prince William of Gloucester, tripped and would have fallen if Princess Margaret, the chief bridesmaid, had not caught him and steadied him. The bride's long, spreading train snagged on the altar steps. The father of the bride and the best man joined forces to free it. After the ceremony, leaving the vestry on her husband's arm, the Princess paused briefly in front of her parents and accorded them a deep curtsey, an unrehearsed touch which moved the King deeply.

There was a captain's escort of Household Cavalry, with nodding plumes and glinting breastplates, for the glass coach in which the bride and groom journeyed to the palace; a sovereign's escort for the bride's parents. At the palace the royal gold had been brought out from storage for the wedding breakfast in the State Supper Room. Bagpipes played and white heather decorated the tables. In contrast to the enthusiasm of Winston Churchill, a few cynics queried whether so festive a display was appropriate to those postwar days of rationed austerity. They were doubtless relieved to learn that the wedding feast consisted of nothing more elaborate than fillet of sole followed by casseroled partridge followed by ice cream.

The speeches, like the meal, were brief and quickly over,

and the newlyweds went out to the open landau which was to take them to Waterloo station where their honeymoon train was waiting. The bride's fifteen suitcases were already aboard the train along with Philip's two.

Unknown to the cheering crowds lining the departure route, the bride was warmly snuggled in hot-water bottles as she waved to them from the landau. Her favourite corgi, Susan, was curled up contentedly at her feet. Surreptitiously, she and Philip held hands, as newlyweds have done from time immemorial.

Their route to Waterloo station took them along Whitehall. An excited Philip, busily acknowledging the cheers of the crowd, was in danger of committing the first *gaffe* of his new royal life when a warning nudge from his young wife acted as a timely reminder. In the nick of time he brought his hand up in a brisk salute as the landau bowled past the Cenotaph.

4

Queen and Consort

I Years of Enchantment

Under the influence and impact of her husband's extrovert and more happy-go-lucky nature, that young royal bride of 1947 was to undergo a transformation. Until she married Prince Philip, Princess Elizabeth had been generally considered, even by some of those closest to her, to be shy, fussy, over-conscientious, a bit on the prim side. That she was cast in such a mould was understandable. She had been brought up in the rather rarified atmosphere and almost total seclusion of royalty. From an early age she was conscious always of the high destiny which lay ahead of her. The years of growing from girlhood to womanhood had been passed with few friends—and perhaps no really close friends —of her own age group. She had had little or no experience of the opposite sex. Instead, she had mixed mostly with people of an older generation whose attitude towards her lay somewhere between loyalty and respect. She was, after all, no ordinary girl and it can hardly be surprising if her thoughts, feelings and emotions were not those of an ordinary girl.

Until, that is, she married Philip. With him, all at once, everything was very different; life was less serious and more carefree. He was young, as she was. He was excitingly masculine. He gave her love as well as loyalty, laughter as well as respect, and exacted love and laughter from her in return. With him, all at once, she found that life was no longer simply a matter of duty and dedication, but fun as well. He piped the tune for their new life together as husband and wife and she was happy to dance to it. Where he led, she followed. He proposed and she responded. He teased and she answered with her rather high, still-girlish laugh. She was head-over-heels in love and had never before known such sheer, unadulterated happiness. Not surprisingly, her femininity blossomed and there were even times when she was coquettish and kittenish, moods hitherto quite foreign to her normally shy and serious nature. But there were equally times when the princess took precedence over the bride. She might laugh at Mike Parker's jokes, as she did on the occasion that she, Philip and Parker were passing through the deserted show-rooms of a departmental store late at night after attending a function on the top floor. The irrepressible Parker slipped behind one of the counters and played the part of a shop assistant. "And what can I get for Modom?" he inquired, grinning. But she could also frown if Parker, in those days when he was Prince Philip's private secretary and equerry to them both, chanced to call her husband "Philip" instead of "Sir".

They were—those first few years of marriage—halcyon, care-free years. The honeymoon was divided between Broadlands, the country mansion in which Philip's Uncle Dickie and his bride of a previous generation had also spent their first night, and Birkhall on the Balmoral estate with its pinewood furnishings and paintings by Landseer, Queen Victoria's favourite artist. At Broadlands, the first day or two of their honeymoon proved to be anything but the quiet weekend the two of them had envisaged. They were regarded as public property and not even on honeymoon were they to be left to themselves. Rubbernecking sight-seers flocked into the area; photographers prowled ceaselessly around with their Long Tom lenses. On the Sunday, when they attended morning service in Romsey Abbey, a mob of people charged wildly to greet them as they drew up at the church and the service which followed was several times interrupted as more and more people streamed in at the door. Those unable to get in humped chairs and ladders and even a sideboard among the tombstones to serve as vantage points from which to peer in through the windows.

Philip had got the girl of his choice. He had also got the beginnings of a head cold and a new and infinitely more public way of life. He can hardly have relished either, and his razor-sharp, slightly acid sense of humour was to be seen in the somewhat ambiguous message of thanks the newlyweds issued before leaving for what they must have hoped would be a rather more private and secluded part of the honeymoon at Birkhall. In it they termed the happenings at Broadlands "an unforgettable send-off in our married life". Having said which, they fled north to Scotland.

Like many newlyweds, they embarked on married life with no real home of their own. Returning from their honeymoon in Scotland, they moved for a time into part of Kensington Palace which was placed at their disposal by Princess Alice and her husband, the Earl of Athlone, while they were away in South Africa. Christmas was spent, as usual, at Sandringham with the rest of the family. Afterwards they returned to Kensington Palace until the end of March when, still lacking a proper home of their own, they moved into Buckingham Palace in readiness for the baby the Princess now knew she was expecting.

Living with his royal in-laws gave Philip no cause for concern. He got along famously with them. After all, he and the King had much in common: the same love of deep-water life, the same bluntness of speech, the same rather slapstick sense of humour, even, it must be conceded, the same quickness of temper. Their tempers, however, never clashed, though it is said that the occasional skylarking in which Philip and Michael Parker were apt to indulge sometimes brought a look of regal reprimand their way.

With his mother-in-law, the Queen, Philip got along equally well and over the years since, whenever the family get together, it has been nothing unusual to find son-in-law and mother-in-law away in one corner of the room, their heads close as they chuckled together over some shared joke. Unlike many a mother-in-law, the Queen Mother (as she now is) has never attempted to interfere in the married lives of either of her daughters. If she did not altogether agree, initially, with the decision to rip her small grandson, Prince Charles, out of the royal nursery and send him away to boarding school, she kept her opinion to herself.

But though the royal newlyweds may have found themselves living with the bride's parents, they did not have the same problems as other young couples who find themselves in the same boat. Mother and daughter, father-in-law and son-in-law were not constantly in each other's way and under each other's feet. Buckingham Palace was more than large enough for the young couple to have their own set of rooms, the small second-floor apartment which the bride had once shared with her younger sister. Here, when they chose, they could be on their own, away from the rest of the family.

Philip went back and forth to work almost, though perhaps not quite, like any other young husband. He had at this time a desk job at the Admiralty. His wife, like any other young bride, watched from a window for his return in late afternoon. In other ways too they behaved like ordinary newlyweds. Philip came home on one occasion with some cans of soup for the larder and on another with news that he was buying them a washing-machine, while his young bride took advantage of a visit by her husband's youngest sister, Sophie, over from Germany, for the two of them to go shopping in Bond Street. Philip, always a staunch believer in physical fitness, pounded round the palace gardens in an outsize sweater, swam in the palace pool, played squash and practised cricket at a net set up in the palace gardens. Lacking anyone else with whom to practise, there was one occasion when he roped in his young wife to act as batsman while he bowled at her with a soft ball.

Weekends were mostly spent at Windlesham Moor, the elegant country home which they rented for a time, though there was also the occasional pleasant weekend with Philip's cousin and her husband, Lord and Lady Brabourne, at their converted cottage near Ashford or, by contrast, with Sir Harold and Lady Zia Wernher at their stately home, Luton Hoo, with its Adam exterior and French-style interior. With Lady Zia, sister-in-law of Philip's dead Uncle George, the young bride found she had much in common, particularly a devotion to horse-racing, and in the years ahead it was to become almost a tradition for her and her husband to celebrate their wedding anniversary by spending the weekend nearest to it with the Wernhers.

In their off-duty moments, like most newlyweds, the young couple were almost inseparable. The only exception was when the Princess went racing at Sandown Park or elsewhere. Philip found racing boring and preferred not to go. There were theatre outings, dances, parties. They donned fancy dress to go to a party given by the American ambassador. They dressed up as maid and waiter. They were similarly decked in fancy dress for a dance at Coppins. The fact that the Princess was now pregnant went unnoticed as she danced in black lace with a large comb and mantilla as the Spanish Infanta. Philip, handcuffs jangling, was done up as a copper. There was, then and later, always laughter, endless practical jokes. The Princess screamed with girlish laughter when she opened a box labelled "Mixed Nuts" and a joke snake popped out. In Canada, later, Philip chased her from compartment to compartment of the royal train with a set of vampire-like mock fangs protruding from his mouth. His humour was perhaps sometimes a shade too sharp. His valet was once standing with a group of maids to watch the royal couple depart. "If you wore a skirt, you wouldn't feel so out of place," Philip twitted him. The unfortunate man blushed beetroot red and the Princess, more sensitive of other people's feelings, was moved to commiserate, "Poor John".

Philip had his first real taste of royal chores. He went to a circus, to Broadcasting House to watch an 'I.T.M.A.' programme being put out, was made a Freeman of the City of London, sat for his portrait, and, with his young wife looking on, took his seat in the House of Lords—not exactly stimulating experiences for a man of his background and outlook. Still it was all something of a novelty and Philip enjoyed it as such. His natural impatience was not yet being stretched, though he was sometimes more nervous than anyone might have guessed and glad of the moral support of his old friend, Michael Parker.

Like Philip, Michael Parker was married by this time. He had married the attractive daughter of a well-to-do Scottish family whom he had met while he was still in the navy and she was serving in the Wrens. When he was invalided out of the navy at the end of the war, his wife's father found him a job in the family rope-making concern. Parker joined the firm's London office and set up home in a cream-painted terrace house in Kensington. But the rather humdrum nine-to-five office life of a rope salesman was not exactly his cup of tea. Bored with it, he had already arranged to return to his Australia with his wife and family when a message arrived for him from Prince Philip.

Would he, Philip wanted to know, like a job as his private secretary?

Can a duck swim? Parker promptly abandoned his plans to

return to Australia, moved out of the rope office which was above a restaurant in Bond Street and into what proved to be a rather more poky office at Buckingham Palace, where a portable screen was used to mask the wash-basin in the corner. For nearly ten years he was to be Philip's number-one trouble-shooter, doing much to smooth his path through the intricate labyrinth of pomp and protocol which lay ahead.

Philip, while performing the traditional royal chores like a dutiful son-in-law, still hankered after his old sea-going life and a remark he made when he visited London docks to see the sailing ship *Pamir*—"I would like nothing better than to make a trip in sail when I go to sea again"—showed clearly the way his thoughts were running. But he was not to go back to sea yet awhile. Instead, he attended a staff course at Greenwich (where, curiously, he decided that it was more convenient to 'live in') and was then placed on half pay so that he should have more time to devote to the royal round.

However, work for the National Playing Fields Association was to prove very much to his liking. Seldom can any organisation have found itself with such a thrusting and conscientious young man at its head. "I have no intention of being a sitting tenant," said Philip at the first meeting he attended in his capacity as president after his Uncle Dickie had vacated the post to make way for him. Nor was he. As though determined to prove himself in his new role, Philip tackled his presidency with the same purposeful tenacity that had characterised both his schooldays at Gordonstoun and his wartime years at sea. Initially, he put in a more or less regular nine-to-five working day at the Association's offices in Ecclestone Square where he helped to address envelopes and lick stamps and drank tea out of thick office mugs. He went through all the old records and accounts he could lay hands on to familiarise himself with what had gone before and then set about putting the association squarely on its feet. He found that it had raised and spent only one million pounds in the previous quarter of a century. He promptly launched what was called 'The Silver Jubilee Fund' with an announced target of half a million. Nor was that the limit of his horizon. "If you can raise a million, I can soon show you how to spend it," he said, in accepting one cheque for the new fund. He was laughing, but not joking.

The Queen on the 1959 Canadian tour during which it was announced
that she was expecting a baby (Prince Andrew)

The Royal Family with baby Prince Andrew at Balmoral in 1960

The number of playing fields opened or planned in the twelve months before he took office totalled no more than thirty. Within three years there was a ten-fold increase and by the end of the decade another million pounds had been raised and spent. Philip was opening playing fields five at a time with the aid of television and the number of new ones had risen to the staggering total of 2,500. "I'll go almost anywhere to see a new playing field opened," he said.

His fund-raising efforts found him visiting a Skegness holiday camp and dining with a group of London pub-keepers; rallying round himself such mixed company as Frank Sinatra, Bob Hope, boxing promoter Jack Solomons and the U.S. 32nd Infantry Band.

He would, of course, be the last person to claim sole credit for what was achieved. Many others played their part. But he was the inspiration and the keystone of the new national thrust towards physical fitness.

In that first year of marriage when the bride's parents celebrated their own silver wedding, the newlyweds also buzzed busily around, placing themselves on public inspection. Everyone was eager to see them. Not everyone could. But they covered as much ground as time permitted, visiting Cardiff, Coventry and Oxford among other places—and Paris.

For both of them, that first visit to Paris, the first overseas assignment they had undertaken together, was more of an ordeal than the second honeymoon it perhaps should have been. Philip was still nervous on public occasions. Pregnancy caused the Princess to feel suddenly faint during a wreath-laying ceremony at the Arc de Triomphe and her husband had to step quickly forward to steady her. Then he himself succumbed to what looked like the beginnings of an attack of jaundice. Neither was feeling up to the mark when they put in a Sunday afternoon visit to the races (where Philip backed a winner) and had a brief session at a nightclub in the evening. London, at that time, had not yet ousted Paris as the permissive centre of the world and the result of such Sunday junketings in the French capital was the almost inevitable public outcry back home. It was the first spate of public criticism which had come their way since marriage, and Philip, for one, did not like it.

For his young wife, pregnancy ran its accustomed course.

Young, healthy and active as she was, there were few problems. Her doctors advised as much light exercise as possible. This was no problem; she had always enjoyed walking and still does. Any free time she had, morning or afternoon, found her happily circumnavigating the 40-acre palace gardens with her corgi, Susan, either frisking ahead or ambling patiently at heel. A moderate drinker though she has always been, she now cut out even the occasional sherry or glass of light wine. The customary royal summer stay at Balmoral gave her an opportunity for long, healthy tramps across the heathery hills, but for once she did no riding. Much as she enjoys it, she decided against it as an ante-natal exercise.

It was at Balmoral during that summer of 1948 that her father first showed signs that his health was perhaps not all it might have been. His legs began to trouble him. He put it down to cramp—he had had it before, he told his wife—and no one at that stage was unduly perturbed. But as the holiday ran its course, so his condition worsened. Cramp became a sort of numbness, first in one leg, then the other, which irked him by day and pained him so much at night that sometimes it kept him awake.

Returning to London at the end of the holiday, the King wisely decided to call in his doctors. Blood tests and X-rays were taken. These, together with a detailed examination by a team of specialists, revealed a more serious state of affairs than anyone could have guessed or would have wished. Indeed, so serious did his condition seem that the amputation of one leg was even a possibility at this time.

Philip was told of the King's condition. But it was equally impressed upon him that he was not to tell his young wife. The King, as mindful as ever of his daughter's wellbeing, wanted her to go into childbirth with an unworried mind and it was not until some two days after Prince Charles was born that the Princess was given her first inkling of the seriousness of her father's condition.

As a result, she moved towards childbirth with a happy, carefree mind. The old cot and baby basket used for her and Margaret in babyhood were brought out of storage and refurbished for use again. The tall, old-fashioned perambulator was similarly renovated and the Princess experimented with pushing it around. She was getting her hand in, she said gaily. Gifts for the expected baby began to stream in. "What a fuss," the Princess commented, laughing but enjoying it all just the same. "Anyone would think I was the only woman who'd ever had a baby."

To her husband, of course, she was. As pregnancy moved into its final stages, Philip proved himself a concerned, dutiful and sometimes worried husband, cancelling various engagements in order to be with his young wife. Like most young husbands whose wives are expecting their first child, he endeavoured to conceal his concern under a bantering exterior, but there was one occasion at least when worry bubbled over into temper.

It happened two nights before Charles was born. The expectant parents had been out to dinner with Philip's cousin, the former Patricia Mountbatten, and her husband Lord Brabourne, at the Mountbatten home in Chester Street. Photographers were lying in ambush for them when they returned to the palace late at night and the united glare of several flashbulbs so blinded and startled Philip momentarily as they drove in through the palace gates that the car swerved fractionally. He was, not unnaturally, furious. "Bloody fools," he stormed as he stalked in. "They might have caused an accident." It was his first real brush with photographers and perhaps marked the start of the running battle in which he has sometimes seemed to be engaged with them over the years since.

Two days later, on 14th September 1948, their first child was born, with a midwife and a four-strong medical team hovering in attendance. The birth took place in that selfsame Buhl Suite at the front of the palace which Philip himself had occupied when he first stayed there. The young husband was chatting with his royal in-laws in their private sitting room when news of the birth was brought to all three of them. He was shirt-sleeved following an energetic game of squash with Mike Parker and a cooling dip in the palace pool to follow.

Told he had a son, he could hardly speak at first for excitement. Then, rather like a conjuror producing a rabbit from a hat, he suddenly unearthed a big bouquet of flowers which he had ordered earlier and had been keeping by him as a "get-well-quickly-you-clever-girl-you" gift for his young wife. He whizzed along to see the baby, took the flowers in to his wife and rounded up everyone he could find—Mike Parker, Lieutenant General Browning, at that time Comptroller and Treasurer to the Princess, and a couple of passing footmen—to join him in the traditional champagne ceremony of 'wetting the baby's head'.

That first-born baby was a prince from birth—but only just. Five days earlier his grandfather, the King, had issued letters patent under the Great Seal granting the style of H.R.H. and the title of prince (or princess) to the children of the Duke and Duchess of Edinburgh. Such style and title had previously been limited to the children of the sovereign and his sons—but not his daughters. In the multiple name tradition of the royal family, he was christened Charles Philip Arthur George. The name of Charles was Prince Philip's idea. He wanted to break away from the more hackneyed family names.

For the first few months after he was born the Princess fed the baby herself. She was, as she said herself, "enormously proud" of him. "I still find it difficult to believe that I have a baby of my own," she wrote to her old music teacher.

With the arrival of the baby, she felt more than ever that she and Philip needed a home of their own. Philip could not have agreed more. "I've never really had a home," he said. "From the age of eight I've either been away at school or in the navy."

Work on the conversion and renovation of Clarence House, just down the road from Buckingham Palace, had already started and as soon as she was up and about again the Princess paid a visit to see how it was coming along. A lot had been done . . . but there was a lot still to do. It had been almost a wreck when she and Philip had first gone to view it, picking their way hand in hand through the dusty rooms and over the rubble. No one had lived there for thirty years, though the Red Cross had used it for temporary offices during the war. The plumbing was hopeless, there were no proper bathrooms, the old-fashioned gas lighting did not work and the makeshift electrical fittings installed in wartime were little better. But it had, the newlyweds agreed, possibilities.

Over the next few months husband and wife visited the house nearly every day—and sometimes twice a day—to see how the work was progressing. Both were forthcoming with ideas to make it the sort of dream-home they visualised. The Princess chose a favourite shade of aquamarine for the sitting room and even helped to mix the actual paint so that she should have the right shade of green in the Adam-style dining room.

Baby Charles was in his eighth month when his parents finally moved into the new home from where an earlier Duchess of Edinburgh, the Russian princess who married Queen Victoria's second son, had once been accustomed to setting forth in the full stateliness of a carriage and retinue even if she was only visiting her next-door neighbours at Lancaster House.

Between the birth of the baby and moving day there had been a busy spate of public engagements for the royal couple, provincial trips designed to let the public see both the Princess and the man she had married. In addition, there had been more worry about her father's health. The King had undergone a right lumbar sympathectomy in March and was still far from well, as was obvious when he attended that year's Trooping the Colour ceremony in a carriage.

Work, worry, the aftermath of childbirth and the problem of moving house combined to give the Princess sometimes rattled nerves and it was perhaps fortunate that Philip, having overcome his own initial nervousness on public occasions, was so often at hand with a quick quip to ease her tension or a brisk intervention to smooth over a gap in the conversation during visits to Lancashire, Wales, Northern Ireland, the Channel Isles and elsewhere.

But if she was sometimes rattled or tense, the Princess was never less than conscientiously dutiful, obstinately determined to do all that was required of her. Despite Bobo's suggestion that she should suck barley sugar, the rough sea crossing to the Channel Isles made her so seasick that she had to have treatment. Yet when it was suggested that she should cut out that part of her schedule which meant a further sea trip to Sark, she would not hear of it. Pale, but determined, she made the further crossing on a couple of pills and a tremendous reserve of willpower and did not flinch even when she had to make three attempts before she could manage to jump from the heaving deck of her torpedo boat to the steadier surface of the quayside.

But now, for the moment, such things were forgotten in the

personal excitement of moving in. Philip, of course, could not simply stand by and do nothing. He took off his jacket and helped the removal men carry some of the things in.

At a cost of something like £55,000, the almost uninhabitable wreck which Clarence House had been earlier had been transformed into a bright, spacious, elegant, labour-saving home with an adjoining house in Ambassador's Court to serve as domestic and secretarial offices. The young couple were both highly delighted as they brought their wedding gifts out of storage and set them out around them. The handsome Hepplewhite cabinet in what was to be the Princess' sitting room had been bought for them by forty-seven members of the royal family who all clubbed together for the purpose. It went well with her Chippendale desk, the damask curtains, the chintz-covered armchairs and Edward Halliday's portrait of the Princess herself. The eight elegant armchairs and two matching settees in the lofty drawing room with its white and gold ceiling and pink and blue Aubusson carpets were similarly a wedding present from the Lord Mayor of London. The eighteenth-century oval-shaped mahogany table and twenty ladder-backed chairs in the dining room came from the Royal Warrant Holders' Association, while the sideboard and side tables of matching mahogany were from Queen Mary. In the entrance hall Philip hung some sea paintings by Norman Wilkinson, one of his favourite artists. His taste was also to be seen in the humorous drawings by such cartoonists as Giles, Bateman and Osbert Lancaster which were scattered about the house, and in the natural leather look which predominated in his 'den' with its walls of Canadian maple, while his love of gadgets was also to be seen here. There was a filing cabinet cunningly built into the rear of a bookcase, wall panels which concealed hidden cupboards and even one which let down close to his desk to serve as an extra work-top.

Upstairs, into the nursery, went the fruitwood table the Princess had had in her own nursery at 145 Piccadilly in childhood, her old rocking horse (its tail long since gone) and a glass-fronted cabinet holding the glass and china miniatures she had collected as a child. A strong guard went around the fire as a precaution against accidents and chintz curtains on which nursemaids pushed prams while children bowled hoops were hung at the nursery windows.

More provincial tours followed the move-in—Dartmouth and Derby, Mansfield and Nottingham, Shrewsbury and Yorkshire. With so much to do by way of royal duty, the Princess could hardly have hoped to bring up her baby herself and that she did not do so is no reflection upon her. She brought up her baby as other young mothers in the upper social stratum bring up theirs, though they sometimes have less reason for so doing. Nursery routine was left in the capable hands of an experienced nanny, Helen Lightbody, an Edinburgh Scot who had previously been responsible for looking after the young Gloucesters. Nursery chores were shared out between a new young nursery-maid, Mabel Anderson, two housemaids and a footman. Additional staff was also required in other directions. The Princess had Bobo as her personal maid and Philip had a valet named John Dean (who later wrote a book about him). Now they also engaged a butler named Bennett and a cook called Mrs. McKee. Mrs. McKee is no longer with them. But Ernest Bennett is. More than twenty years later he still serves the Queen as her principal page.

But if the Princess did not actually bring up her baby herself, she was certainly—except when royal duty took her to the provinces or elsewhere—in and out of the nursery all the time. Once and sometimes twice a day she could be found there, playing with the baby, helping with his feeding. And every evening, when she put on a waterproof apron and took over at bathtime.

Often Philip was with her when she went to the nursery of an evening, boisterously sharing in the bathtime fun, constantly producing novelties which had the effect of turning bathtime into playtime . . . plastic ducks, toy boats and even a toy diver which was operated by squeezing a bulb at the end of a length of rubber tube. Philip, too, was offered a waterproof apron, but masculine pride would not permit him to wear it. The result, particularly when Charles grew to the splashing stage of babyhood, was often wet clothes.

But Philip, much as he loved his young wife and doted on his baby son, was not really cut out for domesticity. Nor, at that time, for the monotony of the royal round, though he has come to knuckle down to it over the years since. He chafed under a growing sense of frustration and longed more than anything to get back to his old love—the sea. That October, at his own wish, he resumed his naval career and found himself posted to Malta as first lieutenant aboard the destroyer *Chequers* on a basic pay scale of £1 6s. per day plus 18s. 6d. marriage allowance. It was a drop in the ocean of royal finances. Parliament had already granted him an annuity of £10,000 and had increased his wife's allowance from £15,000 to £40,000.

Philip's departure for Malta marked the newlyweds' first real separation and the Princess felt the wrench deeply. She was torn two ways. As a young wife, she naturally wanted to be with the husband she loved so much and who had so enlivened life for her. As a mother, she felt that her duty lay with her baby. Finally she compromised. She stayed with Charles over his first birthday on 14th November and then on 20th November she flew out to Malta to spend the evening of their second wedding anniversary with her husband. She stayed on in Malta over Christmas. As it happened, Philip's ship was undergoing a refit and they had plenty of time together.

But if the baby could do without her, monarchy would not. With Philip's destroyer off for a spell of patrol duty in the Red Sea, the Princess returned to Britain with a packed engagement book which included visits to Bath, Bristol and Crawley New Town, the inevitable, unending round of openings and inspections, speeches and bouquets, presentations and handshakes. As in childhood, she again found herself at her father's side and speaking words of welcome in French to a visiting French president. Then it was spring and she was off back to Malta to be with Philip for her birthday on 21st April.

Those spells in Malta still remain in the Queen's memory as among the happiest days of her life. Even today, very occasionally, she will still refer to the Villa Guardamangia, which she and Philip leased for a time, as "our home in Malta". Never before—and perhaps never since—has life been quite so carefree and casual for her. She found Philip, back in the navy and doing the job he loved, a completely contented and fulfilled man who had decorated his spartan, pintsized cabin aboard *Chequers* with photographs of his young wife and baby son. For the Princess, it was perhaps her first real taste of complete freedom, a chance to find out what life was really like beyond the rarefied and secluded atmosphere of the royal circle. She was free to come and go as she wanted, to do as she pleased (or almost as she pleased). She had her own car in which she drove to all parts of the sun-girt island. She gossiped with other naval wives as she had her hair done in one of the local hair-dressing salons. When Philip was off duty, they swam together in the warm, clear waters of the Mediterranean, sunbathed together in the warm sunshine and picnicked together in quiet, rocky coves. She watched Philip display his prowess at water-skiing and aqualung diving. She had given him a polo pony for Christmas and now she watched him play his first experimental, hell-for-leather games, jumping up in white-faced alarm if he was thrown by his pony, as he sometimes was.

Philip knew how she worried for him. "It's nothing—just a graze," he called out quickly as he picked himself up after a tumble which resulted in a cut elbow.

On her birthday, she saw him score a goal—and nearly a second—when playing for Uncle Dickie's team, Shrimps, against the rival Optimists. But despite Philip's goal, the Optimists won.

Of an evening, the two of them would dance together at a local hotel, the 'Phoenicia', and there were romantic tête-à-tête dinners by candlelight without a lady-in-waiting or personal detective within earshot.

They were both young and happy and very much in love, and it was perhaps not to be wondered that during her very first visit to Malta the young royal wife and mother became pregnant for the second time. She was back home at Clarence House when their second child—a daughter named Anne Elizabeth Alice Louise—was born on 15th August 1950. Philip had some leave due to him and flew home to be with her. Again he showed himself a dutiful and concerned husband, having his meals with her as she lay in bed, eating from a tray on his lap.

When he returned to Malta again it was as lieutenant-commander of his own ship, the frigate *Magpie*. His pay had gone up to £1 12s. a day and there was an additional 3s. a day as 'command' money.

Up and about after the birth of Princess Anne, his wife again tried to share herself out as equally as possible between her husband, her children and the continuing demands of monarchy. Again she flew out to Malta to be with Philip over Christmas. Her first, rather unexpected visit to his new command caught some of the crew napping. They were happily sunbathing on the deck in a state of near-nudity when the Princess came aboard. Covered in confusion, if little else, they dived hurriedly for shelter.

She sailed with Philip for Greece on what seems to have started out as a purely unofficial visit to relatives, King Paul and Queen Frederika. But in the way these things happen, the unofficial became the official or, at very least, the semi-official, with no fewer than three ships involved. *Magpie* with Lieutenant Commander Prince Philip on board, another frigate *Surprise* coveying the Princess, and a destroyer *Chieftain* also in attendance. They dropped anchor in Phaleron Bay. It was from here that Philip's dead father had sailed into exile aboard the cruiser *Calypso* a generation before. Now the son of that exiled father returned in triumph as the consort of Britain's future queen, bringing his wife with him. Public buildings were floodlit in his honour and the streets packed with wildly cheering crowds. Such are the twists and turns of fate. Together, the Greek-born prince who was now a naturalised Briton and his radiant young wife visited such ancient marvels as the Parthenon, the palace of Agamemnon, the temples of Poseidon and Apollo, walked the slopes of Mount Parnassos and stood upon that Delphic spot which the ancients thought was the very centre of the earth.

Another visit to Malta by the Princess became the occasion for a side-trip to Rome and Florence. Again, it was supposedly private, but again the private and the public had a tendency to overlap and intermingle. They paid a call upon another of Philip's many relatives, Queen Helen of Romania. But there was also a luncheon given in their honour by the Italian president and, while in Rome, the Princess also called upon the Pope, an action which was to arouse another brief spatter of criticism back home, much to Philip's irritation.

But for both Philip's resumed naval career and his wife's new-found freedom, time—though they may not have realised it—was fast running out. When her father was taken ill with influenza, the Princess had to deputise for him at the annual ceremony of Trooping the Colour. This time he could not be there, even in a carriage. Instead, he stayed at home, where he watched the pageantry on television.

She also hosted the King of Norway for him when he visited Britain. There were more and more provincial tours for her— Norwich and Birmingham, Worcester, Manchester and Portsmouth.

Much she could accomplish without Philip beside her. But not all. In particular, a forthcoming tour of Canada and America required Philip to be with her. Reluctantly he said farewell to the crew of *Magpie*. Today, he does not remember using the phrase, "The past eleven months have been the happiest of my sailor life," and perhaps he did not. But surely his thoughts must have run along those lines. They had been, after all, eleven months in which his love for his wife and his love for his old mistress, the sea, had run closely parallel. Now they were to diverge. The old mistress was to be finally discarded, even if Philip did not realise it. And yet perhaps he did. Perhaps he sensed that this was to be no temporary *au revoir*, but a final farewell.

"It will be a long time before I want those again," he said as he watched his valet packing his uniforms, water skis and spear-gun. It was 16th July 1951.

II Years of Hazard

Never has the Queen needed the support and reassuring presence of her husband more than she did in the autumn and winter of 1951–2. It was a distressed daughter and a worried princess who left Britain for a tour of Canada, with a side-trip to the United States, that October. The tour should have started with a leisurely ocean voyage across the Atlantic which would have eased the effect of the time-change. But at almost the last moment her father's health deteriorated yet further. Cancer had been diagnosed and a lung resection was required. As the next monarch, the Princess could hardly leave the country until it was sure

that he had pulled through. As a daughter, she naturally wished
to be near her father at such a time.

Not until the operation was well over and the King's recovery
seemingly assured did she finally leave for Canada—by air, two
weeks late. Even then, she flew out under the equivalent of
'sealed orders', taking with her a large sealed envelope which
she was told was to be opened "only in the event of the death
of His Majesty". It contained all she needed to know and all
she had to do in the event that she should suddenly find that she
had succeeded to the throne.

Few daughters can have undertaken so much with so much
personal worry on their minds, and if the Princess seemed sometimes stiff and unsmiling in Canada, as it was reported that she
did, this was the reason. And if Philip was sometimes tetchy,
this, too, was the reason. She was naturally worried about her
father; Philip was worried about her. In consequence, his temper,
never very far from the surface, occasionally gave way under
the strain. When it did, it was usually the nearest photographers
or newsmen who bore the brunt of things. At Niagara he sharply
refused to don a waterproof for a second time for the benefit
of photographers who had missed the picture first time around.
"What are they belly-aching about?" he demanded as the camera-
men grumbled among themselves. Organisers of the tour, too,
found themselves similarly caught in the backlash of royal
feelings. In Vancouver, when the inevitable Indian princess
popped up unexpectedly to be presented to the visiting Princess
from London, Philip snapped irritably, "The Indian princess stuff
is out." But his wife disagreed with him and the Indian princess
was duly presented.

Philip's concern was for his wife. He did his best to lessen
the burden on her. He saw to it that she got enough rest. He
buoyed her spirits when they seemed to flag. Every day, without
fail, the Princess put in a telephone call to London to check
on her father's condition. News of an apparent improvement
at one stage did much to ease her concern and, with a square
dance cropping up unexpectedly in the programme, she sent the
indefatigable Bobo out to the nearest department store to buy
her a suitable blouse and skirt. That night she and Philip danced
their feet off. There were other equally lighthearted moments,
for not even a devoted daughter can worry all the time and

there was much about that Canadian tour to excite the interest and stimulate the imagination.

Altogether, they were in Canada for seven weeks before embarking by tender to board the *Empress of Scotland*. That final short trip to the waiting liner was perhaps the roughest of the lot. Philip has denied that it made him seasick, though it has been said that it did. Certainly many of the party were. They had visited every Canadian province, travelling more than 16,000 miles and making over seventy stops, including two days in Washington where they were welcomed by President Truman. "As one father to another", the President wrote later to the King, "we can be very proud of our daughters."

The King was indeed proud of his daughter and delighted with his son-in-law. He showed his pleasure by appointing them both as members of the Privy Council. He was less concerned too about his doctors' refusal to let him undertake his own planned tour of Australia and New Zealand, already once postponed on account of his health. Well, if he could not go himself, Lilibet and Philip could go in his place. They had proved themselves more than able to cope.

As usual, the whole family foregathered at Sandringham that Christmas. It was, though the Princess could not know this, her last Christmas as heiress presumptive. By the time another Christmas came round she would be queen. But if she did not know it, it was almost as though her father sensed it. "It seemed as though the King almost drove himself to enjoy that Christmas as never before," we have been told.

His body may have been almost worn out, but his indomitable spirit refused to be beaten. He made his Christmas Day broadcast as always, but not as usual. Instead of going out live, the broadcast was pre-recorded, laboriously and painstakingly, a few words at a time. When Toc H carol singers from the neighbouring village of Dersingham came to call, he insisted that they should be invited in as usual so that everyone could join in the familiar words and tunes. But he himself did not have the strength to sing. He could not stand to give his Christmas presents to his staff, so he did it from an armchair instead. To save him the effort of going upstairs at night, his bed was moved into a ground-floor suite.

There were a few days following Christmas when it really

seemed as though the King might be on the road to full recovery. He brought his walking stick up to his shoulder as though it was a gun. "I believe I could shoot again," he said. In fact, he did shoot again, travelling from beat to beat in a Land-Rover, wearing battery-heated gloves to maintain the circulation in his hands. He was out shooting only the day before he died, a day of crisp winter sunshine. The late Lord Fermoy was with him. "The King was on top of his form," he told us the next day. By then the King was dead. But the day before he had laughed and joked as though there was nothing wrong with him. It was a day of rough shooting and he bagged nine hares and a wood-pigeon.

Between Christmas and that last day's shooting he had travelled to London and back to see his daughter and her husband off on the first leg of the journey to Australia and New Zealand they were making on his behalf. The Queen, as the Queen Mother still was, went with them, while Charles and Anne stayed on at Sandringham against their grandparents' return. As a farewell treat, the King took the family to see the American musical *South Pacific*. It was the sort of show he and Philip both enjoyed—robust and full-blooded with plenty of belly-laughs.

The next day the young couple took off from London airport, while the King, his face grey and drawn, stood bareheaded at the edge of the runway in the biting wind, waving farewell. Just before the aircraft left, he had taken Bobo quietly to one side. "Look after Lilibet for me," he said to her, almost as though he had a presentiment of what lay ahead.

It was seven days later and Prince Philip was cat-napping in a bedroom of the hunting lodge at Sagana which had been a wedding gift to him and his wife from the Government of Kenya.

The royal couple had flown out to Nairobi and had carried out a light spatter of official engagements before going to Sagana for a few days' rest and quiet before boarding the liner *Gothic* at Mombasa for the next stage of the journey. It was rather like a brief second honeymoon. They went riding and fishing together and had spent the previous night at Treetops, a rest house perched amidst the massive branches of a wild fig tree in the Aberdare Forest. From their perch they had watched elephants and rhino come down to the nearby water-hole to drink. At some point that night, between midnight when the King was heard tinkering with the catch of his bedroom window and half-past seven in the morning when his valet found him dead in bed, the Princess became the Queen.

It was, though she did not yet know it, a strange succession. She was wearing slacks and a blouse and had a movie camera in her hands. She was making a film of the baboons hopping about the tree tops to show to the children when she got back home.

Now, back at the lodge and still unaware that she was Queen, she was catching up with her correspondence when there was a tap at Philip's bedroom door. It was Mike Parker, his face entirely devoid of its usual cheerfulness.

As with so many important moments of royal history—such as that first meeting at Dartmouth and the moment of proposal— some of the facts of what followed are so personal as to be virtually secret while others are confused by memory. But this much is clear. Michael Parker had had the news by telephone from Martin Charteris in Nyeri. Charteris, private secretary to the Princess (now Sir Martin and one of the Queen's two assistant private secretaries) had heard it from Granville Roberts, a reporter on the *East African Standard* who had got it from Reuters.

Now Parker told Philip, "I'm afraid there's some awful news. The King is dead."

Prince Philip's first reaction was to inquire if the news was official. Parker told him it was. He had double-checked and had heard it confirmed on the radio.

As far as the jigsaw of events can be put together, Philip seems to have got his wife out of the house on the pretext of asking her to arrange their horse riding for the following morning while he and Parker briefly discussed how best to break the news to her. So the new, young Queen walked out into the warm sunshine, pausing briefly to chat with Bobo and Philip's valet, John Dean. They were already aware of the news, but said nothing and were careful not to let the fact of their knowledge show in their faces. Then Philip joined his wife, took her into a room where they were alone together and closed the door behind him.

When they were next seen, nearly an hour later, there were signs that the Queen had been crying. She and Philip went walking alone together by the Sagana River. When they returned she was dry-eyed and composed, though very pale. The daughter had wept; now the queen must reign.

So began for the Queen and Prince Philip what was perhaps the most difficult period of their married life. For a time, at least, the years of carefree laughter were over and a period of stressful duty lay ahead. The new life they were required to lead as queen and consort clearly had an effect upon their personal lives. They were no longer simply husband and wife. The wife was also the queen. But the husband was not the king, a fact clearly underlined at the accession ceremony which followed the new queen's return to London. As husband, Philip could be with her, lending her comfort and support, as she walked through from their home at Clarence House to the adjoining Palace of St. James's. But he could not be beside her while she took the Declaration of Accession. That she had to do alone while Philip took his place among the others of the Privy Council who watched and listened.

The ordinary relationship between a king and his queen consort, except in the finer details, is not that much different from the relationship between an ordinary husband and wife. In the average marriage, the husband has his job of work while the wife attends to the home and children. In the same way, the king works at monarchy while the queen runs the palace. That is the way it was with the Queen's parents. But now, with herself and Philip, it was necessarily different. Philip was constitutionally debarred from running the monarchy and could hardly be expected to supervise such royal domestic details as planning the menus and replacing the bed-linen when required. So the Queen did both. Philip found himself in a curiously anomalous position. There were times when he was expected to be at his wife's side, as when she held her first investiture in the month following her accession; others when he could not. He could not be present, for instance, when the Prime Minister called upon her on Tuesday evenings. And he could not, unlike his predecessor in the tricky role of royal consort, Prince Albert, sit beside her to go through the contents of the time-honoured boxes.

In those early days of his wife's monarchy, he attempted at one point to obtain some guidance by a study of Albert's life.

Two journeys to Balmoral
two years apart chart the
growth of the Queen's
youngest children

The Queen and Prince Philip drive past the Berlin wall during the 1965 tour on which the Queen saw her German in-laws in their own homes for the first time

What he read can have afforded him little consolation. The role of Prince Consort, according to Albert's words (though perhaps not his actions) required that he should "entirely sink his own individual existence in that of his wife; that he should aim at no power by himself or for himself; should shun all contention; assume no separate responsibility before the public; make his position entirely a part of hers". It reads as a somewhat shrinking assessment which Albert himself certainly did not abide by and which Philip's yet more thrusting nature would clearly find impossible.

In the comparisons sometimes made between the Queen and Prince Philip and their joint great-great-grandparents, Victoria and Albert, several important points tend to be overlooked. Victoria had already been queen for nearly three years when she married Albert. Indeed, one of the reasons for marriage would seem to have been that she wanted a husband to advise and guide her. Within days of her proposal and his acceptance, he was altering the mistakes she made in letters and, between kisses, blotting royal warrants as she signed them. All this even before they married. On honeymoon at Windsor—and, later, living together at Buckingham Palace—they worked together at two tables by day just as they played duets on two pianos at night. Despite Albert's early lament that he was only "the husband and not the master in the house", he was soon dealing with actual despatches on her behalf, reorganising the palace with Teutonic thoroughness—and sometimes tactlessness—and more and more influencing his wife's ideas, outlook and policy.

The two of them, Victoria and Albert, according to Lord Clarendon, "laboured under the curious mistake that . . . they had the right to control, if not to direct, the foreign policy of England".

In those days, it should be borne in mind, the monarchy had more authority and influence than ever it has today. Queen Victoria, though she did not always get her own way, could and did influence political appointments, government policy and even international affairs to a not inconsiderable extent. The Queen could hardly do the same today. Nor could Prince Philip be a second Albert even if he wanted to. No foreign minister would write to him, as Lord John Russell wrote to Albert, seeking advice on how to deal with Germany. And neither the

Queen nor Prince Philip, in this day and age, would venture to revise a Foreign Office message, as Albert did almost on his death-bed—an action which, as things turned out, perhaps averted war between Britain and the United States.

For the new, young queen, the months and years immediately ahead were to be the busiest she has ever known. There was so much to do; so much still to be learned. She came to her new role with all the conscientious devoutness that a novice enters a nunnery. While the Divine Right of Kings may be an old-fashioned conception, she accepted then—as she accepts now—that monarchy is an almost divine calling. Initially, at least, it was a calling to which she devoted herself if not utterly and completely, at least very nearly so.

For her, there was much to be learned. Despite the training she had undergone with her father, grandmother and others; despite the experience she had gained as her father's deputy, there was much about monarchy that was new to her, much in which she needed help and guidance. And her husband could not be her tutor; he knew less than she did. Necessarily she turned to others, to those who had served her father so well and so loyally: Sir Alan Lascelles, his private secretary; Sir Piers Legh, his Master of the Household; Sir Ulick Alexander, his Keeper of the Privy Purse. Necessarily, too, she was guided by her Prime Minister, Sir Winston Churchill, who may not have encouraged her to rely upon Philip to quite the same extent that Melbourne encouraged the young Victoria to place herself under Albert's guidance.

She spent long hours studying state documents; signing or initialing royal warrants, parliamentary bills. Her personal letter-writing was quickly in arrears and at times she would make frantic efforts to catch up, dashing off letters to friends in hurried, scrawled handwriting, quite unlike her flourishing official signature. But in her official work she would take no short cuts. One rather tedious chore was to sign herself Elizabeth R. on the hundreds of official portraits which were required at the outset of the new reign. It was suggested that she should have a rubber stamp made of her signature to save herself time and fatigue. She shook her head. The photographs would not mean the same if she did not sign them herself, she said.

In five months she carried out no fewer than 140 public

engagements and *The Lancet* cautioned that she was perhaps trying to do too much, as did the select committee which was set up to look into the question of finance for the new reign. "Notwithstanding constant attempts to lighten the burden, the burden of Her Majesty's duties is still formidable and likely to remain so," the committee reported. "Relations between the Sovereign and the Commonwealth are certain to mean a considerable extension in the demands made on Her Majesty." *The Lancet* added that it would "welcome an assurance that by deliberate decisions taken in advance Her Majesty's health and vitality will be protected from her hereditary sense of duty".

Strangely enough, the Queen had never looked better or felt fitter. Just as she had blossomed in the early days of her marriage, so she now seemed to bloom afresh with her new bridegroom—monarchy. She seemed to bubble over with energy and vitality. She seemed virtually tireless as she received the hundreds of official visitors who came to pay their respects to the new sovereign. She posed happily for the many new portraits which seemed to be required. But time was constantly at a premium and more than one royal portrait was finished from a dressmaker's dummy decked out in the Queen's clothes and jewels. Even a painting she wanted for herself—Edward Halliday's family portrait of the Queen, Prince Philip, Charles and Anne and the corgis—had to be painted, in part, with the obliging Bobo substituting for the Queen as a model and a royal footman sitting in for Prince Philip.

Monarchy insisted upon many changes in the royal couple's accustomed way of life, among them a move back to Buckingham Palace from Clarence House. In a way, both the Queen and her husband regretted the necessity for the move. To them, Clarence House had been an essentially happy place, large enough to be royal, but small enough to be homely. But it was clearly not large enough to accommodate all the additional staff and extra work required by monarchy.

At Clarence House, by royal standards, they had made do with comparatively few servants. At Buckingham Palace there were dozens more—pages and footmen, chauffeurs and coachmen, maids, typists and what-have-you. Life was much more complicated and infinitely more formal. At Clarence House there had been a warm degree of informality between the royal couple and their staff. Their principal aides had become accustomed to simply tapping on a door, waiting for someone to say "Come in" and then entering. At Buckingham Palace, Philip, initially tried to keep things similarly informal. If a telephone chanced to ring when he was near, he would pick it up and answer it. He by-passed the old-fashioned chain of command which involved telling a page who would tell a footman who would tell someone else if he wanted even the simplest thing. Instead, he had an intercom system installed and would ring the chef direct if he wanted a few sandwiches sent up or the garages if he wanted his car brought round. If he wanted Mike Parker, he did not summon him to his presence. He simply strolled along to Parker's office. It fidgeted him when footmen rushed around opening doors for him. "I've got hands," he protested. "I can open a door myself." It fidgeted him, too, when he was told that anyone who wanted to see him should be formally announced. "Why can't they just walk in?" he asked. But fewer and fewer did so, and gradually, far from Philip changing the old royal outlook, he found himself being moulded more and more in the traditional royal image.

The Queen made no attempt to change. She was content to do things the way her father had always done them, and the tune for the new reign was perhaps set by Maurice Watts, who had been her father's page and was now her page, when he carefully informed a former Clarence House aide who tried to perpetuate the old tap-and-walk-in system, "Nobody simply walks in on the Queen. You must wait until I have announced you."

To avoid any suggestion that they were pushing the Queen Mother, as she now was, out of her old home, the new Queen and her husband moved initially into the Belgian Suite at the rear of the palace, a set of rooms normally used to accommodate visiting monarchs and presidents. The Queen Mother continued to occupy the first-floor royal apartment while Princess Margaret moved to the front of the palace so as to free the nursery wing for Charles and Anne along with their nanny and under-nanny, nurserymaids and footman.

Soon after the move Philip went down with jaundice. Despite all else she had to do, the Queen continued to show herself a loving and devoted wife. She was constantly in and out of his room, taking her meals by his bedside, and using wifely persuasion to make him stay in bed. Philip, like most extrovert, athletic men, is never a good invalid. There was a subsequent occasion at Windsor when he seemed to be sickening for flu and the Queen, without consulting him, sent for a doctor. Philip was furious and flatly refused to follow the doctor's advice that he should stay in bed for a week. Instead, he was out of bed again the very next day and two days after that he packed his bags and drove himself back to London.

Equally, the Queen contrived to make time for the children. She did not, of course, cook for them or wash and iron their clothes, but then she never had. But she kept an eye on the way the nursery was run, intervening occasionally as when she discovered the children drinking bottled orange juice. In future, she told the nursery staff, their orange juice was to be squeezed from fresh oranges. The children were not allowed to run in and out of her sitting room (which also doubled as her study) during what she came to regard as her working hours. (Years later, more at ease in her role of monarch, she was to relax this rule for Andrew and Edward.) But they were brought down to see her each morning before she started work. Sometimes she would take the lift up to the nursery to see them again at lunchtime, though this was not always possible with a lunch break which sometimes had to be cut to thirty minutes because of the pressure of engagements. Then at five o'clock, when she stopped work for the day, the children came down again to have tea with her and help her in feeding the dogs, a task she always insisted on doing herself. After tea, she would go back to the nursery with them for playtime and bathtime, devoting an hour and a half exclusively to them, even to the extent of asking the Prime Minister to put back his Tuesday evening call to an hour when she had finished with the children. Sometimes, during this family hour and a half, Philip would take Charles off to the heated pool at the rear of the palace to give him his first swimming lessons. In the main, it was Philip who projected the fun into family life. Jumping beans, squeaking fruit, an horrific-looking toy spider—there was no telling what he would produce next from his pockets and the children loved him for it. Mummy, too, had her fun moments, as they found out the day they trotted into her sitting room for afternoon tea and found her sitting there with a real crown on her head, for all the world like a queen in a fairy story. The crown had not been donned simply to amuse the children, of course. With the coronation coming up, the Queen felt it wise to practise moving around with this heavy and unaccustomed weight on her head. According to the Queen's father, the massive Crown of St. Edward weighs 7 pounds; according to the Ministry of Works, it weighs "nearly 5 pounds". Either way, it is a substantial piece of headgear.

If those early days of monarchy were the busiest the Queen has known, they were less busy and certainly less meaningful for Prince Philip. Having abandoned his beloved naval career in order to work alongside his wife, he now found that she no longer required his help to quite the same extent as she had done as a princess. He found himself missing the old freedoms.

While there were things to do in his new role of consort, there was perhaps not enough and certainly not enough of real consequence. He might have inherited the late king's study, but he had neither his desk nor the work that went with it. His wife had both of those. He was simply the Queen's husband, a constitutional non-position which was underlined when the Queen opened the first Parliament of the new reign. Hitherto, there had been two thrones for this ancient ceremony, one for the king and the other for the queen. Now there was only one and Philip found himself sitting on what is known as a Chair of State.

But if he had no proper job of work, he was not the sort of man to stand idly by, twiddling his thumbs. He continued his self-appointed task of supplying Britain with playing fields. He visited, among other places, the atomic research centre at Harwell, the Chemical Research Laboratory at Teddington and the Royal Aeronautical Establishment at Farnborough. He went to Helsinki for the 1952 Olympics. He visited a steel works at Port Talbot, went down a mine in Lancashire and opened a hydro-electric scheme in Scotland. He presided at the annual meeting of the Central Council for Physical Recreation.

Sport, physical fitness, technology—these were the areas in which, gradually, he began to create his own image. With an eye to the future, he also set about learning to fly, something, he said, he had wanted to do ever since he was a small boy. He began his flying training in a Chipmunk at White Waltham in the November of accession year. By Christmas he had already gone solo and four months later he won his wings.

Initially, his flying lessons were inclined to worry his wife. There was more than one occasion when she became quite restless in his absence, asking every few minutes if he was back, brightening visibly when he came in. But in time she learned to live with it. Having mastered conventional aircraft, Philip began to talk enthusiastically about jets. This worried the Queen even more. It also bothered the Government. Winston Churchill had a talk with Philip about it, trying to head him off the idea with the argument that, as husband of the sovereign, he should not take unnecessary risks. This was rather like the pot calling the kettle black when one recalls how difficult it was for the Queen's father to dissuade Churchill from sailing with the invasion forces on D-Day. Philip it was quite impossible to dissuade. He heard Churchill out, then went full steam ahead with his plan for learning to handle jets and, subsequently, helicopters.

Like Albert before him, he developed an itch to reform Buckingham Palace. Like Albert also, he found stumbling blocks in the way. One of Albert's first tasks was to inspect the royal kitchens. Philip went one better. He toured the palace from basement to attics, sometimes losing his way in the process as other royal occupants of that labyrinthine mansion had done before him. On one occasion, searching for the Ministry of Works office, he ended up in a basement fuel store. The royal kitchens, Albert had considered, were "hot, unhealthy and unfitted for their task". But he does not appear to have done anything about it. Philip did. He produced a scheme for a small, new, modern kitchen on the same floor as the royal apartment. Intrigued by the amount of linen that had to be laundered and the amount of bread consumed, Philip also suggested that it would be more economical if the palace had its own laundry and bakery. Both ideas were turned down on the grounds of capital expenditure.

Gradually, however, he did manage to achieve some modernisation of the palace's old-fashioned system. An intercom system reduced the necessity for footmen to trot around with messages; the central heating system was vastly improved; electric typewriters, tape recorders and radio telephones in royal cars speeded the work of monarchy, while the lawn at the back of the palace was shortly to become a landing pad for helicopters. On a more personal note, he had one of the coach houses in the royal mews rigged up as a polo practice pit. An ingenious system of canvas, wire mesh and sloping boards was devised and constructed to return the ball after each shot, with Philip straddling a mock polo pony in the centre of it all. Over the years he has used it consistently to get back in trim for each new season.

At Windsor, Sandringham, Balmoral, he embarked upon rapid fact-finding tours similar to those already carried out at Buckingham Palace. "The Duke's naval inspections," they were nicknamed, jokingly. Philip showed a quick grasp for essential detail even of those things—such as estate management and farming—of which he had no experience, and many changes were made at his suggestion. Among other things, the Christmas tree which an earlier Prince Consort had first introduced into Britain was now to be grown on a commercial basis. At Sandringham, in particular, his suggestions for alteration and modernisation did much to prevent the place being the same drain on the Queen's purse that it had been on her father's.

Inevitably, the new relationship between royal wife and husband which was necessary in their official life tended to overlap also into the private sector. Until now, despite all else she had had to do as a Princess, there had been many relaxed and tranquil spells, as in Malta, when the Queen had been both free and happy to play the wife to Philip's husband. But now she had far less such free time and her mind was constantly pre-occupied with duties of monarchy. Even at Christmas, that first year of the new reign, between making Christmas stockings for the children (and, incidentally, for the dogs) and joining in a family sing-song round the grand piano at Sandringham, the Queen had also to write official letters, sign state papers, decide the final design for her coronation gown and even select some of the dresses she would be wearing on the world tour which was to follow the coronation. It was no longer possible for her to simply drop everything else at a moment's notice in order to go out and watch Philip play polo or plod behind him as he banged away at pheasants or grouse. The contents of the boxes and all the other duties of monarchy must come first. If Philip perhaps did not always understand this, there were equally perhaps times when the Queen laid too much stress upon monarchy rather than marriage. To her, monarchy was all-important, as Philip was to find out during a rehearsal for the coronation ceremony.

The rehearsal had reached that stage where Philip was required to take the Oath of Fealty. Rising, he should have kissed his wife on the cheek, touched the crown on her head as a sign of his loyalty to it and then withdrawn. Whether from embarrassment or joking high spirits, he turned the kiss into a peck while the touch he gave the crown was no more than a casual flick. Like her great-great-grandmother, the Queen was not amused, and her wifely rebuke was heard clearly by many of those present: "Don't be silly, Philip. Come back and do it again."

But if there were new strains in the marriage, there were also gay and happy highlights—bathing the children in the nursery tub with water splashing everywhere, barbecue picnics on the moors at Balmoral with father turning the steaks while mother whipped up the pancakes, Philip and the kids taking a sneaky dip in the fountain at Windsor (which did not then have its own swimming pool), the Queen's laughing cry of "I think you're all mad" as her husband, his nose reddened with grease-paint, and his cohorts tumbled each other into the ship's pool during a quite hilarious crossing-the-line ceremony as they sailed south for Australia and New Zealand.

It was during that tour of Australia that Philip let slip a small remark which gave some indication of his feelings. One couple presented to him were named as "Dr. and Mr. Robinson". Philip raised an inquiring eyebrow and Mr. Robinson hastened to explain that his wife was a Ph.D. and therefore the more important of the two of them.

"Ah, yes—we have that trouble in our family, too," commented the Prince.

It was said in jest, but as so often with Philip, there was a sharp little thorn of truth hidden in the humour.

Life was made no easier for Prince Philip at this time when he and the Queen were both trying to adjust to their new relationship with monarchy by the fact that he found himself cast in the role of royal whipping-boy. No one at this time would have dreamed of criticising the Queen (though this was to come later). Charles and Anne were not yet of an age to warrant criticism (though this too was to come later). In the long-running royal serial story, as Princess Margaret has since pointed out, there has to be a 'baddie' to offset the 'goodies' and the choice, at this time, fell upon Prince Philip.

He was, in a sense, tailor-made for the part. Extrovert, offbeat, outspoken, sometimes witty, sometimes tetchy, he had all the attributes . . . and still does. Indeed, then as now, there were even times when he seemed to be enjoying the role and playing up to it, as though he was employing shock tactics to make people aware of his existence. Then, as later, his speeches were often controversial and sometimes tended to verge on the political, which royalty is traditionally supposed to avoid (though heaven knows why). A speech in which he extolled national service as a character-building experience was held to be advocating conscription, and he was promptly labelled a "royal meddler" by one Scottish newspaper waxing indignant about what it called "this intolerable intrusion into political affairs".

More sensitive to criticism than he appears—or would perhaps care to admit—Philip at times reacted sharply. He was the first member of the Royal Family to reply to criticism in public. "You know what I am doing?" he inquired of an audience in Birmingham. "I'm twiddling my thumbs"—a dig at a newspaper which had referred to the royals as under-employed thumb-twiddlers. In both his speeches and his clearly audible asides, he was frequently sour to the Press and some newspapers have been a long time forgiving him for it. He was sometimes blunt almost to the point of rudeness. "It is no good shutting your eyes, saying 'Britain is Best' three times a day and expecting it to be so," he told a gathering of manufacturers. Yet sometimes he seemed to see further ahead than most people and when he blamed the inefficient use of fuel for "Some of the muck which passes for fresh air in our cities" he was ventilating a problem which others since must have wished had been tackled at the time Prince Philip first raised the subject.

He was criticised for the things he said, the things he did, the things he didn't do. His tendency to play games on Sunday brought him under attack from Dr. Donald (later Baron) Soper. "It is no good saying that a man in his position can play games on Sunday without interfering with anybody else. However discreet he is, it becomes a public occasion, and even a commercial occasion, whether he likes it or not." In saying which, Dr. Soper seemed to overlook the fact that the majority of Britons behaved likewise without being able to say, as Philip could, that they had gone to church first.

Then and later, nothing seemed to raise so many people to such fury as his seeming fondness for guns. "Loathsome," snapped one M.P. of Philip's deer-stalking activities. "Trigger-happy," the League Against Cruel Sports called him. Even foreigners joined in this new national sport of baiting Prince Philip. "Butchery", shrilled an Italian newspaper after Philip had been out for a day's shooting with sewing-machine tycoon Vittorio Necchi and others which resulted in 650 birds in the bag.

Yet the curious thing is that Philip would perhaps not have taken up shooting to the extent that he did—any more than Charles, later, would have played rugby—if he had not felt that it was expected of him. When he first went out shooting with the Queen's father, at Sandringham and Balmoral, he was a mere beginner who missed as often as he killed. He had done a little rough shooting before, in boyhood and while on leave from the navy, but nothing more. But shooting, he found, was expected of him in the new royal stratum in which he now moved and, a man who will not do a thing if he cannot do it well, he resolved to become good at it. So he shot and he shot and he shot, even if at times he found it almost as boring as watching horseracing.

There is in his view, as he has made clear in his speeches, shooting *and shooting*. He has defended his own exploits with a gun as the rational control of certain species of wildlife while not hesitating to condemn the indiscriminate killing of such rarities as the North American golden eagle and the Arabian oryx. But his condemnation of Australians for killing the kangaroo brought a quick riposte from one Down-under politician who urged him equally to decry what went on nearer home . . . "Children taught to shoot stags and coverts beaten so that pheasant fly over hidden sportsmen to their deaths by the bagful."

In fact, even in those early days, Philip had little real love for the big organised shoots. More to his liking were those more solitary occasions when he could pit himself against the wily zigzag flight of the woodcock or go after duck flying high on the cold, windswept marshes. Better still if the sport was truly adventurous and with a hint of danger to it, as in crocodile hunting. There was one occasion, on the Gambia River, when a crocodile he and Mike Parker thought they had killed between them thrashed about so violently as it was being lashed to the boat that it threatened to overturn them before it was finally despatched with a knife.

If the criticism which came Philip's way from so many different quarters was sometimes justified, it was sometimes also considerably unfair. The new royal yacht *Britannia* may have been the "costly toy" one politician labelled it—it depends upon your viewpoint—but to nickname it "Philip's Folly" was unjustified. The proposal for a new yacht to replace the old, unseaworthy *Victoria and Albert* was already in the planning stage as far back as 1951, which was before the Queen had succeeded to the throne and before Philip could have had any real say in things. Later, after the Queen's accession and as the new yacht reached the fitting-out stage, he did have a say in things. Characteristically, he shipped a load of palace servants out to the yacht to test things out. To check whether kitchen and dining room were adequate, he had them cook a meal, serve it, eat it. The dining table, he found, seated only thirty-two people. On his suggestion, removable wings were added to bring the seating capacity up to sixty.

With the cost of construction having jumped from an estimated £1,750,000 to £2,139,000 by launch time, and a further £200,000 forked out in the rush to get things done in time for the yacht to collect the Queen and her husband from Tobruk at the end of their 1953–4 world tour, it is perhaps no wonder that it was looked upon by some people as the most controversial royal possession since Charles II acquired Mistress Nell Gwyn . . . and Philip became a convenient scapegoat.

In the sometimes confused overlapping of public and private lives which is one of royalty's biggest bugbears, nothing was to so confound those early years of the Queen's monarchy as the business of Princess Margaret and Peter Townsend. Like it or not, this was destined to be a situation in which the Queen and her husband were involved on both levels, public and personal. Neither of them wanted the throne rocked again as it had been in the weeks leading up to the abdication of the Queen's uncle. Yet personal feelings came into it, too. Margaret was, after all, the Queen's sister, and a sister to whom, through childhood and later, she was extremely devoted.

The attachment between the younger sister and the ex-fighter pilot royal equerry had blossomed long before the elder sister succeeded to the throne, even if the Queen, happily preoccupied with her own courtship, betrothal and marriage, had taken little notice of what was going on. Indeed, her own absorption with the monarchy following her father's death had perhaps combined with her mother's grief to push Margaret more and more towards Townsend. Both were too involved to pay much attention to Margaret and so the younger sister, 21 at the time in actual years but perhaps emotionally still a teenager due to the seclusion of her royal upbringing, turned elsewhere for comfort in her own grief. But from that autumn day in 1952 when the Queen Mother and her younger daughter moved into Clarence House, with Townsend going along with them as Comptroller instead of staying on at the palace as Deputy Master of the new Queen's Household, neither the Queen nor her mother can hardly have failed to be aware which way the wind blew.

The full story of what went on behind the scenes during the emotionally-charged period which followed will necessarily not be known until some future royal biographer, privileged to root through present-day royal archives, diaries and correspondence, reveals at least some of the sidelights. But it is a perhaps not unreasonable assumption that while the Queen's continuing use of the name of Windsor may have originated at the instigation of Winston Churchill, the role she played in the matter of Townsend and Margaret was her own with her husband as the main supporting character.

It is a matter of record that Townsend, in Margaret's absence, was banished to Brussels. For two years more the unhappy situation was to drag on, kept alive publicly by the newspapers and privately by tender letters passing back and forth between Margaret and Townsend, until the approach of Margaret's twenty-fifth birthday in August 1955 brought things finally to a head.

For members of the Royal Family, the twenty-fifth birthday is an important personal milestone, a sort of second coming-of-age. That it is so goes back something like two centuries to the

Royal Marriage Act of 1772. Upset because two of the family had contracted marriages with commoners, the Duke of Gloucester marrying Lady Waldegrave and the Duke of Cumberland allying himself with a Mrs. Horton, that good and frugal—and, eventually, unstable—monarch, George III, had it passed into law that, "No descendant of his late Majesty George II (other than the issue of princesses who have married or may marry into foreign families) shall be capable of contracting marriage without the previous consent of His Majesty, his heirs and successors, signified under the Great Seal." Marriages contracted without such consent are void in law, though the fact does not seem to have prevented George III's own son contracting an alliance with the widowed Mrs. Fitzherbert.

Today, when marriages between royalty and commoners are no longer deemed quite so undesirable, that Royal Marriage Act of 1772 is still in force. But for Princess Margaret, as she celebrated her twenty-fifth birthday, the next section of the Act offered a possible way out if she should decide to take advantage of it: "But in case any descendant of George II, being above 25 years old, shall persist to contract a marriage disapproved of by His Majesty, such descendant, after giving 12 months' notice to the Privy Council, may contract such a marriage and the same may be duly solemnised without the consent of His Majesty, his heirs and successors, and shall be good except that both Houses of Parliament shall declare their disapprobation thereto."

So the question posed itself: would Princess Margaret, now "being above 25 years old" give the required 12 months' notice of her intention to marry Townsend in the hope and belief that both Houses of Parliament would not "declare their disapprobation thereto". With Townsend's return to London a bare seven weeks later, their reunion at Clarence House and their subsequent weekends spent together in the country, it seemed possible, even probable, that things were moving in that direction. The problem, though long public property, was one which could be resolved only on a personal level.

In the emotional tug-of-war which ensued, hardly anyone in the family was on Margaret's side. The Queen, devoted though she was to Margaret, was devoted even more to monarchy. And if Margaret had hoped that Philip, with his more informal background and more free-and-easy outlook, might see things her way, she found herself mistaken. He was firmly on his wife's side. The Queen Mother, much as she loved her younger daughter, much as she desired her happiness, was not of a nature to stand out for long against two such firmly-held opinions, backed as they were by Church and Government.

How far the ultimate decision was Margaret's own and how far she was talked into it, it must be left to some future biographer to reveal. Certainly that final poignant statement would seem to have been her own, issued against the wishes of the Queen and the Queen Mother, though they may have had different reasons for wanting nothing so public.

Either way, she renounced Townsend. But not before the whole unhappy business had made tall headlines around the world and, in combination with other things, helped to set the stage and induce the climate which was to make subsequent rumours about a rift in the royal marriage of the Queen and Prince Philip briefly believed in some quarters.

III   Years of Adjustment

"It is quite untrue that there is any rift between the Queen and the Duke of Edinburgh."

This terse statement emanating from Buckingham Palace in the February of 1957 nailed, if it did not finally end, the spate of unhappy rumour about the private life of royal husband and wife which was currently being headlined in newspapers and magazines around the world.

How did the rumour start? How much fire, if any, lay behind the smokescreen of gossip? What effect did it all have on the Queen and her husband?

It started with tittle-tattle on the part of those few who like to pretend that they are in the know. Royal marriages, as Princess

Margaret and Lord Snowdon have had every cause to know in more recent times, afford excellent fuel for the human weakness for gossip. The smallest things—small areas of disagreement which would pass unnoticed in any ordinary marriage—become exciting topics of interesting, and sometimes slightly malicious, speculation once they become public. The tiniest titbit is seized upon, perhaps misconstrued, added to, passed on, added to again, passed on again, to emerge finally in quite different form, just as "Send reinforcements; am going to advance", passed on by word of mouth, can finally become "Send three-and-fourpence; am going to a dance."

An example. One evening, somewhere between the birth of Prince Andrew, the Queen's third child, and the marriage a few months later of Princess Margaret, someone inside Buckingham Palace chanced to overhear that Prince Philip "and the princess" had gone swimming together. He mentioned it to someone else who talked about it outside the palace. It came finally to the ears of a gossip columnist. By this time "the princess" had become Princess Margaret and the published story made no bones about who had been swimming with whom. Prince Philip was not unreasonably incensed at the idea of the public being told that while his wife was nursing the new baby, he was gallivanting around with her young sister. It was true that he had been swimming in the palace pool on that particular evening. It was true that he had been with "the princess". But not the princess of gossip column assumption. The princess with whom he had been swimming was, in fact, his sister Sophie, who was staying with her brother and sister-in-law at the time.

The gossip flames of early 1957 were probably fuelled in much the same misconstrued fashion. There was, at the time, plenty for them to feed on.

There was the known fact that Philip had been away from his wife, his children and his palace home for four months. It was, in fact, the longest spell he and the Queen had been apart in all their married life. Not even when he was in the navy, in Malta, was there a separation quite so long. There was his background of restless, bored frustration. There was his earlier attendance at the Thursday Club, an all-male luncheon club meeting above Wheeler's Restaurant in Compton Street, to which he had been upon occasion to enjoy good food, fine wine and perhaps a few stag party jokes. There was, in addition to all this, the matrimonial situation of Mike Parker and his wife, Eileen, estranged and contemplating divorce.

Inevitably there was gossip, restricted at first to the few and concerned perhaps more with what was going on between Parker and his wife than with the Queen and her husband. Equally inevitably, in hinted remarks left unfinished and overheard by ears for which they were not intended, there was confusion as to who was being talked about, who was supposed to have done what and when and where. So far, however, no real harm had been done and the whole business might well have died a quick natural death, as gossip so often does, if a report had not gone to the *Baltimore Sun* in America from its correspondent in London beginning: "The whisper started last summer . . ."

Not every foreign correspondent bothers to report whispers of personal gossip when they are still no more than whispers. Not every newspaper bothers to print them. This correspondent and newspaper did, the correspondent subsequently defending her action with the argument that "if you are a foreign correspondent, it is your duty to report rumours. I was most careful to point out that they were just rumours."

Others were rather less careful once the rumour was fully airborne and actually in print. Other American newspapers picked it up from the *Baltimore Sun*, reprinted it, set their own correspondents to work to salvage more gossipy titbits, and, in case these established correspondents should themselves have succumbed to the British atmosphere of royal veneration, in some instances even flew the untainted, homebred product over to London to dig deeper in search of yet juicier worms. So the story grew, spreading out into two overlapping circles. One circle had the Thursday Club as its centre, and this version of the story had the Queen allegedly incensed by Philip's patronage of such stag parties. The other story centred around parties which were alleged to be not quite so exclusively stag. Either way, Philip's Antarctic trip, it was suggested, was because he had been "got out of the country to cool off" and Winston Churchill was on the point of returning home from the Riviera to sort it all out.

Newspapers in Canada, Australia, Europe, picked up and

built up the story and published it in turn. But in Britain, to their credit, the newspapers did not touch it—not for three days.

Then came the official denial from Buckingham Palace. Now the British newspapers joined in, dismissing the rumours out of hand, attacking those who had spread and published them in the first place, condemning the Queen's advisers for "ineptitude" in simply looking down their noses and hoping that the rumour would go away, urging Philip to "fly home". But Philip, having reached Gibraltar at the end of his long trip, having accepted Mike Parker's resignation and said his goodbyes, stayed where he was.

He had been away from his palace home since the mid-October of the previous year, engaged in an extremely offbeat royal tour which originated with an invitation to open the 1956 Olympic Games, being held that year in Melbourne. Philip accepted the invitation, looked at the maps and came up with an idea. Why not, if he was going to that part of the world anyway, visit some of those places and people which the Queen, as a woman, could hardly hope to visit: rough, tough, out-of-the-way spots, small islands and isolated communities, survey teams in the Falklands and the transantarctic expedition? It would be a royal trip with a distinct ring of adventure to it and, as such, it appealed strongly to the young man of 35 Philip still was. And if it enabled him to again enjoy, however briefly, the company of his old mistress, the sea, and escape for a time from the rather enervating atmosphere of the traditional royal round, so much the better. For perhaps the first time since his wife's accession, Philip had a project of his own over which he could really get excited, something with a distinct challenge to it. For the first time he could feel that he was doing something worthwhile and meaningful. So the royal yacht was made ready.

It would have been easier and simpler, of course, as Philip himself was to remark later, to merely have flown out to Melbourne and back. And to have done so would perhaps have killed the subsequent gossip before it had even started. But it would have been less of a psychological safety valve, of which Philip was perhaps in need at the time; and not even a royal consort has the ability to foresee future events.

So off he went on a trip which was to enable him to recapture something of his days in the navy, taking charge on the bridge of the royal yacht just as he had once done aboard *Magpie*, surrounded by the all-male atmosphere in which he is in his element, able to express himself freely (except when either of the two girl secretaries were around) in blunt, sea-going language. He photographed sea birds, had a dab at oil painting under the expert tuition of artist Edward Seago, talked with Sir Raymond Priestley who had been with Scott on his expedition to the South Pole, grew a beard again, saw icebergs and whales, skylarked with Mike Parker and issued certificates of the "Order of the Red Nose", designed by himself and Seago, to commemmorate the crossing of the Antarctic Circle. It was just like the old days. But all this, of course, was but a sideline to the real purpose of the trip which was to show the royal banner in lonely and out-of-the-way spots where it could not otherwise be seen. On both counts—as a royal tour and a counter-balance to Philip's frustrations—it was very much worthwhile.

But, back home, the gossip was beginning and the royal yacht had only just berthed at Gibraltar at the end of its long and arduous voyage when the storm finally broke.

To those closest to the royal couple—Bobo MacDonald and others—the newspaper stories seemed to depart so far from the facts, as they knew them, that they might have been referring to two quite different people. The Queen herself was understandably upset and, for once, even perhaps a trifle bitter—an emotion normally foreign to her nature—about the "terrible things" being published about herself, her husband and their marriage. To her, there seemed no basis in fact for even the slightest gossip. She and her husband were on the best of terms, she felt. Only the previous March the two of them had briefly recaptured something of the halcyon atmosphere of those pre-monarchy days when she was a naval wife. She had flown out to join Philip (who had been attending Fleet exercises in the Mediterranean) aboard *Britannia* and together the two of them had explored Corsica and Sardinia. As in Malta, there had been quiet picnics in rocky coves and informal sightseeing with the Queen clad in slacks, blouse and head-scarf. She was dressed like this the day a Corsican peasant woman stopped her and asked in halting English if she could direct her to "the Queen of England's big ship" which she very much wanted to see.

The Queen showed her which way to go, but shyly, did not reveal who she was.

The Queen had understood and agreed with the motivations, both public and personal, which had prompted her husband's long Antarctic trip. They had parted on an affectionate note, he excited about the adventure ahead, she content to have her work, the children and a few close friends to speed away the long weeks of his absence. Then as now, they were not a couple who found it necessary to live in each other's pockets. But neither, by contrast, are they a couple to whom out of sight is to be also out of mind.

Philip had been gone some five weeks when their ninth wedding anniversary came round, but the customary big box of white blooms was there to greet his wife when she came through to breakfast that morning. For Prince Philip there was a similar happy surprise aboard the royal yacht, some 1,300 miles from the nearest land, on Christmas Day. Unwrapping a mystery parcel carefully labelled "Not to be opened until Christmas Day" which had arrived in the mailbags at the last port of call, he found a tape recording among the Christmas gifts his wife had sent him. A reproduction of Edward Halliday's portrait of his royal wife looked down on him as he played back the tape in the privacy of his teak-panelled cabin. He had spotted the picture in a New Zealand hotel, fallen in love with it afresh and 'borrowed' it in true naval tradition. Now, from the tape recorder, came his wife's voice tendering her love and good wishes at Christmas, an excited chorus of "Happy Christmas, Papa" from Charles and Anne, and the eager-beaver background yapping of the royal corgis.

And at Sandringham that afternoon, soon after the Queen had finished her Christmas Day broadcast, there was a radio-telephone call from her husband aboard *Britannia*. Charles and Anne stood beside her as she took the call, both eager, as she was, to talk with the absent husband and father.

In fact, there were many such calls from Prince Philip during his four-month absence and one of his later laughing complaints about the trip was that Mike Parker always seemed to be hogging the radio-telephone when he wanted to use it himself. Philip's calls were usually timed to reach his wife around lunchtime on Sunday at either Windsor or Sandringham, according to where she happened to be, though it was not always possible, of course, to make exact allowance for the difference in time between London and that part of the world where *Britannia* was. There was one Sunday morning at Windsor when the Queen, just out of church, called at Royal Lodge for a few minutes' chat with her mother to find that the expected call had already come through and Philip was waiting on the line.

The royal Christmas broadcast, that year, gave a rare public glimpse into personal feelings. Prince Philip, introducing his wife's broadcast from his cabin aboard *Britannia*, concluded with words clearly intended as a personal message for her: "The Lord watch between me and thee when we are absent one from the other."

And the Queen, in her own message, had this to say to her millions of listeners: "You will understand me when I tell you that of all the voices we have heard this afternoon, none has given my children and myself greater joy than that of my husband."

Those who knew her best were in no doubt that she missed Philip during the weeks and months he was away. Perhaps fractionally more than he may have missed her. After all, he had the freshness of new places and new people to take his mind off things while she plodded the same old round. For the Queen, her working days were as busy as ever. During the early part of the evening and at weekends there were the children to keep her occupied and take her mind off things. She filled in the balance of many an evening with a rare spate of theatre-going in the company of close friends such as Lord Rupert and Lady Nevill. But there were inevitably still times when she felt her husband's absence keenly.

In the weeks which followed Christmas, as the Queen prepared for her forthcoming state visit to Portugal, she was noticeably more lighthearted. The state visit had been planned for some time past and it had been arranged that she should meet Prince Philip in Portugal at the end of his long haul. In laying these plans, allowance had been made, of course, for the possibility that so long and unpredictable a trip might not be completed on time and *Britannia*'s stopover at Gibraltar had been included in the schedule to allow for this. Against all expectation, Philip's Antarctic voyage was completed to the exact day of the original estimate—"perhaps rather unfortunately as it turned out", as Philip himself commented later.

The Queen's whole attitude, as she prepared for that visit to Portugal, was far too bubbling and buoyant to be accounted for simply by another in the succession of state visits she had undertaken since succeeding to the throne. There had to be another factor to account for the happiness she radiated . . . and it can only have been the joy she felt at the prospect of being reunited with her husband. Hers was the sort of effervescent gaiety you see in a woman who misses her husband and is overjoyed that she will soon be seeing him again. In her whole demeanour there was not the slightest hint of any sort of a 'rift', marital or otherwise. The successive fittings for the new royal wardrobe she would wear in Portugal seemed to fidget her a lot less than usual, as was clearly noticeable the day she returned to the palace from a busy round of public engagements to find the dressmaking team awaiting her yet again. Someone suggested putting off the fittings until another time when she was less tired. She would not hear of it. "Oh, no", she said, gaily. "This is for Portugal." Those were her words, but for "Portugal" one can perhaps read "Philip".

It is easy to be wise after the event, and, looking back, it seems clear that the rumours of a 'royal rift' would perhaps have gained less credence if Prince Philip had simply flown home from Gibraltar. Arriving there, as he did, "to the day of our original estimate", found him with a clear week in hand before going on to Lisbon to meet his wife. The very fact that he stayed on in Gibraltar, seemingly kicking his heels, served to add fuel to the flames.

Why, then, did he stay on in Gibraltar?

Was it, as one American newspaper suggested at the time, a form of princely protest following the resignation of his old friend, Mike Parker? Was it, as has been suggested to us, because the crew of *Britannia* were not similarly free to drop everything and fly home to their wives and children, and he did not wish it to seem that he was 'deserting ship'? Was it perhaps because he feared further criticism of royal extravagance if he flew home only to fly out to Portugal again a few days later? Or was it a stubborn disinclination to toe the sort of line the newspapers were advocating?

It could have been for any one of these reasons or a mixture of all of them. But whatever his reasons, whether staying put was his own idea or someone else's, it was clearly a nine-days' blunder. Had he flown home, there might well have been less gossip and fewer headlines. As it was, the story went round the world, gathering momentum until it finally collapsed with the clearly happy reunion aboard the Viscount aircraft which took the Queen to Portugal. Some 150 newsmen and photographers, drawn to Portugal in the aftermath of the 'royal rift' headlines, jostled one another at the Montijo military air base as the Queen's Viscount touched down and Philip, his sea-going beard shaved off, went aboard to greet her. Two minutes later the pair of them left the aircraft for the official reception. The Queen was smiling radiantly and an eagle-eyed newsman claimed to have spotted a tiny smudge of lipstick on Philip's mouth. Whether he did or not, the news went round the world and the 'royal rift' rumours were finally nailed as the Queen and her husband enjoyed a happy private weekend aboard the royal yacht as a prelude to the state visit proper.

Twenty-four hours after their return to London at the end of that four-day visit it was announced that "The Queen has been pleased . . . to give and grant unto His Royal Highness the Duke of Edinburgh the style and titular dignity of Prince of the United Kingdom." Thus she made good the omission of which her father had inadvertently been guilty when heaping honours upon his prospective son-in-law in the days immediately preceding the royal wedding. But was this all there was to it or was it perhaps also the Queen's regal way of 'cocking a snook' at the world and showing the newspapers what she thought of them and their 'terrible' stories?

In the weeks and months which followed the royal couple's reunion in Portugal, it seemed as if something—either the four months of separation or those hurtful 'royal rift' headlines—had caused the Queen and her husband to take a long, fresh look at each other and at the monarchy to which they were both bound, and, gradually, a delicate shift and change of direction became apparent in the threefold relationship of husband, wife and monarchy. It was as though the husband—now undeniably *Prince* Philip—had come at last to understand his wife's deep and unswerving devotion to her hereditary role and to a proper appreciation of his own slightly subsidiary role. It was, equally, as though the Queen had come finally to realise that absorption in monarchy can be less than total. So a new relationship developed and the adjustment they achieved in their public roles was perhaps true also of their personal relationship one to the other.

It was now just over five years since the Queen had first succeeded to the throne. In a sense, they had been, if not five years of further apprenticeship, perhaps years which lay somewhere in the hinterland between apprenticeship and complete qualification. For it is ridiculous to pretend that a monarch, through some sort of divine intervention, becomes automatically qualified the very instant that he or she succeeds to a throne. Whatever advance training the Queen may have had—and it had been considerable—monarchy remains one of the few top jobs in the world, perhaps the only one, which is fully learned only by actually doing it. Only experience can teach a monarch. Nothing else, though others can help with the process of learning. Philip, at the outset of his wife's reign, can clearly have been of little help in this connection. He may have had, as he did, ideas for modernising and up-dating the monarchy, for hauling it willy-nilly out of its Victorian slumbers and into the twentieth century, but who was to judge how far his ideas were valid; how far they might advance the ancient system and image or whether perhaps they might not bring the whole business tumbling down upon its own neck? He could hardly judge validity himself. He was too close to his own ideas to see the wood for the trees. The Queen, at this early stage, could hardly judge either. She was not yet sufficiently experienced. Her main idea, in those early days, was to do things the way her father had always done them. A customary remark when some problem of procedure arose was, "What did my father do?" Told, she would reply, "Then I will, too." For advice and teaching she relied, for the most part, on those who had served her father before her and whose ideas and outlooks were too often rooted in the past. Commander (later Sir) Richard Colville, her then Press secretary, for instance, made no secret of the fact that he saw his job as one of maintaining royal privacy and upholding royal dignity rather than providing information for press and public. In consequence, there were those who labelled him uncooperative and the editor of one national newspaper went so far as to comment in print that he had finally come to accept that the policy of Colville's department was "to ensure that an absolute minimum is published about anything of interest concerning the royal family. In our experience, they have always performed this function with unfailing and melancholy efficiency". And what was true of Colville was equally true of other royal aides whose work was less public.

Philip, in many ways though perhaps not in this question of press relations, was more forward looking. He has never liked the unending publicity which is inevitable for royalty and even today has not really come to live with it. "I fully appreciate the problems which arise under the heading 'The Royal Family and the Press'," he told a dinner of newspapermen back in 1955. "Some will be solved in time, while others will always remain a headache." But, in other areas of royal life, he had long wanted to be more progressive. Until now, however, he had not had his wife's ear and had been unable to play the Albert to her Victoria. Now, at last, he could.

That the Queen was now more willing to listen to her husband in matters of monarchy as well as in matters of family life is clearly seen in the changing pattern of the next few years. Philip's role was to change too, to grow in extent and importance. Hitherto he had seemed a man who does not like playing second fiddle, but knows that he must. Now it was as though he realised that he need not always chug along in his wife's tracks, but could branch off on another line running almost parallel. Things he had previously considered drawbacks in his nebulous role as the Queen's husband, he now perhaps saw as advantages. As he was to phrase it himself later, "The fact that I do not always have to toe the party line is sometimes an advantage." Just as on his Antarctic trip he had been to places the Queen could not hope to visit, so he could say things the Queen could not say. If he had no real official standing, neither had he any constitutional restrictions (or very few). No longer was there any need to be submerged as a mere royal patron of this or that. Instead, he could move forward in the updating of monarchical thinking and equally bring royal influence to bear on those areas of national life which he considered to be important.

All this, of course, was a gradual process of thought and development which had perhaps not fully crystallised when Philip made his first television appearance, talking about his Antarctic adventures. It was entitled 'Round the World in Forty Minutes'. In fact, he spoke for fifty-five minutes. "Overtime as usual," he joked as he finished. A second television appearance, in a documentary entitled 'The Restless Sphere', introduced the International Geophysical Year. In Paris, that year, a new, very much more with-it Queen, was to dazzle the French by discarding the traditional and bulky royal crinoline in favour of a pencil-slim gown of silver lace with a square, low-cut neckline, though the transformation was perhaps as much to do with Norman Hartnell, who designed the dress, and Bobo, who finally persuaded her royal mistress to wear it, as with Philip. "Ravishing", one French newspaper styled her, a new adjective in the royal vocabulary. In Canada, later that year, the Queen gave her first press conference—"I'm shaking like a lily," she confessed in a personal aside as she took her seat—and followed that up by appearing on television, speaking in both English and French. Initially, in front of the cameras, she was clearly terrified with nerves. Then she received a message from her husband. "Tell the Queen to remember the wailing and gnashing of teeth." It was a private joke between them. The Queen smiled when she was told what he had said and relaxed somewhat, though not entirely. That Christmas the traditional royal broadcast became a telecast transmitted live from the Long Library at Sandringham. Again the Queen was nervous—so much so that Christmas lunch, as far as she was concerned, was wasted; she could do no more than pick at it. But with an occasional sideways glance at her husband, standing just out of camera range, she steeled herself to go through with it and another step into the new royal age had been taken.

That telecast also saw a small departure from the usual royal platitudes. For once the Queen had something of moment to say. As though foreseeing the permissive age which loomed ahead, she took advantage of the opportunity to chide "unthinking people who carelessly throw away ageless ideals as if they were old and outworn machinery". Such people, she said, "would have religion thrown aside, morality in personal and public life made meaningless, honesty counted as foolishness and self-interest set up in place of self-restraint. . . . It has always been easy to hate and destroy. To build and to cherish is much more difficult."

There were changes, too, on the level of family life. Charles was ripped away from the petticoat government of the royal nursery and buzzed off glumly to Cheam accompanied by a leather trunk labelled H.R.H. Prince Charles and a consoling box of chocolates. If the boy's mother had some slight misgivings, his father had none. He was quite convinced that life in a boys' boarding school would prove as beneficial and enjoyable for Charles as it had been for him. Enjoyable it may not have been; beneficial it certainly was and not only in the academic sense. Among other things, Charles found himself folding his own clothes at night instead of having a nanny to do it for him, cleaning his own shoes and waiting on table; a tendency to nibble his nails was also checked, and, at Gordonstoun later, he even found himself helping to empty dustbins.

Philip was perhaps helped around this time in the fresh, forward-looking attitude he was encouraging his wife to take by the publication of two articles on monarchy, one in England, the other in the United States. Both were easily the most critical reviews of the subject yet published, though neither was actually as devastating as those who did not actually read them were perhaps led to believe.

In Britain, Lord Altrincham, writing in the *National and English Review* (August 1957) dragged monarchy down from its Olympian heights for perhaps the first time since Victorian days with the perhaps slightly too realistic view that, "The Monarchy will not survive, let alone thrive, unless its leading figures exert themselves to the full and with all the imagination they and their advisers can command."

So far, so good. It was not so far removed from what Philip himself was thinking.

"When she has lost the bloom of youth," Altrincham's article continued, "the Queen's reputation will depend, far more than it does now, upon her personality. It will not be enough for her to go through the motions; she will have to say things which people can remember and do things on her own initiative which will make people sit up and take notice. As yet there is little sign of such a personality emerging."

For once, Philip was not the whipping boy. The difference between this article and any that had gone before was that this was not criticism of the Queen's husband or royal advisers, but of the Queen herself. The criticism, as the article ran its course, became more pointed.

The Queen and Princess Margaret, Altrincham opined, "still bear the debutante stamp". Royal presentation parties "are a grotesque survival". The composition of the Court "emphasises social lopsidedness". Those who serve the Queen "are almost without exception people of the tweedy sort". The Court "has lamentably failed to move with the times". The Queen's style of speaking "is frankly a pain in the neck". The personality she conveyed "is that of a priggish schoolgirl".

Fighting talk. Strong meat, taken out of context, though time has witnessed the bringing about of many of the things Altrincham advocated. Presentation parties have long since come to an end. People of a non-'tweedy' sort have been introduced into the circle of those who serve the Queen. Even the Queen's tone of voice and style of delivery when speech-making have changed. Nor was this mere coincidence. It was something deliberately accomplished with her husband's advice and help. It was Philip who showed her the difference between 'making' a speech and simply reading it parrot-fashion. It was Philip who encouraged her to try rehearsing her speeches in advance with the aid of a tape recorder, as he did himself. The resultant play-back, with the addition of Philip's helpful and sometimes joking comments, produced the change.

The second attack came from America, though the author of the article was another Briton, Malcolm Muggeridge, one-time editor of *Punch* and latter-day TV pundit. It was provocatively entitled "Does Britain Really Need a Queen?" and was published in the *Saturday Evening Post*, at that time one of America's most widely-read and most authoritative magazines. It was published on 19th October 1957, and it was perhaps more than mere coincidence that publication synchronised with a royal tour of Canada and the United States.

According to Muggeridge, the Queen, Prince Philip, their family and doings had come "to constitute a sort of royal soap-opera". The monarchy provided "a sort of substitute or ersatz religion". It had become "a pure show".

Duchesses, he reported, found the Queen "dowdy, frumpy and banal". There were equally those who found "the ostentation of life at Windsor or Buckingham Palace little to their taste" while "a more valid criticism of the Monarchy is that it is a generator of snobbishness and a focus of sycophancy". Like Altrincham, he saw the Queen's entourage as "exclusively upper-class".

Apart from the few essentially personal references, both articles were reasoned arguments which if published today, whether one agreed with them or not, would excite much less stir than they did at the time. But at the time of publication Prince Philip's ideas on monarchy and the Court had not yet taken proper root and the so-called permissive society was not yet upon us. So feelings ran high. Muggeridge was spat upon in the street and had his contract with a Sunday newspaper abruptly terminated. Altrincham was struck in the face, even if lightly. His views, in particular, seemed to bring a rush of blood to certain noble heads. The Duke of Argyll would not have been averse to seeing him "hanged, drawn and quartered" while the Earl of Strathmore reportedly gave it as his opinion that "the bounder" should be shot.

Even Prince Philip, not realising at first what additional ammunition the two articles gave him, was somewhat incensed when the *Saturday Evening Post* and its contents were brought to his attention during the U.S.–Canadian visit. "If they must print such things, does it have to be while we are here?" he demanded, truculently.

But if these two critics of royalty provided Philip with both extra ammunition and an additional spur, if spur was needed, in some respects, at least, events had moved ahead of criticism.

It had already been announced from Buckingham Palace that the Queen, in order to achieve more flexibility in the royal round, would no longer feel duty-bound to attend the same time-honoured functions year after year. The Royal Film Show that year was among the first casualties. To give her more time for a private life, the Queen also cancelled a number of portrait sittings. Other changes were to follow in fairly rapid succession.

The traditional welcome-home luncheons at the Guildhall were curtailed in what was now clearly an era of increasing royal travel. The laying of foundation stones, that traditional royal chore, was likewise reduced. There were other less noticeable changes. Royal footmen, on official occasions, were no longer required to whiten their heads with a messy mixture of flour, starch and soap, a practice Philip had long considered "ridiculous, unmanly and unhygienic". It was at his suggestion too that state liveries were lightened by the removal of the heavy—and expensive—gold trimmings which had long adorned them. The anachronistic presentation parties of ostrich-plumed debutantes, as we have already stated, were finally abolished. They were replaced by additional garden parties and by the now-familiar palace luncheon parties. Cocktail parties in the Bow Room of an evening for selected guests from the worlds of business and show-biz, art and letters, politics and sport were to be another innovation.

The royal luncheon parties are as informal as any function can hope to be in the rather awe-inspiring setting of Buckingham Palace. Sherry and martinis are handed round to put the guests at their ease and an equerry moves among them, introducing those who do not already know each other. Presently the royal corgis rush in as a sign that their royal owner is not far behind. The Queen enters, usually with Prince Philip or perhaps with Prince Charles or Princess Anne or others of the family. There is half an hour of light preliminary chat. Then the palace steward announces, "Luncheon is served, Your Majesty." The Queen leads the way to the table and sits, not at the head, but midway along it, facing her husband, the two of them thus occupying vantage points from which it is easier to keep the conversation flowing amongst their sometimes nervous guests, talking mainly to those on their right hands during the early part of the meal and switching to those on their left later.

Initially, the palace luncheon parties were not perhaps distinguished for the breadth of their guest-lists. They started at a time when the education of Prince Charles was uppermost in the minds of the royal parents. In consequence, educators and others who might have helpful ideas on the subject were prominent among those who first sat down to enjoy prawn cocktail or melon, roast lamb or veal, a suitable sweet, biscuits and cheese, fruit, coffee and brandy (or a liqueur of their choice) in the 1844 Room at the palace. But over the years the guest-list has been widened and extended to include not only the more obvious politicians, trade unionists, bankers and business-men but also such popular idols as footballer Billy Wright, boxer Henry Cooper, jockey Doug Smith and racing driver Graham Hill as well as such occasional sex symbols as Julie Christie and a pop star or two. Luncheons and cocktail parties alike, whether intentionally or otherwise, thus come to serve a dual purpose. They help to keep the Queen in touch with public opinion (though only up to a point, of course, with the more controversial topics of the day seldom given an airing) and also link the still somewhat remote royal image with the far less remote images of public celebrities, a gimmick which politician Harold Wilson was also to adopt in the days of his premiership.

The deftness of touch Prince Philip had developed in anything and everything to do with monarchy was also to be seen in the constitutional gimmick which highlighted the 1958 Com-monwealth Games in Cardiff. It happened at a time when the Queen was undergoing a rare bout of poor health. As far back as childhood, she had had a tendency to succumb to feverish chills and flu-like colds and that year of 1958 she was plagued with one after another. She suffered from them at Sandringham just after Christmas, at Windsor in April, and again in Scotland in the July. A whole load of engagements, public and private, had to be cancelled one after the other. A weekend with Philip's relatives, the Brabournes, went by the board. So did a visit from the Prime Minister and his wife, another planned trip to Sandringham, a dinner party following the Ascot Horse Show and a visit to the Cup Final. Prince Philip was naturally worried, particularly when, still not really well, she insisted on taking part in the annual Trooping the Colour ceremony on a day of pelting rain. He suggested postponing the ceremony in the hope of better weather on another occasion, but the Queen shook her head. Subsequently, during a royal tour of Scotland and the North-East, she was again taken ill aboard the royal train as it journeyed south from Largs to Carlisle. This time Philip insisted that she should continue on to London while he carried out the rest of their engagements on his own. He returned to London to find her still in bed with a sinus operation in prospect. While she was ill, he did some of her work as well as his own (among other things, he helped to receive the last annual crop of debutantes), but adjusted his evening engagements so that he could sit at her bedside of an evening, eating with her and chatting to her. The operation for sinus was completely successful, but the period of convalescence which necessarily followed meant that the Queen had also to cancel a planned tour of Wales and a visit to the Commonwealth Games. Once again her husband had to go it alone, but his deft Philippian touch was surely to be seen in his dramatic production, on the final day of the Games, of the secret and surprise recording his wife had made for the occasion:

"I intend to create my son, Charles, Prince of Wales today." Pause for applause and effect. Then: "When he is grown up I will present him to you at Caernarvon."

If any one occasion can be said to have epitomised the new relationship between husband and wife, then this—starring the Queen and presented by Prince Philip—was surely it.

IV   Years of Contentment

A gap of nearly ten years separated the birth of the Queen's second child, Princess Anne, in the August of 1950, from that of her third, Prince Andrew, in the February of 1960.

On the basis of a casual remark the Queen made in her courting days, saying that she looked forward to a family of four children—"two boys and two girls"—this ten-year gap has been interpreted by some as a deliberate sacrifice made at the altar of monarchy. Perhaps it was; perhaps in those earlier years there was no time to think about having more children. Or was Prince Philip perhaps drawing upon an example from his own experience in the remarks made in a more recent interview?

"People want the first child very much when they marry," he said. "They want the second child almost as much. If a third

Schooldays: (*right*)
Prince Charles at
Timbertop, Australia and
(*below*) Princess Anne at
Benenden

Prince Charles at Cambridge, as student and sportsman

child comes along they accept it as natural—but they haven't gone out of their way to try to get it."

Whatever the answer, the birth of the third baby was to mark the beginning of a new phase in royal life—a phase which started even before the baby's birth with the Queen's decision to link her husband's name with her own in the joint surname of Mountbatten-Windsor to be borne by some of her descendants.

Prince Philip had not been long back from another of his globe-trotting tours, this time one encompassing the Far East and the Pacific which started in New Delhi at the beginning of February, 1959, and ended up in the Bahamas and Bermuda nearly three months later, when the Queen found that she was expecting another child.

She was 33, and ahead of her lay the biggest tour of Canada ever contemplated by a reigning monarch, a planned 16,000 miles of travel and some forty-five overnight stops. Many a woman of her age, in her condition, would have baulked at a much shorter trip with no over-night stops. But just as she had refused to postpone the Trooping the Colour ceremony on a day of pelting rain, so she now refused to consider cancelling the Canadian tour. Initially, indeed, she would not even permit her Canadian hosts to be informed of the happy condition in which she found herself. Not until she had been a week in Canada (her entourage augmented by an additional seamstress to let out the royal dresses if required) did she confide her glad tidings to Mr. Diefenbaker, the Canadian prime minister. Coincidentally, one of her private secretaries was flying from London to Ghana to inform Dr. Nkrumah that the royal visit planned for November would not now take place, and the reason why.

Mr. Diefenbaker, of course, promptly suggested abridging the current tour of Canada to ease the strain on the Queen. In her dutifully obstinate fashion, the Queen shook her head. Everything was to go ahead as planned, she said. No one was to be told.

Inevitably, of course, it was the sort of royal secret which could hardly hope to be kept and certainly not in the circumstances of so strenuous a tour. The Queen had already flown from London to St. John's, St. John's to Gander and on to Deer Lake, Deer Lake to Stephenville and Schefferville and then on to Sept-Isles where she boarded the waiting royal yacht.

13

She had inspected guards of honour, signed visitors' books, taken part in slow drives, opened the new air terminal at Gander, toured a paper mill, an air base and an iron foundry. Now it was on to Gaspé, Port Alfred and Quebec. She visited a sanitorium and an aluminium plant, attended a banquet given by the Quebec Government and played hostess at a return function aboard *Britannia*. Then on to Trois Rivieres, and Montreal, watching folk dancing, walking round hospitals, attending another official dinner and even a celebration ball. All this in the space of a week, in temperatures which went as high as 82 degrees on a day in Schefferville, with her body suffering the combined effects of early pregnancy and the Atlantic time-change. It was bound to have an effect and when word leaked out that she was being attended by the doctor accompanying the royal party, the shrewder reporters covering the tour were quick to jump to the correct conclusion, however often it was officially denied.

Yet despite everything, at first pregnancy seemed to give her a new bloom of beauty. "My, I've never seen you look so beautiful," Mrs. Eisenhower, the wife of the President of the United States, exclaimed impulsively when the two women met at the opening of the St. Lawrence Seaway.

But, inevitably, the strain began to tell. The Queen, as the tour progressed, became more and more tense. Philip, as always, did his best to help. "You must try to relax," he told her. She couldn't. Minor upsets did nothing to help. In Chicago, on a side-trip to the United States, a lost dental filling had to be replaced. In Port Arthur, travelling in an open car, she was drenched by a rain squall which unexpectedly blew up. In both Nanaimo, where she was installed as an Indian princess, and Whitehorse she looked so exhausted that Philip was frightened that she was going to faint. Worried for her, as he had been on a previous visit to Canada, he was again tetchy. Finally he persuaded her to stay in bed while he went on alone to Dawson City. Up again, though looking far from well, the Queen coped with engagements in Edmonton, but wisely let Philip go it alone in Yellowknife and Uranium City. Towards the end of the tour she was again so bad that the planned sea trip back to Britain, with visits to the Shetlands and Orkneys on the way, had to be cancelled and she flew straight home.

A few days of real rest worked its customary cure and by the time she was safely esconced at Balmoral for the long summer holiday, Lord Evans, her number-one medical adviser could truthfully report: "The Queen is in the best of health." As with her previous pregnancies, she again gave up riding. But she walked more than ever and even went stalking on one occasion with no small success. She bagged a twelve-pointer.

Returning to London, she rose at eight o'clock each morning as usual, worked away at her desk as usual. Each afternoon she walked in the palace gardens. She developed a number of unusual tastes, as mothers-to-be often do. In the Queen's case, it was an unaccustomed longing for sweet things. She liked Philip to be with her as much as possible and he did his best to oblige. But he could not be with her all the time and at Sandringham, that Christmas, when he had to leave her in order to attend the wedding of his cousin, Lady Pamela Mountbatten, she became quite restless and uneasy at one stage of his absence.

Mindful of the public rejoicing outside the palace which had so disturbed her rest at the time she had Prince Charles, the Queen, returning to London, decided that this time she would move into the Belgian Suite at the rear of the palace. And it was here, on 19th February 1960, that the baby was born. The delighted parents named him Andrew Albert Christian Edward—Andrew after Philip's father, Albert after the Queen's (who was Albert in the family circle before switching to George for the purposes of kingship), Christian after that King of Denmark from whom the Queen and her husband are both descended, and Edward after King Edward VII, whose wife was sister to that Greek king who was Philip's grandfather.

The Queen had taken her paperwork downstairs to the Belgian Suite with her. The day before Andrew was born she was working at a desk looking out on the palace gardens. The day after she was back at work again, her dispatch box on a table on one side of the bed, a telephone on the other.

While the Queen continued to cope with her paper work as industriously as ever in the months immediately following Andrew's birth, she had her public engagements kept to a reasonable minimum. Most of the extra free time thus gained was devoted to the new baby. Each morning, between breakfast and the time the Queen started work, he would be brought down from the nursery by his nanny, Mabel Anderson, so that his mother could have him to herself for half an hour. Later, as he grew from babyhood to childhood, these morning sessions constituted his first lessons. Each morning when breakfast was over a small blackboard fitted with a clock face and counting frame was carried into the royal dining room and set up close to the table. The Queen would settle Andrew on her lap to give him his first lessons in spelling, counting and telling the time.

Like any other mother, the Queen was quick and happy to show the new baby to friends when they came to call. "A fine little boy," American president Dwight D. Eisenhower commented when he lunched at the palace and Andrew was brought down for him to see at the end of the meal.

Her day's work over, the Queen would ride up to the nursery in the lift, donning a waterproof apron, as she had done with Charles and Anne, to bathe him, checking his increasing weight on the nursery scales, fluffing his hair with the same silver-backed brush that had been used on her own head in childhood.

Father, too, would often go bounding up to the nursery at this time of day. As with most fathers, his visits tended to be more boisterous and his playfulness more robust. Andrew responded in kind and occasionally there were small accidents, as when chocolate-sticky fingers explored the clean white shirt Philip had donned in readiness for an evening engagement he was due to attend. As a result, another quick change was required before he went out. Later, when Andrew was somewhat bigger, he poked a finger in father's eye during a boisterous bedtime romp and Philip turned up for a film premiere that evening with an eye which had all the makings of a Cockney 'shiner'.

Almost as though the birth of Prince Andrew had triggered off a flurry of birds and bees in the royal atmosphere, marriage and motherhood seemed suddenly in the air on all sides. Princess Margaret married her photographer; the young Duke of Kent married Sir William Worsley's daughter, Katharine; while his sister, Princess Alexandra, allied herself to the Earl of Airlie's son, Angus Ogilvy. Princess Anne was bridesmaid at all three weddings. The Queen was reported as looking straight-faced and solemn at her sister's wedding. Maybe so, but it was not the solemnity of disapproval, as was apparent to anyone who was privileged to be at Buckingham Palace after the ceremony, when an excited elder sister joined her husband, mother and daughter in a spirited race across the inner quadrangle to shower the newlyweds with rose petals as they set off on their honeymoon.

With Andrew's birth, the Queen and her husband had come to an important personal decision. Their private life, they were resolved, was going to be rather more private in the future. Looking back, they were inclined to feel that they had made mistakes in the upbringing of their first two children. In particular, they regretted the public spotlight which had shone so fiercely upon Charles and Anne over the years. They planned to do their best to reduce the glare for the future. As a first move, no photographs of Andrew's christening were released for publication—the royal parents looked upon the occasion as a purely private family affair—and not until he was sixteen months old was the new baby seen in public for the first time when his mother had him with her on the palace balcony following the Trooping the Colour ceremony that year. In other directions, too, a new hankering for royal privacy was to be seen. The Queen declined to let Anne present the prizes in a children's cookery competition and, equally, turned down a request that Charles, as Duke of Cornwall, should open a new bridge linking Devon and Cornwall. "Public life is not a fair burden to place upon them," she said of her children, a theme which Prince Philip was to elaborate upon later in a B.B.C. interview. The problem was, as he recognised, not a simple one.

"You can't have it both ways," he admitted. "We try to keep the children out of the public eye so that they can grow up as normally as possible. But if you are really going to have a monarchy, you have got to have a family and the family's got to be in the public eye."

But if there was a clamp-down on publicity where the children was concerned, there was, at the other end of the scale, a widening of the horizons of childhood. The Queen's own childhood had been secluded in the extreme and Philip's influence was to be seen in the parental decisions to let Anne got off to France for a short holiday, while Charles went to Switzerland to learn to ski.

As in all families, there were occasional mishaps and occasional health worries. The Queen's own health was much improved following the sinus operation, but Philip's hell-for-leather brand of polo resulted, in successive years, in a torn thigh muscle, a broken ankle, and a gashed arm necessitating stitches. At Cheam, Charles was taken ill, with what turned out to be appendicitis. He was promptly whipped into a London hospital where the offending appendix was speedily removed. His mother drove there to see him immediately afterwards, taking along a get-well gift of fruit and flowers, while his father, away on a tour of South America, put in a long-distance call from Caracas to chat with him.

One of Philip's polo mishaps resulted in a rare public display of his wife's impish sense of humour. It happened at a royal garden party. Philip emerged, hobbling. The Queen Mother emerged, also hobbling after a slip on the steps at Windsor. The sight of them both so tickled the Queen's sense of humour that she could not resist the brief temptation to feign a similar hobble.

While taking steps to ensure more privacy for their children and family life generally, the royal parents were by no means unmindful of the public life which inevitably lay ahead for the youngsters and perhaps for Prince Charles in particular. In a number of small ways they began breaking the ice for him. During one of the traditional Christmas visits to Sandringham they allowed him to read a short lesson during a carol service held in the nearby church at West Newton. With his father away, his mother also had the boy join her for one of the informal luncheon parties which were now part and parcel of royal life.

It was also time for the schoolboy prince to take another educational step forward. Father's old school again seemed a suitable instrument for producing a chip of the old block—at least in Prince Philip's view, though not everyone agreed. Among those who disagreed was Charles himself, though at 13, as can be imagined, he had little say in the matter. His mother, who might have had a say, had no real views on the matter and was quite content to let his father decide. So Charles went to Gordonstoun. But, as subsequent events have shown, he was not really a chip of the old block, and now, for a time, he was to be as unhappy at Gordonstoun as he had been initially at Cheam. Indeed, he was so unhappy there at one stage that he asked his grandmother to intercede with his parents to let him return home. But the Queen Mother, as a wise mother-in-law, has always made it a policy never to interfere. So Charles had to stick it out. His parents visited him only once in his first year, when the school staged a handicrafts exhibition in which Charles had several pieces of pottery on show. To have visited him more frequently would only have resulted in focusing the public spotlight upon him more strongly and would hardly have helped their new policy of keeping personal publicity to a minimum.

Inevitably, as the boy's years at Gordonstoun ran their course, there was to be publicity, including two spates of world-wide headlines, one when Charles downed that history-making glass of cherry brandy and another when a book of his essays came into the wrong hands and ended up in print. As though publication of the essays was insufficient in itself, an American magazine came up with a story that the schoolboy Prince had sold the book of essays to augment his pocket money. Reacting as indignantly as any other parents would have done in a like situation, the royal couple had their Press secretary write a letter to the magazine which said, in part: "There is no truth whatever in the story that he [Prince Charles] sold his composition book. . . . The suggestion that his parents keep him so short of money that he has to find other means to raise it is also a complete invention."

It is a curious anomaly that Charles, the shy, quiet one, should have found himself more than once at the centre of such a storm in schooldays, while those of his sister, clearly the more extrovert and outgoing of the two, should have passed off so much more quietly. Perhaps the answer lies in the fact that the spotlight followed Charles, as heir to the throne, more constantly and thereby revealed more.

The Queen, when she took Anne to Benenden at the start of her first term in the September of 1963, was again pregnant. "When the fourth child comes along, in most cases it's unintentional," said Prince Philip in the same interview quoted at the beginning of this chapter. In this instance, he was clearly not drawing upon his own experience, as the Queen herself had already made plain. With a gap of nearly ten years between Andrew and the younger of her other two children, she saw clearly the dangers of loneliness and precociousness which lay in wait for him if he was brought up as virtually an only child. "We'll have to think about a little playmate for Andrew," she remarked with a smile not long after his birth, though, as subsequent events now showed, she was not entirely joking.

Previously, she had had no one with whom to share the joy and discomforts of pregnancy. But now, all at once, she had plenty of company. Coincidently, her sister, Princess Margaret, her cousin, Princess Alexandra and another cousin's wife, the Duchess of Kent, were all in the same state of expecting a happy event. For Alexandra, it would be her first child; for Margaret and the Duchess of Kent a second to go with the small son each already had.

Years ago, in her courtship days, as we have said, the Queen once told a friend that she looked forward to a family of four children, two boys and two girls. Now, with Edward's birth on 10th March 1964, she finally came close to realising that courtship wish. And if that fourth child turned out to be another boy instead of a girl, she was no less delighted. Her obvious happiness is to be seen in the batch of family photographs taken around that time and which, like Charles' essays, were subsequently to find their way into print in magazines and newspapers around the world. All who have seen those photographs will recall the radiant smile which suffuses the Queen's face as she sits up in bed with the new baby in her arms and the rest of her family around her. Nor, as we know, was this any put-on smile for the benefit of professional photographers, but the natural reflection of a mother's happiness. These were private photographs intended for the family album, not for publication, and the non-appearance of Princess Anne in some of them and the proud father in others indicates clearly who the photographers were. That they were finally published on a world-wide basis a full four years after they were taken—and when Edward's birth could scarcely any longer be termed news—indicates the measure of interest which so constantly surrounds the royal couple and their family and which has always been among the most tormenting of the problems they have had to face.

The Queen had been on the throne now for just over twelve years. Of those twelve years, when the weeks and months were totted up, she had spent more than a year abroad, visiting more than thirty countries and travelling a distance equivalent to nearly six times the circumference of the earth. In Britain, she had visited another 210 different places, held 111 official banquets, presided over 150 meetings of the Privy Council and granted 2,236 official audiences. It was time for a bit of a rest or, at very least, a change of pace.

Indeed, a change of pace was already apparent. As small children in the days when their mother first succeeded to the throne as a new and inexperienced young monarch, Charles and Anne were not permitted to invade her sitting room during what the Queen came to regard as her working hours. But more experienced by now in the workings of monarchy the Queen found that there were times when she could be both monarch and mother simultaneously. As Andrew grew from babyhood to childhood, household officials and royal servants became quite accustomed to the sight of him sitting on the close-carpeted floor of the sitting room, playing happily with building bricks, pull-along trucks or a set of toy soldiers, while his mother worked away at her desk in the bay window. A royal page, entering the room on one occasion, failed to notice a rubber ball with which Andrew had been playing. Setting his foot firmly and unexpectedly upon it, he found himself bounding and leaping across the room in the Queen's direction in a desperate endeavour to maintain his balance. Every morning, before starting work, the Queen would have the new baby brought down to her sitting room, with Andrew, now 4 years old, sometimes providing a lively and noisy escort, so that she could enjoy half an hour of motherhood. She would see the children too at intervals during the day, sometimes slipping out of the palace on fine afternoons to join them and their nannie for a picnic tea in the gardens. And always, except when overseas tours or provincial visits took her away from London, she would go up to the nursery regularly at half-past five each afternoon to bath and feed Edward and put him to bed, to play with Andrew or read him a bedtime story.

Charles and Anne were growing up fast, as children seem to at this stage of their lives. Both had still been very much children that August in 1959 when the Queen broke the news to them at Balmoral that she was expecting another baby. But with Edward's birth in March, 1964, Charles was 15 and in his second year at Gordonstoun while Anne, at 13, was in her second term at

Benenden. Tall for her age, she seemed already on the verge of womanhood. Indeed, within the year, helping the Queen to host the five monarchs, six other heads of state and sixteen Prime Ministers who journeyed to London for the funeral of Sir Winston Churchill, the daughter was noticeably already fractionally taller than the mother. Charles, too, was shooting up and showing promise of matching his father's height when father and son played polo together for the first time—and occasionally revealing himself a hitherto unsuspected chip of the old block. A visit to Athens for the wedding of King Constantine was a case in point. Charles and others were sun-bathing on a raft at the Astir beach club when some French photographers moved in on them for some close-up shots. What happened in the next few moments is not 100 per cent clear. Different people give different versions of the incident. But it seems that Charles along with one of his German cousins and Crown Prince Carl Gustaf of Sweden were instrumental in precipitating the photographers and their kit into the water.

The fact that the two older youngsters were children no longer was perhaps one of the reasons which persuaded the royal parents to break with the family tradition of trekking all the way from London to Sandringham at Christmas, though there were others. With so many new babies in the family, so many additional nannies and other servants, Sandringham, big though it is, could no longer accommodate them all in comfort. Either way, the switch to Windsor was undeniably welcomed by some royal relatives who had long tired of the hundred-odd mile haul to Sandringham, sometimes for only a few days, each Christmas. Advantage was also taken of the change for Charles and Anne to throw their own Christmas dance for teenage friends, with their parents and such older relatives as the Queen Mother, Princess Marina, Princess Margaret and Princess Alexandra on hand as chaperones. The exuberant Anne was quickly in the swing of things. Charles, though older, was longer in taking to the dance floor. Asked by his mother what he was waiting for, he replied that he was working out "which are the prettiest girls".

It was surely with a heartfelt sigh of relief that the Queen welcomed the advent of 1965 with its attendant state visit to Germany. Now, at last, her in-law troubles were at an end and she could step down from the tricky tightrope swaying to and fro between private and public life along which she had had to tiptoe throughout the nearly eighteen years of her marriage. Old enmities were to be officially forgotten by the governments on both sides and the Queen, who had herself forgotten them long since, could finally feel free to call upon her husband's sisters.

Hitherto, though she had entertained them often enough in Britain—though always, it was stressed, in a purely private capacity—she had been forced to carefully sidestep their return invitations to visit them in Germany. But now she could take advantage of a leisure weekend in the course of her official visit to Germany to go to Salem, where Philip's widowed sister, Theodora, lived along with his youngest sister, Sophie, and her second husband, Prince George of Hanover, Salem's headmaster (Sophie's first husband, Prince Christopher of Hesse, had been killed in a wartime air crash). She could likewise make an evening side-trip to call on Philip's eldest sister, Princess Margarita of Hohenlohe-Langenburg, a widow like Theodora.

In fact, all three sisters were there to welcome her warmly when she and her husband pulled into Salem station on the first passenger train to stop there in ten years. Others of the family were there, too. Theodora had her two grown-up sons, Prince Max and Prince Ludwig, with her. Sophie and her husband had their three children in tow, including Prince Guelf, at school with Prince Charles at Gordonstoun. Margarita had travelled over from Langenburg with her eldest son, Prince Kraft. To make the family reunion complete, Prince Philip's mother, now at the gateway of her eighties, was there too.

It was a happy family group of sisters-in-law, nephews and nieces who showed their brother's wife round castle and school, and we can imagine with what amusement the Queen saw the battered desk on which her husband had cut his initials during his brief period of schooldays at Salem. Then it was down to the cellars to sample the local wine followed by a brief, casual walk round the nearby village—until the Queen was spotted and the inevitable crowd began to gather—and a pleasant jaunt through the surrounding countryside in a horse-drawn carriage, the Queen perhaps enjoying everything all the more from having waited so long.

For royal husband and wife, as for any other married couple, it was a time of life when the years seemed to fly by with increasing pace and the children to shoot up. They travelled north to Scotland to watch their eldest son, just turned 17 and resplendent in a false beard which must have reminded Philip of his wartime days at sea, take the title role in a Gordonstoun production of *Macbeth*. At the Badminton horse trials they watched their teenage daughter do a clear round on a gelding named High Jinks to win a prize of £5. In many ways, it was a time of complete contentment, though not without its problems, as there always are for parents. Charles was not making out at Gordonstoun as well as his parents would have liked. It was neither his fault nor that of the school. It was more that the son was not the sort of youngster the father had been and what was right for the one was not necessarily so for the other. A change of atmosphere, the boy's parents felt, would do him no harm and might do a lot of good. So it was off to Australia for two terms at Timbertop on the lower slopes of the Great Dividing Range. Flying out there, he was waylaid in Honolulu by an American teenager who garlanded his neck with the traditional *lei* and also succeeded in snatching a kiss. "He is growing up, isn't he?" chuckled the Queen when she heard of the incident.

The break with the old secluded way of royal upbringing was now virtually complete. Boarding school was now an accepted thing for the royal children and there was little excitement, compared with the furore there had been when Charles first went to school, when Andrew was hauled out of the royal nursery and buzzed off to Heatherdown. The second-floor nursery schoolroom seemed a deal quieter without him, as did the palace generally. Stocky, sometimes precocious, always high-spirited and mischievous, he was fast proving himself the sort of youngster Anne might have been if she had been born a boy, a young man who would perhaps require firm handling in the future. If he tended to irritate his older sister sometimes when they were at home together, it was perhaps because they were two of a kind.

With the death of Miss Katharine Peebles, governess to the royal children since Charles first started lessons, a new governess, Miss Lavinia Keppel, took over with Edward, the youngest of the family and now of an age to begin his education. There were other changes in the nursery schoolroom too. Charles had had his first lessons entirely alone. Anne, when her turn came, had had two small girls for company. But now, as though moving with the times, the nursery schoolroom became co-educational, with two small boys, one of them Princess Alexandra's son, James, and two small girls, one of them Princess Margaret's daughter, Sarah, to keep Edward company.

By the autumn of 1967 Charles and Anne were of an age to join their parents for the state opening of Parliament. For Charles, the schooldays he had so rarely enjoyed were now behind him. He was now at university. He had gone to Cambridge amidst the usual hullabaloo that seems to accompany almost every new step the Royal Family attempts to take. Examination results at Gordonstoun did not justify a place at university, it was said. He was taking advantage of his royal prerogative. As it turned out, Cambridge was to do him more good than anything that had gone before. There, for the first time, there were signs that he was emerging finally from his shell of shyness and developing into the more confident young man we know today. Anne has never shown such shyness, though, like her father, there have been times in public when she has felt more nervous than she would perhaps care to admit. At Benenden, the outcome of her A-level examinations proved worse than what Charles had achieved at Gordonstoun. So for her there was to be no spell at university. Not that she was disappointed. "I'm academically lazy", she confessed. But that was only part of it. Lacking her brother's plodding and painstaking patience, she also found the act of learning boring and tedious.

The extent to which Charles had matured during his years at Cambridge, and his parents' wisdom in postponing his investiture as Prince of Wales until he was of an age to endure it with equanimity, was clearly seen at Caernarvon in the summer of 1969. The last incumbent of that historic post, the youngster who became, in turn, Prince of Wales, briefly King Edward VIII and Duke of Windsor, has confessed that the ceremony found him half-fainting with heat and nerves. Charles, three years older than his great-uncle when he underwent the same ordeal, was clearly nervous from time to time but gave no signs that he was "half fainting", though he perhaps had more cause.

For once, it was the Queen who was nervous, the mother

in her making her so. She is never worried about herself. "There's no need to worry," she reassured her entourage during a visit to Quebec at a time when that French-Canadian city was tight with tension. "I'll be as safe as houses." But with Wales now showing similar signs of tension, she had a hand-picked team of detectives assigned to guard her son not only during the actual ceremony but during the preceding months when he was brushing up on the Welsh language at the University College of Wales in Aberystwyth. His arrival at Aberystwyth had a twofold effect. Four students supporting the Welsh Nationalist cause went on hunger strike and there were 1,000 extra applications for copies of the university prospectus.

His investiture as Prince of Wales was perhaps the most controversial royal ceremony since kings wore armour and princes wielded battle-axes. A public opinion poll carried out three months ahead revealed that 76 per cent of the Welsh people were in favour of it—but the minority were to make their opposition felt in noisy and violent fashion. Among other things, a satirical pop song poking fun at "Carlo Windsor" was briefly top of the Welsh hit parade. In contrast, souvenir tea towels bearing the Prince's likeness enjoyed a ready sale, as did a whole range of other souvenirs, some well designed, some rubbishy . . . goblets and vases, mugs and money boxes, pencils and calendars, ash trays and key rings, Welsh dolls and toy dragons.

The anti-investiture pop song found a more violent echo in the homemade bombs which exploded here and there. As a result, the great day itself found stringent security precautions in force. Armed Special Branch men and thousands of extra policemen were drafted into the tiny township of Caernarvon. Frogmen guarded the royal yacht which was berthed off Holyhead in readiness for an investiture party in the evening. Special locks were fitted to the doors of the ruined castle which was the venue for the ceremony and there was a Guy Fawkes check of the place ahead of the event. Even so, the train bearing the royal party was delayed for fifty minutes by a mock bomb made of candles which was found fixed to the bridge over the River Dee at Chester, a real bomb exploded near the railway sidings while Charles was actually travelling to the castle, eggs were hurled at the Queen's carriage, and 35 miles away, at Abergele, two would-be terrorists blew themselves to bits with their own bomb.

For all that, the actual ceremony went off without interruption, violent or otherwise. The Duke of Windsor, when he was invested as Prince of Wales, found himself togged up in old-fashioned knee breeches of white satin, "a preposterous rig" he was quite sure his friends would laugh at. There were some among the planners who would have liked to have seen Charles decked out in similar outlandish fashion. Others went to the other extreme and plumped for an ordinary suit. His appointment as Colonel-in-Chief of the Welsh Guards enabled him to duck either extreme and wear uniform, a happy compromise which was augmented at one stage of the proceedings by an ermine-trimmed cloak and a custom-built coronet studded with emeralds and diamonds. To ensure that the coronet fitted, the Queen had briefly borrowed a curious contraption of springs and rods, looking like nothing so much as a medieval instrument of torture, which Locks the hatters use to measure the heads of their customers.

The impression has sometimes been given that the investiture of the Prince of Wales is an age-old ceremony. In fact it is not. The previous one, for all its attempt at medieval pomp and pageantry, would seem to have been the first of its kind, an invention of the wily Lloyd George with more than an eye to retaining his own parliamentary seat. The 1969 repetition proved to be a ceremony in which the medieval was mixed with the twentieth century, sometimes compatibly enough, sometimes a shade incongruously, a mingling of what one newspaper was to call "pomp and Perspex". The "Perspex" was a reference to the canopy beneath which the Queen stood to invest her son, part of the somewhat theatrical setting Princess Margaret's husband, Lord Snowdon, had designed for the occasion.

He also designed his own outfit, a sort of battledress in hunting green. Prince Philip, by contrast, thought an ordinary suit more fitted to the extraordinary occasion. The Queen wore a knee-length outfit designed by Norman Hartnell with a pearl-embroidered hat; no robes. Anne, for her part, took full advantage of her youthfulness to move right into the twentieth century and wore a mini skirt. The royal charter proclaiming Charles Prince of Wales was read in both languages, Welsh and English, while the television cameras caught Philip in the act of flashing his eldest son a quick grin of reassurance. Charles himself spoke in both Welsh and English, not nervously as the Duke of Windsor had done in his day, but clearly and confidently, even to the extent of tossing in a joke about his favourite comedians, the Goons. "I was amazed", commented a Welsh-born student who had been at Cambridge with him. "He said he was going to learn Welsh, but I didn't really believe he would get the pronunciation as well as he has done." But a Welsh girl who spoke to Charles in her own language a year later was to grumble that he didn't seem to understand what she was saying.

Advantage was taken of the occasion to turn it into a royal television spectacular. Thirty cameras were looking in from various vantage points and the six-hour transmission which was evolved around the few minutes of actual ceremony was seen by 19 million people in Britain and an estimated 500 million others around the world.

The American show-business publication, *Variety*, awarded it the accolade as "The best commercial produced to attract the tourist trade since that coronation in London several years ago", adding, "It is quaint native ceremonies of this type, seen so seldom in the U.S.A., that makes you want to fly to places like Caernarvon for your holiday instead of just taking a bus to Kokomo, Indiana."

Be that as it may, it was a ceremony not without its moving moments for televiewers and royal parents alike, and mother and monarch were surely inextricably mingled at that moment when the Queen led Charles to Queen Eleanor's Gate and presented him to the people as "My most dear son".

The investiture of Charles as Prince of Wales was a very special once-in-a-lifetime ceremony. Other, more regular ceremonies—like Trooping the Colour and the state opening of Parliament—continued to come and go with clockwork regularity. Along with birthdays and wedding anniversaries, they marked the passage of the years and underlined the fact that those royal newlyweds of 1947 were now a middle-aged mum and dad. A few months after the investiture ceremony the newly installed Prince of Wales celebrated his twenty-first birthday. Two months later his sister also attained her majority, though it was not her birthday and she was, in fact, not yet twenty.

Prince Charles in the regalia for his investiture as Prince of Wales

(*above*) Princess Anne confidently carrying out one of her many public engagements. (*left*) The Queen's youngest child, Prince Edward, arrives at school for the first time

This seeming anomaly was brought about by Parliament's decision to reduce the age of majority to eighteen. Anne could not have been more delighted. For her, it meant an official £6,000 a year income of her own instead of relying upon handouts from her mother whenever she went shopping for clothes, make-up and other things dear to the feminine heart.

Inevitably, death too was to make its mark upon these middle-age years of the royal marriage. Philip's cousin, Princess Marina, who had been of such help to the royal couple in their days of youthful courtship, had died at Kensington Palace in the August of 1968. Another year was to witness the death of Philip's sister, Theodora, fifteen years his senior. And now, in the December of 1969, came the death of his mother, perhaps not altogether unexpected; she was 84 and had been in failing health for some time past.

Her death marked the end of a full and eventful life, if not always a completely happy one. For her, life had always been something of a struggle from the very moment of her birth. She was born deaf, yet such was the inner strength and determination of this amazing woman that before she was out of her teens she could converse in both English and German, lip-reading the replies. She was 18 when she married Philip's father. We have related earlier what she went through in those agonising days when her husband was on trial for his life. Exile and separation were to follow. Then came World War II with the emotional torment of knowing that her daughters were married to Germans while her son and brother were fighting for Britain.

In the years following her son's marriage and her daughter-in-law's accession to the throne she was a frequent visitor to Buckingham Palace, staying sometimes for several weeks at a time, and in 1967, when she came out of hospital, the Queen gave her her own apartment there, curiously enough that self-same Buhl Room suite in which Philip spent his first night at the palace. Day and night nurses were engaged to care for her, and her son, his wife, their children were frequently with her. Nor were these mere duty visits. They were also vastly entertaining, for Philip's mother had a rich store of reminiscences to relate of life at the court of Queen Victoria in the days of her girlhood. Christmas 1968 found her strength failing and

14

she could not accompany the rest of the family to Windsor. But she was not forgotten. On Christmas Day the Queen and Prince Philip drove back to London in the afternoon to have their Christmas tea with her and give her their Christmas gifts. She did not quite live to see another Christmas.

So the years continued to roll by. Margaret and Tony celebrated their tenth wedding anniversary, thereby confounding those prophets of woe who had wailed that their marriage would never last. The Queen Mother, as smiling and as seemingly indefatigable as ever, celebrated her seventieth birthday . . . and her seventy-first, with the audience rising to applaud her when her two daughters went with her to the Royal Ballet as a birthday treat. Anne celebrated her twenty-first birthday aboard the royal yacht and a welcoming crowd burst spontaneously into "Happy Birthday" when she went ashore at Thurso to visit her grandmother at the Castle of Mey. For Anne, there was no title of Princess Royal to mark the occasion, as had been rumoured in some quarters, and the official allowance originally due to her on her twenty-first birthday had actually started some nineteen months earlier when the new lowered age of majority applied to her equally with other young people.

Edward, the 'baby' of the family, though a baby no longer, started his schooldays at a day school in Kensington, where he had Princess Alexandra's son, James, another 7-year-old, as one of his classmates. Prince Philip notched up his half century, and one sign of middle age was the announcement soon after that he was giving up polo because of recurring inflammation of his right wrist. In other respects, he continued to be as active as ever and certainly as outspoken, saying what he felt needed to be said, acting as Britain's public conscience.

"As it is very much more difficult to recapture markets than to keep them," he told the Institute of Marketing, "we shall have to look forward to even more bankruptcies and even higher levels of unemployment if we continue to lose overseas markets at the present rate."

Even stronger stuff was contained in an interview with him published in *Industrial Management*. He was quoted as saying: "Now everyone is mouthing what is basically true, that for a number of reasons . . . the stuff we produce is not quite so reliable. It is not made with such great care, it doesn't arrive at the right time, there is a bit of a muddle about how it is put together and things of that sort."

Charles, as the next stage in his training for future kingship, went to the R.A.F. College, Cranwell, to learn to handle jets, where he also made minor history as the first of the royals to make a parachute jump. So has royal thinking changed with the years. The Duke of Windsor, when he was heir to the throne, had to give up steeplechasing because it was deemed too risky. Today, even a princess can take those selfsame risks, as Anne did to be voted Sportswoman of the Year, and the heir to the throne can bale out by parachute. Sensible precautions were taken, of course, when Charles made his jump from an Andover transport flying at some 1,200 feet above the English Channel. He was equipped with two parachutes—one for emergency in case the other failed to open—and Royal Marines were on the spot in a matter of seconds to haul him out of the water and into a rubber dinghy.

All in all, 1971 proved to be a proud year for the royal parents. A delighted Prince Philip journeyed to Cranwell to see his eldest son awarded his R.A.F. 'wings'. Charles had a natural aptitude for flying, said his college report, and excelled at aerobatics in jets. His father was so bucked he was even affable to the press photographers. Would he shake hands with his son for the purpose of a photograph? "I'll stand on my head if you want me to," he quipped.

An equally delighted Queen had the pleasure of presenting her daughter with the championship trophy at the end of the European Three-Day Event at Burghley. Thus, Anne amply substantiated an earlier claim that riding "is the one thing I do really well" with a victory rendered all the more impressive by the fact that she was not long out of hospital for the removal of an ovarian cyst. Even the fact that her hands and muscles went soft during her spell in hospital did not deter her. She hardened her hands again with incessant games of deck tennis aboard the royal yacht; toughened her legs by marching up and down Scottish mountainsides with her dad for company.

"She has steely determination," her trainer, Alison Oliver, said of her. She she showed, though she was not included in Britain's official team for Burghley. Hers was an individual entry. She ended up beating not only the members of Britain's official team, but the cream of riders, male and female from four other countries, France, Ireland, Italy and Russia. Throughout the three days and three sections of the championship, she never looked like being beaten. Riding Doublet (bred by her mother), she was already leading at the end of the dressage section. She went on to return the best time in the stiff cross-country speed and endurance section, taking risks and cutting corners but never losing her blonde head. "She showed that when Doublet was struggling to get out of the water and up a steep bank," Alison Oliver said afterwards. "She never panicked. She stayed still in the saddle and gave him his head, stopping what might have been a dangerous fall for both of them." Anne cemented her victory by clearing the twelve fences of the show-jumping section without incurring a single penalty point. While a smiling Queen presented her daughter with the championship trophy and £250 prize money, a grinning Prince Philip proclaimed that he was "only here for the beer"—a wisecrack which did nothing to conceal his obvious pride and pleasure in Anne's success.

But like almost any other royal year, 1971 was not without its alarums and excurions. Royal finances were yet again a focal point for controversy. With Philip's "next year we shall be in the red"now in the past, the Queen made a formal approach to Parliament for more money, a royal move which Richard Crossman, M.P. and Privy Councillor, was to denounce as "truly regal cheek" in an editorial in the *New Statesman*, which he edits. In the course of a sharp dig at the "entire royal apparatus—the clutch of palaces, the powdered footmen, the racing stables and polo ponies, the fleets of luxury cars, the squadrons of aircraft and helicopters, the yachts, the elaborate apparatus of consumption at its most conspicuous level", the editorial pointed out that the Queen's wealth was not subject to death duties; that on much of her income she paid no tax; that she appeared to pay no surtax whatever. It rumbled on: "The Queen, in short, is the beneficiary of a complex system of tax privileges and exemptions which has never been fully disclosed, but whose value to her in terms of hard cash must be enormous. The only thing private about it is the element of concealment. The Queen, in fact, is trying to get it both ways, pressured, to judge by his ill-judged public utterance on this subject, by the Duke of Edinburgh."

To all this, the Queen made no direct reply. Others did,

however, among them Professor Roger Fulford, former Liberal Party president. "We pay the Royal Family, in real money, less than we did a century ago," he wrote. "Should we grudge a tiny fraction of Britain's £13,000 million annual expenditure to the monarchy which brings colour, dignity and unselfishness to our life at the top."

There was also a reply to the *New Statesman* attack in the form of a seemingly inspired 'leak' which provided a rare glimpse into the private finances of the Royal Family. John Colville, the Queen's private secretary in the days when she was Princess Elizabeth and today a director of Coutts & Co., where she banks her money, revealed that her private fortune was nowhere near as large as was generally imagined. He dismissed the idea that the Queen's fortune is in the region of £50–100 million as "just guesswork"—and guesswork which sometimes upsets the Queen. Her father, it was revealed, paid the Duke of Windsor something like £200,000 for Sandringham and Balmoral at the time of the abdication. The late King, though Mr. Colville did not mention this, also dipped into his private pocket to the tune of around £190,000 to meet the mounting costs of monarchy during the last five years of his reign. As a result, he left his daughter "about half-a-million" and if she had "more than two million today", not counting such things as the royal art collection and her own jewel collection (which she could hardly dispose of even if she wished to), then Mr. Colville was prepared to eat his hat.

Parliament had already appointed a Select Committee to look into this matter of royal finances and, almost inevitably, its recommendations were to result in renewed controversy. Nor was the committee itself by any means unanimous. If it had been hoped to silence the sometimes vociferous criticism of Willie Hamilton by appointing him to the committee, then it was a move which did not succeed. He issued his own minority report in which he lambasted the whole business as "the most insensitive and brazen pay claim made in the last 200 years". Other Socialists on the Committee, while not going as far as this, favoured an idea by Douglas Houghton, Chairman of the Parliamentary Labour Party, that the monarchy should be run and financed as a special government department, in some eyes a somewhat drastic proposal which escaped acceptance only by eight votes to seven.

The committee's final majority recommendations included a

big increase in the Civil List (in effect, the running costs of monarchy) from £475,000 to £980,000 a year, with other similarly big increases for individual members of the Royal Family: Philip —up from £40,000 to £65,000; Anne—up from £6,000 to £15,000; the Queen Mother—from £70,000 to £95,000; Margaret—from £15,000 to £35,000; the Duke of Gloucester—from £35,000 to £45,000; plus an increase from £22,000 to £60,000 in the sum which the Queen shares out each year between others of the family, such as the Duke of Kent, Princess Alexandra and Princess Alice. Prince Charles did not come into the committee's report. He has his own not insubstantial income from the Duchy of Cornwall, half of which he was already surrendering to the Treasury.

In an era of mass unemployment, continued pay claims and continued inflation, the recommendations did not please everyone, of course. But with Members of Parliament also voting themselves substantial increases around the same time, it seemed extremely unlikely that they would not be approved as this book went to press.

Margaret and Tony were again in the news when Lord Snowdon appeared in court on a driving charge. The prosecution was a private one brought by photographer Ray Bellisario, a self-confessed "treader on royal toes" in his pursuit of candid camera shots. On a more serious level, 1971 was also a year of assassination threats. There were anonymous threats to the Queen's safety when she visited Essex and Suffolk at Whitsun and, later in the year, on a visit to York. Both lots of threats could well have been the work of cranks, but no one was taking any chances and strict security precautions were taken on both occasions. Whether for this reason or not, the visits passed off without incident.

Then in the November, less than three weeks ahead of the Queen's twenty-fourth wedding anniversary, a still more massive security operation was mounted to safeguard her when she climbed into her great-great-grandmother's creaking coach and set forth to perform the annual ceremony of opening Parliament. This time there had been no specific threat made against the Queen herself, but the Post Office Tower had been bombed and there was a threat to do the same to the Victoria Tower through which the Queen would have to pass. In consequence, the vaults of Parliament were subject to their most thorough search since the days of Guy Fawkes, some 6,000 police lined the route of the state drive from Buckingham Palace, Special Branch men mingled with the crowds along the route and armed marksmen kept watch from rooftops. The Queen was undoubtedly aware of all this, but gave not the slightest hint of apprehension as she drove from Buckingham Palace to Parliament. On the contrary, as pictures in the next day's papers clearly revealed, she was as smiling—and seemingly as young—as she was in that famous photograph of her when she opened her first Parliament nineteen years before.

Anne, at the time, was away in Hong Kong, visiting the 14th/20th Hussars of which she is Colonel-in-Chief. But the Queen's husband and eldest son rode with her on that apprehensive state drive to Parliament. Father and son were both in naval uniform. Having gained his 'wings' at Cranwell, Charles had gone on to the Royal Naval College, Dartmouth, where his father first met his mother, for a six-week cram course in such nautical subjects as navigation and marine engineering. He finished top of his class in navigation and seamanship and subsequently flew out to Gibraltar to join the guided missile destroyer *Norfolk* as a sub-lieutenant.

Three weeks later the Queen and Prince Philip celebrated their twenty-fourth wedding anniversary. It fell, happily, on a Saturday. The previous evening, royal husband and wife—proud parents of a 23-year-old son in the Navy, two younger sons now both at school and a 21-year-old daughter who had been elected Sportswoman of the Year by the British Sports Writers' Association—flew from Cardiff to Luton Airport. From the airport they drove to Luton Hoo, where they had spent so many happy anniversary weekends, to be again with their old friends, Sir Harold and Lady Zia Wernher.

It was a quiet weekend, with no crowds, no photographers, nothing much in the newspapers afterwards . . . the sort of weekend the Queen and her husband enjoy most.

5

Family On The Throne

Prince Philip was talking about the Queen's Christmas telecast.

"Television," he said, "is a difficult medium in which to deliver this kind of message.

"In the old days, when it was just a spoken message, people turned on the wireless and it was fine. But somehow it's not the same just to have the Queen looking into a television camera.

"It's hard to know how we can get over this. Perhaps the alternative is to dress it up and call it 'The Queen Show'."

Perhaps the last sentence was just another example of his famous instant wit, not to be taken seriously, intended as joke. Certainly, to some people, it must have conjured up visions of the Queen and Princess Anne singing a duet together, Charles and Philip engaged in a quickfire crosstalk act and a grand finale in which the whole family join in a sort of royal dance spectacular around a papier-mâché throne against a background of gilded crowns.

Well, they did not go quite as far as that, of course. But for the Christmas of 1970, after a year's absence, the royal Christmas message was back on television in what was undeniably a type of 'Queen Show', with the Queen (in trousers and head scarf at one point) as the star and her husband, daughter and eldest son in supporting roles. Princess Anne, in the opinion of one TV critic, stole the show, and the parts of the show in which she was concerned came fairly close to a crosstalk act.

Those who watched saw shots of the Royal Family in Australia, in Scotland and in Canada's Far North. What they also saw, without perhaps realising the fact, was a perfect example of Walter Bagehot's concept of "a family on the throne".

"A family on the throne is an interesting idea also," wrote Bagehot, the eminent Victorian historian, in his book *The English Constitution.* "It brings down the idea of sovereignty to the level of petty life."

He gave as an example the marriage of the then Prince of Wales (later King Edward VII) to Princess Alexandra of Denmark. It was, like many of the marriages of Queen Victoria's children, an arranged match. The Queen, having decided upon Alexandra as the most suitable choice, arranged with her daughter, the Princess Royal, for the couple to be thrown together in a seemingly chance encounter. The Queen's subjects, of course, were quite unaware of this and the resulting marriage, at St. George's Chapel, Windsor, in 1863, was a signal for tremendous public rejoicing.

As Bagehot put it, "No feeling would seem more childish than the enthusiasm of the English at the marriage of the Prince of Wales. They treated as a great political event what . . . was very small indeed. But no feeling could be more like human nature as it is or as it is likely to be." Women, he added sagely, care "fifty times more for a marriage than a ministry".

But Bagehot's concept of a family on the throne never worked out in his day. The widowed and autocratic Victoria permitted her son and heir to play very little part in things.

Today, things are very different. Not only the Queen and her husband, but Charles and Anne have a part to play—and the two youngsters are encouraged by their parents to play it to the utmost. Monarchy today, as Philip himself has said, "involves the whole family, which means that different age groups are part of it. There are people who can look, for instance, at the Queen Mother and identify with that generation, or with us, or with our children."

So Bagehot's Victorian concept of "a family on the throne" has been finally realised. At the head of the family, in public though not in personal life, stands the Queen, ploughing through her boxes, seeing her ministers, holding audiences and investitures, opening Parliament, carrying out an endless round of public engagements with much more apparent enthusiasm than her great-great-grandmother ever displayed. The Queen Mother stands for what has gone before. Charles represents the future. Anne provides a touch of much-needed youthful glamour, while father acts as the, sometimes controversial, spokesman for the whole family.

Charles, currently in the Royal Navy, has not yet fully entered into his heritage of ship-launchings and tree-plantings, though he has done his bit. Anne has been carrying out a more or less continuous round of public engagements from the age of 18. Her first go-it-alone engagement, like that of her mother before her, was of a military nature. She handed out leeks to the Welsh Guards at a St. David's Day parade. Over the next year or so, arrayed in a fetching selection of dolly-bird outfits and eye-catching hats, she dashed busily around on a royal work schedule which was at times more jam-packed even than her mother's and almost as frenetic as her father's. She visited horse shows (perhaps no real hardship to someone of her equine inclinations) and children's homes. The children she visited took an instant liking to her, a fact she is said to have found a bit puzzling. At home, she said, her own small brothers, Andrew and Edward, were inclined to fidget her at times. Nevertheless she allowed the children at one home to stuff her mouth so full of sticky sweets that she was finally forced to sort the resulting mess out with her fingers while the attendant photographers obligingly looked the other way.

She visited youth clubs and police cadets, the Cup Final and Wimbledon, launched her first ship and named her first hovercraft. At a transport training centre she took the wheel of a double-decker bus and at a police training school she further exhibited her driving prowess by slewing a car round a greasy skid-pan. Switching from her customary mini-skirt to an equally fetching trouser suit, she boarded a helicopter to drop in on a gas rig out in the North Sea. She also flew to visit British troops in Germany, where she added a 52-ton tank to her other driving experiences and clapped a sub-machine gun to a shapely hip with all the aplomb of a heroine in a James Bond movie and scored eleven bulls with a burst of twenty rounds. A speech she made at a London shopping festival which turned into a succession of free plugs for some of the stores at which she shopped proved to be almost as controversial as anything uttered by her father. She was, it seemed, destined to be a rip-roaring royal success.

Then, for a time, it all seemed to go sour on her. Perhaps she was too anxious to justify herself and tried to do too much too soon. She was, after all, still only a teenager at the time for all that a new Act of Parliament suddenly made her—along with thousands of other youngsters—an adult at 18. Whatever the reason, subsequent overseas trips were destined to be rather less successful. Visiting Australia in company with her parents, she was accused of being impatient and there was one occasion, when the Sydney wind whipped the streamers on her hat into her eyes, when she was heard to mutter what sounded extremely like her father's favourite adjective. Did she use the word "bloody"? "Quite likely" she admitted with characteristic frankness.

A subsequent visit to Washington, D.C., in company with her brother, Charles, was even less successful on a public level. There she was labelled "snobbish, pouting, spoiled, bored, sullen and disdainful"—surely an overlong string of critical adjectives to apply to a girl who was still only 19.

It seems to have been generally assumed that she behaved as she did out of nothing more than pure princessly cussedness. Nobody paused to think that there might perhaps be another reason—her youth, nerves perhaps (it is said that she is sometimes more nervous in public than she would care to admit), tiredness, tension or merely the time of the month. In assessing royal behaviour patterns, plain everyday facts of life are sometimes either overlooked or ignored out of a mistaken sense of good taste.

By contrast, Charles went down well in America, and in Canada before that. Gone completely was the old princely image of dullness and stuffiness. "The Prince comes out a winner", said an Associated Press report circulated to some 1400 American newspapers. "The press and apparently the public deemed him charming, sexy and adroit." Princely adroitness was skilfully displayed in Canada when he was asked if he would kiss the winner of a beauty contest at Yellowknife.

"May I see her first and may I choose where I kiss her?" Charles inquired, grinning.

The excellent balance he has achieved between regal dignity and down-to-earth good-fellowship reflects credit on his parents and the upbringing they have given him. Anne, though the more colourful of the two, would seem to lack, as yet, the same fine degree of balance. She can swing one way or the other, sometimes without warning. Yet her very unpredictability will surely make her the most stimulating and exciting of all the Royal Family for years to come.

For her, the problem is the same problem that her father has always had and Princess Margaret has always had . . . that any worthwhile serial story must have a 'baddy' to offset the 'goody'. In the non-stop chronicling of royal affairs the Queen is clearly a 'goody'—all things to all people. So Prince Philip and Princess Margaret, by turn, have served to fill the role of the 'baddy'. The emphasis, where they are concerned, is nearly always on the controversial, the temperamental, the outspoken and the off beat. Equally, Prince Charles, as the future king, qualifies as a 'goody'. So Anne must be the 'baddy' and it remains to be seen whether Andrew or Edward may yet be cast to share the role with her.

"There are always people around waiting for me to put my foot in it, just like my father," Anne has said, and there is a measure of truth in that. If in her case, as in her father's, her allotted role comes close to type-casting, she can console herself with the thought that things would have been no different had it been otherwise. Had she been of exactly the same nature as Prince Charles—a bit shy, rather serious, patient and painstaking—in her it would have been said that it was too much of a good thing. She simply cannot win, and she might as well resign herself to the fact and continue to be her naturally temperamental and outspoken self, as her father has done.

Indeed, if anything, Prince Philip would have seemed to become a shade more temperamental with the march of the years and certainly more outspoken. Nothing could have been much more outspoken than the gauntlet he threw down to the Australians in March 1967 (when he told them that there was no point in them keeping the monarchy if they felt they were getting nothing from it) and again to the Canadians in the October of 1969.

"The monarchy exists in Canada for historical reasons," he

told Canadians. "It exists also because it was thought to be of benefit to the country and the nation. If at any stage people decide that the system is unacceptable to them, then it is up to them to change it.

"It is a complete misconception to imagine that the monarchy exists in the interest of the monarchy. It does not. It exists in the interest of the people in the sense that we do not come here for our health, so to speak."

For perhaps the first time, a member of the royal family was saying, quite openly, that they do not necessarily enjoy some of the things they are called upon to do.

"We can think of other ways of enjoying ourselves," said Prince Philip. "Judging by some of the programmes we are required to do here and considering how little we get out of it, you can assume that it is done in the interests of the Canadian people and not in our own interest."

And he flung down this challenge: "If at any time, any stage, people feel that it [the monarchy] has no future part to play, then for goodness sake let's end the thing on amicable terms without having a row about it."

Whether he was echoing the Queen's views also, it is, of course, impossible to say. Perhaps he was speaking only for himself. Perhaps his wife and the eldest son who will one day succeed her would not necessarily agree with all he said.

There have been times, however, when he has clearly been speaking for his wife as well as himself, as when he first dragged the question of royal finances into the open. It was in America in November 1969 on television.

"We go into the red next year," he admitted openly, "which is not bad housekeeping when you come to think of it. We have in fact kept the whole thing going on a budget based on the costs of some eighteen years ago. So there have been considerable corners which have had to be cut."

He went on to give examples of what he meant, some perhaps merely flippant, but one at least factual.

"We may have to move into smaller premises. . . . We had a small yacht which we have had to sell. . . . I shall probably have to give up polo fairly soon."

Joking he may have been, in part at least, but he was also making it very clear that the Queen, just as much as the dockers and dustbinmen, the railwaymen or post-office workers, was in need of a pay rise.

Again and again, over the years, Philip has acted as a front-man for monarchy, its principal mouthpiece and public relations officer. Sometimes, as on American TV, with wit. Sometimes, as in Canada, with a touch of asperity. In public as in private he is a man of many parts. He can be, by turns, witty, blunt, angry, sensitive. And one facet can switch quickly, almost without warning, to another, as was seen at a luncheon given by the Small Businessmen's Association in the autumn of 1969.

He was good-humoured enough over pre-luncheon drinks, crinkle-faced and witty. A bit restless perhaps, as he so often is, spinning abruptly on his heel to move on from one group to another. Over lunch the conversation became more serious, turning on the problems of the small businessman. Someone said something about a man no longer being able to make a fortune in Britain.

"What about Tom Jones?" Philip queried, having heard the singer at the Royal Variety Show the night before. "He's made a million and he's a bloody awful singer."

He was grinning and cheerful as he said it, completely at home in the all-male officers' mess atmosphere of the luncheon, clearly enjoying himself. Then, all in an instant, his good-humour vanished completely as he spotted a reporter taking notes of what he had said.

"What the hell are you doing?" he demanded, scowling and clearly angry.

He pushed his chair back, came to his feet and began to stalk out while his aide, Admiral Sir Christopher Bonham Carter, looked as surprised and confused as most of the others around the table. Officials of the association hurried after him, assuring him that they would 'stop' the report.

"You'd bloody well better," Philip flung back at them.

In the lobby he spotted another reporter already on the telephone. Abruptly he jerked open the door of the telephone box, and demanded to know "what the bloody hell" he was doing. Later, however, there were princely apologies to the press and a note of 'explanation' to Tom Jones who was moved to comment, "I was singing for charity—not auditioning for Prince Philip."

It was not the first time—nor, presumably, will it be the last—that Prince Philip has been at the centre of an unregal scene or put his foot in things by something he has said. Yet, over the years, he has also said many things which have very much needed to be said and has sometimes seemed to see further ahead than most. Pollution, for instance, is one of the big issues of the seventies. If Philip had had his way, it would have been a big issue of the sixties. As far back as 1962 he was already forecasting what would happen "If we take action now, we can—indeed, must—prevent some of the worst tragedies mankind is committing in its thoughtless progress. If we don't, future generations will have cause to feel more ashamed of us than of any other generation in history."

Finding himself in unexpected hot water—or dowsed with cold—has not prevented him from again saying frankly what he felt and thought next time out. Politicians, priests and press have all had a go at him at varying times. He was quickly taken to task by one national daily for saying that he was "sick and tired" of making excuses for Britain on his trips abroad.

"The country needs neither Prince Philip's lectures nor his excuses," the newspaper flayed him. "It is hard to imagine any Jack being more all right than the Prince. If he finds making excuses for us abroad wearisome he should spend more time in his adopted country."

But not all the newspaper's readers agreed. "Three cheers for Prince Philip! He took off the kid gloves and told us in plain English what is wrong with the country."

"Prince Philip is bravely stating publicly what everyone abroad and in the Commonwealth has known for a long time."

"While Prince Philip must be subject to some criticism to hold him in check, he is trying hard to provide the leadership this country so desperately needs."

It is usually the attacks on Prince Philip which make the headlines. But there are perhaps more people than you might think who agree with his views and attitudes, or so it would seem from a poll one newspaper conducted a few years back. Subject of the poll: Who would you pick for president if Britain became a republic? It was, of course, no more than another newspaper gimmick, but that does not necessarily negate the fact that Philip topped the poll, coming out ahead of Edward Heath, Harold Wilson and the controversial Enoch Powell.

But being a prince consort is a long way from being a president. As prince consort, Philip has no direct power, though he may have considerable influence. His speeches and personal contacts represent one sort of influence. Another form of influence is through his wife, the Queen. He cannot, as Albert did, sit beside his wife as she tackles the duties of monarchy, drafting replies for her to fair-copy. But there is no reason to think that she does not listen to his views and sometimes, even, seek his advice. Such things are part and parcel of any husband-wife relationship. But any influence he may exert through the Queen can be no more than fractional for the simple reason that the Queen's own influence, in this day and age, is no more than fractional. She has no direct power of her own and her indirect power is far less than Queen Victoria's was. She cannot juggle with governments or interfere in foreign affairs as her great-great-grandmother did. Indeed, it is perhaps true to say that she is the only person in the country who cannot hold political views, much less act upon them. Or if she does hold them, it is only to Philip, in the privacy of her own apartment, that she can express them. True, no Act of Parliament becomes law until she has given it her royal assent, yet, by a curious contradiction in terms, she cannot withold her assent from anything Parliament has determined.

Yet it is a strange thing that the more power has swung from monarch to Parliament, the busier the monarch has become. The Queen is surely the busiest ever. Changing outlooks, the growth of population, increasing speed and ease of travel, new forms of communication—all these things have contributed to this seeming anomaly. There was a time when Queen Victoria hardly carried out a single public engagement from one year's end to the next. Her great-great-granddaughter thinks nothing of flying across the Atlantic to Canada or tripping halfway round the world to Australia and New Zealand.

It is not always, as Prince Philip said in Canada, the enjoyable task it may seem. Like any other job, it can be sometimes tiring, sometimes boring, sometimes tricky. Yet it is perhaps true to say that the Queen, in her quiet, usually serious fashion, does enjoy it most of the time. Certainly she derives satisfaction from what she considers a job well done, a duty painstakingly performed.

Which brings us to the point: will she one day abdicate in favour of Prince Charles?

One well-known astrologer has gone out on a long limb by predicting that she will and even going so far as to forecast the year—1978.

By then, the Queen will have been twenty-six years on the throne. She will be only 52.

Some years ago, visiting the United States, where the most pointed questions are always tossed at him, Philip was asked when Prince Charles would succeed to the throne. Doubtless the question took him by surprise. His reply was short and sharp: "Are you asking me when the Queen is going to die?"

That, at the time, as Philip knew, was the Queen's own attitude to monarchy. She had been 'called' to the throne on the death of her father and would similarly hand it on to her son on her own death.

She may still feel the same. But times and attitudes may also change. When a somewhat similar question was again put to Philip in the November of 1969, it brought not a short, sharp reply, but a chuckle.

"It has its attractions," he said of the possibility that the Queen might abdicate. Then, more seriously, he added: "I don't think it has been thought of very seriously and I am not sure that the advantages necessarily outweigh the disadvantages."

Question and answer resulted, almost inevitably, in yet another newspaper opinion poll. This time the question was: should the Queen abdicate in favour of Charles? Answers revealed a distinct divergence of views between the generations. The younger generation—those under the age of 24—were in favour of abdication by an approximate ratio of five to four. But the overall figures were against the Queen abdicating in roughly the same ratio: 40 per cent for abdication and 49 per cent against.

Failing abdication, Charles could be almost an old-age pensioner before he succeeds to the throne. Only two monarchs have ascended the throne in recent times while in the first flush of youth. Victoria was a youthful 18 when she took over in 1837. The present Queen was a hardly less youthful 25 when she succeeded her father in 1952.

15

Queen Victoria lived to the ripe old age of 81 and her son, Edward VII, was rising 60 when he finally succeeded her. The present Queen apart, successive monarchs have all been in their middle or early middle years. George V was 45 when he became King, Edward VIII was 41, George VI was 40.

The Queen's health would seem to be quite exceptionally good. She could live as long as her great-great-grandmother. If so, then Charles, like his great-great-grandfather, would be not far short of 60 before becoming King.

Does it matter?

"The idea that he [Charles] would only be able to make a contribution as Sovereign is really not true," Philip has said. "There have been many cases where the heir has had a particular ability to do things he would not have been able to do otherwise."

Our old Victorian friend, Bagehot, would not have agreed.

"The only fit material for a constitutional king," wrote Bagehot in *The English Constitution*, "is a prince who begins early to reign—who in his youth is superior to pleasure—who in his youth is willing to labour—who has by nature a genius for discretion. Such kings are among God's greatest gifts, but they are also among his rarest."

To date, Prince Charles has shown himself superior to the kind of pleasures Bagehot had in mind. He has proved himself willing to labour and shown himself to be discreet. But whether he will begin "early to reign" remains to be seen.

Even if he does not, his mother—"terribly sensible and wise", as Charles himself has termed her—will certainly not freeze him out of royal affairs as the autocratic Victoria did the son who was destined to succeed her. On the contrary, she will afford him, as her father did her, "every opportunity of gaining experience" in the duties which will one day fall upon him as king. His father, too, will offer advice and guidance as he has always offered all of his children advice and guidance. And the combination of royal wife and husband working together to prepare their son for future kingship may well prove to be the greatest thing to come out of their years of marriage.

Royal Wedding Anniversaries

1948   Princess Elizabeth and Prince Philip spent what is traditionally known as their cotton wedding anniversary together at Buckingham Palace where they were then living with the bride's parents and where Prince Charles had been born only six days before.

1949   Prince Philip was back on active duty with the navy, stationed in Malta, serving aboard HMS *Chequers*, and on 20th November—their second (or paper) anniversary—the Princess flew out there to join him.

1950   They were apart on their third (or leather) anniversary. Prince Philip was still in the navy, still in Malta, now in command of HMS *Magpie*. The Princess was living now at Clarence House, where Princess Anne had been born the previous August. She spent part of her wedding anniversary visiting the annual exhibition of the Royal Society of Portrait Painters in company with her mother. But five days later she again flew out to Malta to join Philip for a belated anniversary celebration.

1951   Philip had left the navy and they were just back from a tour of Canada undertaken together. They spent their fourth anniversary quietly together in London.

1952   Their fifth (or wooden) anniversary. The Princess was now the Queen and they had moved back into Buckingham Palace from Clarence House. A rare visitor to the palace was the Duke of Windsor who joined them for a family luncheon party. In the evening they went to the Coliseum to see the American musical *Call Me Madam*. The following weekend they went to Luton Hoo, the first of many anniversary weekends they were to spend at this Bedfordshire stately home of Sir Harold and Lady

Zia Wernher. (Lady Zia's sister was the wife of that 'Uncle George', second Marquess of Milford Haven, who took care of Philip in early boyhood.)

1953   They celebrated their sixth anniversary by revisiting their old home, Clarence House, where the Queen Mother, who was now living there, gave a dance in their honour.

1954   Their seventh (or woollen) anniversary was spent at Barnwell Manor in Northamptonshire with the Queen's uncle and aunt, the Duke and Duchess of Gloucester, and in the evening Philip attended the Balaclava Centenary Dinner at Deene Park. But three weeks later they were again at Luton Hoo for the weekend.

1955   They spent the weekend immediately preceding their wedding anniversary at Luton Hoo, including the morning of 20th November. They then drove to Windsor where they spent the night.

1956   They spent their ninth wedding anniversary thousands of miles apart. Prince Philip was in Australia and bound for the Antarctic, though he had arranged for his customary anniversary box of white flowers to be delivered as usual. The Queen was at Buckingham Palace, where she held an investiture in the morning. In the evening she went to see a performance of *The Chalk Garden*.

1957   Their tenth (or tin) anniversary. They celebrated with a dinner party at Buckingham Palace and again spent the weekend at Luton Hoo.

1958   They celebrated with a luncheon party at Buckingham Palace and again spent the weekend at Luton Hoo.

1959   Their twelfth (or silk) anniversary found the Queen again pregnant after an interval of nearly ten years. They spent the weekend at Luton Hoo, driving there along the M1 for the first time in Philip's Lagonda.

1960   The Queen was now the mother of three, Prince Andrew having been born the previous February, and yet again they spent their anniversary weekend with the Wernhers.

1961   Their fourteenth wedding anniversary found them engaged on a tour of Ghana, Sierra Leone and Gambia which had been previously postponed on account of the Queen's pregnancy, and they were together in Ghana on their actual anniversary.

1962   They were again apart on their fifteenth (or crystal) anniversary, Prince Philip having just arrived in Australia after a visit to San Francisco. The Queen spent the weekend preceding her anniversary with the Wernhers and on 20th November went to a concert at Festival Hall in aid of the Musicians' Benevolent Fund.

1963   Philip was in the middle of a three-day visit to Wales. The Queen, who was by now expecting Prince Edward, went to Covent Garden to see *Marguerite and Armand*. But they were together again at Luton Hoo the following weekend—a weekend darkened by the news of President Kennedy's assassination.

1964, 65 & 66 Ananniversary weekend spent at Luton Hoo was now a regular part of the royal calendar.

1967   Their china (twentieth) anniversary. They were together in Malta just before the anniversary—from 14th to 17th November. It was an official visit, but perhaps one which also enabled them to recapture, however briefly, the halcyon days of early marriage. Returning, they spent the weekend with the Wernhers, then drove to Windsor on 19th November for the Devaluation Council. They stayed the night at Windsor and returned to Buckingham Palace on the actual wedding anniversary.

1968   They were back home only just in time for their wedding anniversary, arriving at Buckingham Palace at midnight on 19th November following a royal tour of Brazil and Chile. Philip had a meeting the following day. Apart from that, they had no engagements and celebrated their anniversary quietly on their own.

1969   Prince Philip was in Geneva on their actual wedding anniversary. The Queen was in London, where she opened the new ITN studios. But they were reunited at Luton Hoo for the weekend, Philip flying directly to Luton Airport from Switzerland.

1970   Again they spent their anniversary weekend with the Wernhers at Luton Hoo.

1971   On the Friday evening of their twenty-fourth wedding anniversary the Queen and Prince Philip flew from Cardiff to Luton Airport to again spend their anniversary with the Wernhers before returning to Windsor on the Sunday.

Index